GERALD BENNEY
Goldsmith

GERALD BENNEY
Goldsmith
The story of fifty years at the bench

Graham Hughes

For Serena

First published in 1998 by Starcity Ltd., Publishers, Burnt House
Cottage, Dukes Green, Alfriston, East Sussex, BN26 5TS

ISBN 0-9526653-1-X

British Library Cataloguing in-Publication Data. A catalogue
record for this book is available from the British Library.

© Graham Hughes

Designed by Isambard Thomas.
Printed and bound in Italy by
Mariogros Industrie Grafiche, Turin.
Distributed by Art Books International,
1 Stewart's Court, 220 Stewart's Road, London SW8 4UD.

FRONT COVER: detail of large silver coffee pot by Gerald Benney
1990. The taut curves of the spout and the texturing on the
surface of the metal are characteristic of Benney's strong, original
designs, and of his innovative personal approach to modern
technology.

FRONTISPIECE: Gerald Benney at his drawing board.
Silver designs are partly a matter of creative originality, partly
of practical function, partly of craft technique. Benney often
makes a prototype to test his initial drawings. Mental
concentration is a necessary prerequisite of artistic success.

Introduction

Overleaf
Heads of stakes. Silver sheet is
hammered over the specially
shaped surface which is made
of Meonite or malleable iron.
Gerald cast these stakes from
wood patterns he made to suit
the shapes he wanted

Gerald Benney may be the outstanding goldsmith of the century. Nobody else has made so many important pieces for such a range of important people. Peter Carl Fabergé of Russia, Georg Jensen of Denmark, Philippe Wolfers in Belgium and René Lalique in France may have been more prolific and famous than Benney but most of their gold and silver was sold ready-made. Most of Benney's masterpieces, by contrast, have been commissioned for special purposes by his personal clients, both private individuals and public institutions. Fabergé, Jensen, Wolfers and Lalique were active creators for not much more than two decades each. Benney's astonishing creative spark has enriched us all continuously for half a century. His career is without parallel.

It is sad how few art books deal with artists while they are still living. There is a poignant contrast, for instance, between the healthy on-going industries today built round Van Gogh or Charles Rennie Mackintosh, and the neglect from which they suffered while they were alive. This is because the living are always changing. The dead, by contrast, can be inserted into their pigeon holes and they won't then move. Historians prefer to record what is static rather than to follow what is moving.

Writing about someone who is still alive and developing can be embarrassing. You are tempted to record flattering opinions in an attempt to gain more commissions for an outstanding creator. But that route leads nowhere. Superlatives soon become counter-productive, and literature degenerates into public relations of which the world is tired. Honesty is the only worth while aim, and that is what I have tried to achieve. Even if this text does hurt a few feelings in its attempt to scale the lower slopes of Parnassus, at least it will not have been influenced by trivial motives.

I hope this survey of Gerald and his times will help living craftsmen and their patrons to appreciate some aspects of their calling, and that historians in future may use these pages to suggest what silversmithing was like in the half century before the Millennium.

There is one verbal detail which usually causes confusion, and that is the word Goldsmith. It is the old word for craftsmen who worked both in gold and in silver. The medieval guild which features large in this story as Gerald's first patron, is called the Worshipful Company of Goldsmiths, not silversmiths, because in the Middle Ages most silver was gilded or gilt to look like gold, and it was called gold, not silver-gilt.

I love modern art and the artists who make it. I admire the direct ways and words of living artists, and I try to understand what they are trying to express. So I thank my friend Gerald for allowing me to dissect him: it has been fun for me, and I hope not too painful for him.

Graham Hughes, Burnt House Cottage, Alfriston, Sussex, June 1998

1 Beginnings & Craft training

Beginnings. Born 21.4.30. Discipline from father, interest in making hand-work from mother. Bad at school work – meets girls – makes machine guns from motor armatures – real warplanes flying overhead in Brighton – crashes. Craft training – Dunstan Pruden – church plate – drinking. Gerald's family life – motor cycles

Gerald in Hull in 1933, aged three. At this time, he stuck a garden fork through his boot and his foot, and still retains the scar

Aged eight

Gerald Benney has shown flashes of brilliance throughout his long life, but initially the brilliance was often interpreted by his elders as tiresome conceit, a meaningless wish not to conform. He was born in Hull, Yorks on 21.4.30, where his father, Sallis Benney, was head of the art school, having previously been appointed to those at Salisbury and Cheltenham. Gerald's rather strict, conventional upbringing began at Withdean Hall Prep School nearby, from 1935–38. Then his father became head of Brighton College of Art, and at the age of eight, Gerald moved to Brighton, and went to Brighton, Hove and Sussex Grammar School 1938–45, followed by Brighton College of Art 1946–48. During all these two decades he was thought by his teachers to be bad at everything, and his exam marks were certainly depressing. He says his teachers "accepted pretty early on that I was going to be a complete dunce". He even nearly failed Art in his School Certificate exam. He says he was bottom of the class all the time at everything. This is because he was constantly inventing, thinking for instance about how to make machine guns out of motor armatures, and not listening to the trigonometry, which was "just going straight in, was barely understood, and then went straight out".

School work was not fun for Gerald, but he made up for that in his own way by getting into trouble. "Thunderflashes" he recalls "which the Army used, were like imitation hand grenades which made a really loud bang … I was completely fearless, I mean in the sense that if I got caught I didn't mind … it wasn't dangerous, I don't think … once I went down the lift shaft in my school, until I got level with the Headmaster's study, and I hung the thunderflash and lit it, shinned up the rope into the chemistry room at the top, and it blew the doors in! Terrible! And I was found out of course, because they're not daft. The Headmaster just hared up the stairs, he realised what I had done, which room I was going to appear in, while I was still going up the rope. And I nearly got expelled for that. It was constantly happening … Every time I threw a snowball, some member of staff would appear from behind a wall, and it would knock his hat off or something … whenever any trouble occurred, if I was there, I was the one who was hauled in … and I got rather fed up with this … it made me pretty determined not to get caught" …

"Later, at art school, I met my first girl. I didn't know what was what at all: nobody told me about sex, until a dashing girl introduced me to it when I was maybe sixteen. We had some girls for modelling in the studio who were amazingly nice-looking, but we weren't allowed to fraternise; it was actually forbidden to talk to them … at one time they weren't even allowed to move. It was absolutely comical. There was one particular girl who I went in for in quite a big way … I had to be discreet about it, so I'd take her away from the area, to Lewes … about twenty miles away … On Guy

Fawkes night, a big occasion in Lewes, when I was in absolute cahoots with her, I was caught and threatened with the boot. So I just went underground with anything I did that was supposed to be naughty. I just wasn't found out: I became perfect at it." Great designers are always original characters, but not all of them have to win their independence from such restrictive conditions as these.

There were more serious temptations, too. You could not get bicycles then, so bike parts were in demand. But they were still being made for the army, and some of the factories which made them were in the Brighton region. Somebody whose brother worked in one of the factories, offered Gerald what he called a fantastic break: a three-speed bicycle gear box costing almost nothing. The friend had "got" it and brought it out of the factory in parts. Gerald just didn't think about it and said 'Gosh, very kind of you'. Then he realised this wasn't right at all, much as he wanted the three speed. So he returned it and got his money back, less a little bit. 'We were all very sharp weren't we' was his verdict in retrospect. That was a definite decision not to steal.

He used to lead a mob of local boys. The whole scene was exciting. There were huge transport planes crashing into the Sussex Downs, the hills round Brighton, with Dakotas, Spitfires and Messerschmitts being shot down in the middle of the road just outside his house. Sometimes if the aeroplane had crashed up on the Downs, about ten of these boys would immediately get on their bikes and go out there even if it was dark. They just "messed about in the wreckage" and, however macabre their experiences were, they didn't turn a hair. Once he picked up a flying suit which was heavier than it should have been, and lots of human body fell out. "It didn't upset me: kids have rhinoceros hides".

While living at Brighton, Gerald trained as a silversmith with the Roman Catholic craftsman Dunstan Pruden at the Guild of St. Joseph and St. Dominic. This had been founded by Dunstan's master Eric Gill near Ditchling, at Folders Lane, Burgess Hill. It was and still is a semi-religious community of craftsmen and women who lived in cottages and caravans close to each other, sharing their skills and opportunities, helping each other, and training their apprentices. Dunstan taught at Brighton College of Art, which was his link with Gerald. He gave Gerald the opportunity to get practical work experience at Folders Lane in a rather informal way, as time allowed, in holidays, evenings and weekends from about 1946 to 1949. Working there was probably the most useful single experience for Gerald before he got to London.

There was a steady trickle of commissions through the workshop, one of many new experiences there for him. The Buckfast Abbey collection, which is still at the Abbey, was a typical large job. It was the sort of challenge which taught him some of the practical limitations of silver design. Dunstan would do his own sketch designs, then he would ask Gerald to draw them out in detail – Dunstan knew that Gerald was already the better draughtsman, so his presentation drawings were valuable to the workshop practice. Buckfast was Dunstan's concept, but it was Gerald who put the ideas on paper and then made most of the pieces, a practical and generous sharing of aptitudes of the sort which Gerald was later to use with his own craftsmen in his own workshop.

As well as the special commissions, usually for Roman Catholic churches, there was batch production of chalices and monstrances and reliquaries, all of them things with which Gerald was not then familiar. Perhaps most exciting of all was the quantity production, mostly of small pectoral crosses. Dunstan was very good at selling these. He would give Gerald a sack of fifty or sixty rough castings of them, to file up and emboss or chase until the surface was perfect. Gerald used often to have to file as many as fifty of them every day. They were then sold direct to young trainee priests, or through the church furnishing firms and church establishments who equipped priests for their future careers.

The coffee break in Dunstan's workshop was memorable and pleasurable. All the craftsmen used to come inside to enjoy the well-made coffee. There were the stonemasons and engravers and carpenters and letterers, as well as silversmiths, probably not more than about twenty, and they all seemed quite ancient to Gerald. There was a lot of talk about work, and a lot of gossip about who was sleeping with whom that week, which Gerald took for granted as normal, though it didn't seem much like home. Fiona MacCarthy's book about Eric Gill describes accurately all this colourful activity. Many good craftsmen were trained there by Dunstan and his colleagues, and Gerald knew them all.

Dunstan was quite a man of the world, with an extrovert love of women and wine, both of which had been neglected in Gerald's other schooling. Dunstan seemed to have had quite a number of wives and girl friends, who all seemed to be around at the same time – they all knew each other. It was from him that Gerald learned how to buy wine in bulk, and how to keep it from going off, mainly, he says, a question of drinking it as fast as possible.

It is quite a long way from Brighton to Folders Lane, about sixteen miles, which Gerald had to cycle over the Downs every morning. Then Dunstan would send him off to Burgess Hill to get the meat and various vegetables for lunch, and bring them back again to put them on ready for cooking. One of Gerald's unsung creative gifts is his cooking; at first rather reluctantly, he had to cook for Dunstan, with the happy result that Dunstan ended up by teaching him to be a good cook. This was a rare accomplishment in those days of food rationing: the poverty of English kitchens meant that baked beans and fried bread were the norm.

Gerald knew where to get the best draught beer. In the evening, before he cycled home, Dunstan and he would go off on their bikes and play shove ha'penny for beer. They were invincible, and their reputation soon spread from pub to pub. At each new place, they would take on the local team for a pint of beer, which they never had to pay for because they always won.

Gerald always speaks kindly of Dunstan. His Neo-Romanesque style was light-years removed from Gerald's sinewy modern line, and he may not have been a great stylist in his own right – his silver sometimes resembled that of Eric Gill. But he showed an unusual blend of idealism, kindness and business judgement. He had a sensitive feeling for the metal, he always insisted on a careful professional finish, an important lesson for the quick-moving, impatient young Gerald, and he introduced Gerald to the essentials of Christian symbolism.

Dunstan helped to educate Gerald. He gave him personal and technical guidance which formed useful adjuncts to Gerald's armoury of professional craft equipment for the future. His pay as apprentice disciple went up from twelve shillings a week to fourteen, a symbol of hard-earned success which must have seemed to be the voice of the real world outside, as opposed to the artificial assessments applied at school.

Gerald at this time felt he was a really "constipated" designer – ideas just didn't come, and that worried him. He said to his mother quite seriously that if his designing didn't go any better, he would open a garage and do his motor cycles full time. But he was underestimating his ability: he was soon able to prove that he could be a motor cycle mechanic and a silversmith at the same time, each activity helping the other.

He has a strict sense of self discipline and personal integrity. He does what he says he is going to do, he starts work punctually every morning, and he expects perfection not only in his own work, but from those around him. If they are late or slovenly, he will tell them and the relationship between them might become strained; if their silver is not up to the standard he requires, then he may scrap it. His present exigencies about the craft can easily be traced back partly to Dunstan, and through Dunstan to Eric Gill.

But this sometimes frightening work ethic cannot be due entirely to the good-living Dunstan. More likely, it also came from Gerald's father Sallis Benney. Sallis became head of Brighton College of Art, and usually walked to work at the college every morning, leaving home at about eight o'clock. Gerald himself had already walked off to school – he normally walked three miles to school, and three miles back in the evening, six miles a day in all, quite a show of energy on today's standards. Sallis always presided over the college evening classes, so he did not leave college till about nine o'clock, and got back home late. Gerald therefore hardly ever saw him.

Tea and hot water pot still showing pre-war influences, made by Gerald at Brighton College of Art c. 1947 for the wife of the brother of the band leader Henry Hall. Gerald was already developing a clientele from among his many friends from all walks of life. The bigger pot was sold at auction in London in April 1998 for £3,000, proving that silver by living craftsmen can now fetch high prices when sold second-hand

Despite these pressures, somehow they did make time to wander together through the antique shops in the Lanes in Brighton about 1937 and 1938, when Gerald was seven or eight years old. They liked to buy Japanese prints. They would try to find one each, costing maybe sixpence apiece, from the big unlabelled folders where the prints were unsorted and unknown: some might turn out to be important and were later established as by Hokusai, Utamaro or Toyokuni. Eventually they came to embellish the walls of Gerald's homes. So Sallis helped to nourish Gerald's passion for the unusual.

Sallis' teaching aims were difficult to fulfil during the war. His reaction to what we now call stress was remarkable, and must have stiffened Gerald's own capacity to resist hardship. He reminisces that Sallis was "very strict … He was always throwing things at the wall, throwing down his food and plates, and sometimes jumping up, throwing his plate, and walking out of the room … He was grossly overworking. The Philistines in Brighton on the Council were always trying to close the art school, because they didn't agree with art … he got landed with two thousand students from the American and Canadian forces who were stationed in the South … from a rather nice job it became a nightmare, … I think it really knocked him out actually, he didn't last very long after … I could be pretty certain when there were going to be ructions … it was awful really, he used to have nightmares and things like that … he did frighten me … but he was all right when he wasn't cross … we used to go out drawing together … I got petrol coupons for my motorcycle … these emotional outbursts required my brother Derek and me to be rather better behaved than one would normally expect any boy to be." Sallis had a difficult relationship with his wife and he caused a harsh emotional climate at home.

Apart from teaching, Sallis' main interest was painting in water colours –

The local Grammar School OTC (Officers' Training Corps) at Marshall House in 1946, dressed as war-time heroes. The adjustment to peace-time habits in1945 after the excitements of war, was slow and sometimes difficult. Gerald discovered that if he ran very quickly from one end of the line to the other in formal group photos like this, the long photographic exposures which were then necessary, made it possible for him to appear twice in the same photo, an exciting trick for him, a bewildering phenomenon for the school staff. Here he appears only once (seven from right, main front row)

he was specially well known for his studies of trees: Gerald admired Sallis' work and now has about twenty of his paintings. Visitors today to the splendid new Sallis Benney Hall in what is now Brighton University, one of the best art schools in Britain, might be surprised to know how Sallis' distinction and popularity in school, was the outcome of such pain at home.

Gerald's mother was very supportive. He was not frightened by the war: he found it exciting to be machine-gunned, as long as he was not actually hit. Walking home, he might see little tufts of smoke in the road, and he would go along with a pen-knife and dig out the bullets, and go home to show her. She almost used to pass out. But even when he was emptying hand grenades to get the explosive out to make rockets, she remained calm. She was probably a frustrated farmer, but she became a good silversmith – she made many teapots, coffee pots, bowls, and cutlery, some in the family home in Brighton, some at the art school under eminent silversmiths. Her silver was in a sort of Art Deco style, strong in design and well made. Fortunately for her reputation, Gerald still possesses and treasures some of it at home. But hers was a short-lived craft career: when he started his own silversmithing, she decided to drop hers.

He thought his mother was an extremely good cook. Cooking in England was so awful at that period of food shortages, that standards may not have been high. Anyway, whenever he and Sallis went anywhere, they would bring her back presents of cooking instruments. When he finally went abroad as far as France about 1948, he brought back a whole collection of French cooking things, and gave them to her, and she said 'Oh, God, not more cooking instruments. Do you know, I hate cooking' ... that really upset him. For all those years he had thought she was so marvellous partly

Armoured car c. 4 inches long, made in his bedroom at home when aged c. 12, out of anti-aircraft shell cases found lying out in the fields near Brighton

His first workshop built by him in his bedroom at the top of the Benney family home, 19 Cornwall Gardens, Brighton, painted in 1942 by his brother Derek, who became a distinguished calligrapher

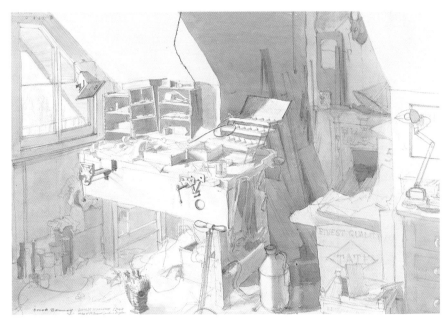

Beginnings & Craft training

because he thought she loved cooking. And she didn't, and had never told him this disappointing truth. It made him feel rather sad to think that he loved his mother so much, yet knew her so little. Gerald's brother Derek was in the RAF for several years during the war, one and a half of them in Ceylon, so the emotional maladjustments at home must have seemed all the more powerful and uncomfortable to Gerald who was the only child there. Parental matrimonial tension may have helped to propel him away from the domestic home life of books, into his private empire of the workbench.

His father's mother, "Grannie", also lived in their home in Brighton during the war, another source of family tension. She was very humourless, not a very attractive personality, he remembers. She used to boil the water for Gerald and his friends who were already starting to make things in his mother's kitchen. He thinks Grannie's idea was not so much to help her grandson, as to irritate her long-suffering daughter-in-law, who doubtless wanted to use her kitchen for her own cooking, not for what seemed like Gerald's weird manufacturing fantasies.

He already knew that the "primary importance" in his life was motorcycles, even though he wasn't supposed to have one at that age. It is impossible to explain some of the strongest instincts in life, but some recent writers have tried to analyse the motor bike: one writer guessed that riding a motor bike is the best fun you can have with your clothes on, despite the dangers and inconveniences. This enthusiast decided that for the true rider, the motor bike is transcendental. Only sex, religious rapture or intoxication can compare. Another fantasist aficionado invited fellow riders to "experience the thrills of motor-cycling in summer by sitting in front of a hair dryer and getting a friend to fire bees into your face with a spud gun."

I doubt if the young Gerald would have rhapsodised about his motor bikes quite like this, but he did certainly respond to the magic of motor bikes, as well as to their mechanics. Indeed, one of the ways he resourcefully discovered of getting his motor bike repaired, was to use the equipment at the local art school. So away he sped to study silversmithing there, but he was determined to learn there also how to repair mudguards, handlebars and all the other hardware necessary to propel him along the road literally, and over the horizon metaphorically into a bigger life.

Gerald in 1950 indulges his passion for motor bikes on an ex-army WD (War Department) American Harley Davidson machine which he had bought in a box and assembled himself in an Ariel SQ 4 frame: evidence of his mechanical ingenuity. Sometimes he sold the assembled machines at a good profit

2 The Maker & Personal Development

The maker – soldering – model aircraft sold – Brighton College of Art – early products – making things constant theme throughout life – bikes, rockets from grenades, model cars. Early disappointments in army – no commission – remained a Private – slow to win admission to RCA – poor exam results. Personal development. Royal College of Art– John Donald – David Mellor – Robert Welch – Geoffrey Bellamy – serious aftermath of war – house in Gunter Grove – Patrick Guest – Helen Hamlyn – Molly Parkin – collecting cars and motor bikes – student fun – list of more amusing cars and bikes – on-going links with RCA as Professor.

Making things has been the basis of Gerald's life from early days. "I don't do anything except make things" he once said to me. Possibly it was with petrol lighters at about the age of twelve that he first found himself as a compulsive creator. He used to collect cartridge cases for .303 rifles and Sten Guns from the Downs near Brighton. These shell cases were left by the Canadian and American armies from their fire practice on the nearby Downland ranges. With the addition of a spring and wheel, he found he could make reliable lighters from them which he sold mostly to masters at his school and to friends of his parents.

Still around the age of twelve, the maker in him began to graduate into being an inventor and a craftsman. Toyshops in those war years, he remembers, were badly stocked. So he hit on the idea of making model aeroplane kits. He found four or five boys to work with him. They made Messerschmitts and Heinkels, Mustangs and Supermarine flying boats – his ability to identify the different types of plane, foreign as well as British, is evidence of his early interest in precise line and form.

They had to find and use unwanted scrap. Soft balsa wood was valuable for war factories, so he had to use the easily available hard woods instead, an early sign of his determination and versatility. Builders' lead came from discarded electric cabling, usually as much as two foot lengths, in a new housing estate nearby in about 1940. Boiled up in an old tin like a petrol can, the softened wire came out and the rubber came off. Inside was left the lead, which they made into tiny model undercarriages and into machine guns. Old dynamos taken to pieces yielded exotic purple wire, which was unwound and then rewound to form the coil springs round the machine gun pods beneath the wings. Bunsen burner tubing was rolled with a pencil over a tiny piece of bamboo, a quarter inch in diameter, and became a miniature tyre with a hole through it for the air. The results of these improvisations always looked realistic and were sometimes profitable as well.

From car dumps he and his young friends picked up old Triplex windscreens made from glass and plastic. With a knife and hot water, he learned to prise the glass off from the plastic, splitting what was useful to him from the useless. He then softened the plastic in boiling water, formed it into shape on wooden dies made from Beech wood (the male) and plastic wood (the female). When pulled apart, the plastic wood shrinks, leaving just enough space to insert some hot plastic. Then he pressed it and, when it had cooled, cut it to shape with a pair of scissors. To be precise, he got Grannie to do this cutting to shape, because she had the time and patience to wait for ages while it cooled. Eventually, this improvised process became a routine. Behold! The result was a tiny aircraft cockpit or gun dome. Probably the only ready-made part in the whole creation was the transfers for the Royal Air Force markings on the wings or fuselage.

He evolved a price list and an instruction kit to explain the mysteries of assembly, and he printed it on a jelly mould, a sort of primitive litho method. The editions were only about fifteen, which was as many as this early technology could manage. Like most artists, he always disliked the act of selling, so he found a partner to handle the sales and together they did well, as well as having a lot of fun. Their main sales outlet was Halfords, a big company already burgeoning into new fields of consumer demand which it has since conquered. The Halfords business was related to cars and mechanics, far removed from the type of art which was Gerald's main concern. But he sensed that the world was changing, that, if he was to survive, he must identify with the newly emerging mass markets. He made enough out of these models to buy a new pre-war Enfield Bullet motor cycle which had arrived in a crate in 1939 and never been unpacked by its first owner, probably his first big commercial success.

He had to improvise his own making techniques, but initially some inspiration came from the garage of a neighbour of his father, in which Gerald probably first became in thrall to the magic of the motor bicycle – in this case, a Vincent Black Shadow, the memory of which still sends shivers of excitement down his spine.

He loved soldering, so even as a child he had made model armoured cars out of anti-aircraft shells, which he still possesses today . He could not think of anything else. His mother did try, since he was interested in metals, to get him a job in ICI, because they had some family connection with ICI originally when it was founded. But he did not really like that, because at ICI the only subject of conversation seemed to be metallurgy. That did not interest him: he probably did not even know how to pronounce the word, let alone what it meant. Knowledge of metals came to him through the workbench, with blowlamp, hammer and file, and through his hands and fingers, not through the textbooks.

He and his friends in Brighton were "sort of mad". They used to buy American motor bicycles in crates ex WD (ex War Department stock) for about five pounds including the tyres. The next three months went on assembling the bikes, the next six months on riding them around. There was a good market for made-up motor bikes and eventually they did quite well selling them.

During the war, new cycles were unobtainable, so Gerald used old parts instead. He cycled to old dumps in the country and pedalled back home with salvaged old frames, wheels, saddles, dynamos, 3 speed gears, which he stored in his bedroom workshop. He would then find or buy the necessary chains, tyres and brakes, paint and assemble them till he had a complete bike, sometimes with smart saddle bags which he made of scrap linoleum and wood. They sold well, another early commercial achievement.

Mug made at Brighton College of Art c. 1947. The applied patterned wires on the knop (the central hand-hold) were a typical decoration used by the pre-war Arts and Crafts movement

He had fun with the girls, too, the main idea being to find an excuse to get closer to them, usually in somebody's house. The beach was attractive, also. Most of the mines there had gone off by then and the shingle had been de-mined, so he bravely says "there wasn't a great deal of danger walking about". Old Forte's ice cream palace on the sea front was a favourite at lunch time, run by Charles himself (later Lord Forte of the hotel group); Rocco Forte started work there soon, when he was about 14, and they all became quite friendly with Gerald.

His energy was already impressive. He remembers he thought nothing of cycling to Cornwall and then up to Wales, a thousand miles bicycling … and they would take girls with them, too. There were Youth Hostels; they cost a shilling a night, about 5 p or less today, which they could easily afford. The low price included some sort of meal, too. Together, they might do ninety miles a day, and they covered most of England and Wales.

His family chose Brighton College of Art for him, because it was obvious, useful and near, even if its course was limited in scope. For instance, there was no instruction there in how to run a workshop, how to design or sell. Nevertheless Brighton provided what he needed. On his silversmithing course there, he learned "how to make things by hand – a sort of Greenpeace course". He learned how to hammer things properly and how to solder them, which led to an instinctive appreciation of real quality.

He went to Brighton College of Art from 1946 – 48, and he says he did not do well there. After scoring the highest marks ever recorded for the Intermediate exam, 93%, from no less an outside examiner than Henry Moore, he determined to do his final exams in one year instead of the usual two. For that, he got the lowest marks ever, about 13% . He went out of the college with "not very flying colours".

He thinks he must have been a real art philistine, not going to galleries, not discussing art, only interested in motor bikes and making or repairing parts for them. "I think I must have been a nasty, over-confident person" he says ruefully.

His busy hands continued to make all sorts of things, but the momentum was reduced by conscription into the army 1948 – 50. One of his friends had what sounded like a marvellous Sikh battalion in India, and told Gerald he had trucks and tanks and big tank transporters and motor bikes made by the big old names. Gerald thought "Right" and went straight into the Army, volunteering for the British Army Service Corps. "I didn't know anything about it" he says. He began with all the joys of Spring. He describes with glee one of his jobs, pulling tanks out of holes in Germany. Another was more amazing but less fun: the huge transporter he was driving ripped across a fuse-box and blacked out the whole base.

In Place de la Concorde, Paris, with fellow art students from Brighton College. Speed and mechanics were important to them all

The Maker & Personal Development

The shock of reality was not long in coming. He was immediately transported to Aldershot by what he calls "one of those extraordinary, dramatic people, Sergeant-Major Britton, who eventually became quite famous. I could just about stick that, but it was an amazing experience to be bullied by paratroop sergeants and people who really seemed to want to kill you, to hurt you, to take your confidence away so that you would be a good mouldable soldier".

Gerald discovered that his hard-earned Brighton art degree was not then recognised as an academic qualification, so it did not help him to win the commission as an officer which he badly wanted. He had assumed he would more or less automatically receive a commission. Optimism has always been one of his endearing characteristics, but at this age, he seems to have shown some over-optimism which appeared to his selection boards to be unpleasantly close to arrogance. He failed three attempts to become an officer through the WOSB (War Office Selection Board), ending up in Aldershot and then Farnborough. There, still a Private soldier, he got a job as painting instructor, and started this new career with huge murals in a REME (Mechanical Engineers) barracks, only recently demolished.

Some tough, rough acquaintances once asked him to join their gang, stripping lead off barrack roofs and selling it. "We're going to take the lead off the Tank Barracks roof tonight, and you've been a good bloke, so come and join us" they said. He saw the red light and refused; but he noticed to his surprise how many of his friends at that time had a criminal record. This sort of friend seemed to him to be more fun than the soldiers who aimed at orthodox success, an early example of his independence in personal judgements.

Eventually, he was offered the lowest possible promotion – to the rank of Lance Corporal. He felt so insulted that he threw his hat at the Captain. Luckily he missed his target and somehow avoided being put on a charge for insolence. He consoled himself on his twenty-first birthday by taking the local NAAFI (Navy, Army and Air Force shops) girls for a drive in his vintage Chrysler car. An exciting moment was when he sold this Chrysler – a wooden-artillery-wheeled dream of a car – to his Commanding Officer, a Lt. Colonel. But to everyone's dismay, the Colonel was soon arrested, nobody knew why; his brothers were diamond dealers, which may have had something to do with it. He vanished, the deal collapsed, and Gerald lost a useful contact at the top.

In an effort to relieve the monotony, he started an education centre before the formation of the Army Education Corps. But he soon got depressed and decided to try to streamline his life. He eliminated his name from the lists for roll-call, guard duty, morning parade and other unwelcome chores. The result was that he was required to put in a formal

Private Benney at Farnborough in 1950 (right), smoking in a grown-up way, wears dark green Canadian army uniform which it was then possible to buy and wear, and which was generally considered smarter than the British. Gerald hoped to become a commissioned officer. He never did. He used his bicycle to tour far afield to Wales and beyond, usually with girls from Brighton College of Art, but motor bikes were more fun than the simple cycle

appearance only on Saturday mornings, when he would receive his meagre pay as what was called attached personnel.

He was living in a deserted sergeants' mess in the Farnborough swamp with no arduous duties to perform, so he started to make some serious paintings. These sold well – another unexpected commercial success – until he was able to construct from spare parts the object of his dreams, a very fast Ariel Square Four motor bike with a Harley Davidson engine. He learned to live in Brighton during the week, speeding back to camp only on Saturday to collect his pay.

He enjoyed the fruits of his ingenuity until the day of fire drill for the whole camp, when the official system proved too thorough for even his practised technique of bending the rules in his favour. The roll-call for this occasional imaginary crisis was taken from a master list kept, unknown to him, in a fire proof safe. He had tried to penetrate all the lists in order to type his name off them, but this one had naturally eluded him because he did not know it existed. When his name was called out, he was not there to reply "present" so he was posted AWOL (absent without leave). A friendly Sergeant phoned him in Brighton with the unwelcome news, and he returned to camp in uniform PDQ (pretty damn quick, in the slang of the time). He explained that he had been painting some murals in an army hall in Aldershot, which was true not of that moment but of a few weeks earlier. He survived, and was demobilised soon after in time to prepare for joining the Royal College of Art.

Derek, Gerald's brother, got straight into the Royal College of Art after his several years in the RAF. Their father had been there as a student under Sir William Rothenstein, and was short-listed to be head of the RCA when Robin Darwin got the job. Gerald's godfather R. R. Tomlinson, later Principal of the Central School of Arts and Crafts, had been there. Gerald himself knew Jowett (Darwin's predecessor) and knew of Rothenstein, so the RCA was already part of him.

Gerald loved old cars. Here is one of his first, his 1928 wood-spoked Chrysler with external contracting hydraulic brakes. He sold it to his Lt. Colonel at Aldershot, who proved unable to pay and for mysterious reasons went to prison. Gerald thus lost his chance of quick promotion and high influence

On leave from the British Army, up the Eiffel Tower 1951

He failed in his first attempt at entry into the RCA in 1949, despite the rare distinction which had been given to him by Henry Moore as outside examiner at Brighton. Eventually he passed the entrance exam in 1950 and won the Prince of Wales Scholarship in his first year, mainly for one particular silver tea set which he still possesses. Soon after, he won a travelling scholarship to Italy.

But he was often being marked down for trying too many things at once. Cast aluminium was one of the techniques he studied. Industrial glass fascinated him, too. He went to Stourbridge, where the technical college ran a special glass activity, and he did glass blowing there quite often. Then there was furniture: he designed a lot of it, and that was useful because he was able to continue with it after the RCA. So there was furniture, glass, cast

Silver and ivory salad servers inspired by Dunstan Pruden, designed and made by Gerald in 1950 just before he joined the Royal College of Art and was inspired by the direct lines of creative modern design

Silver tea box 1952, made by Tom Boucher and Gerald in his first year at the RCA, the first of many such boxes with swoop lid and high polish to give rich reflections

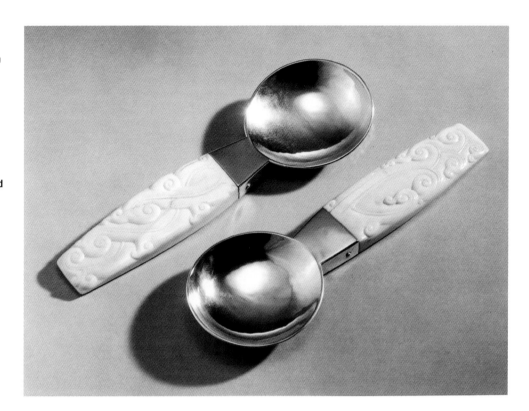

Overleaf
Silver teapot with laminated bent beech wood handle, part of the set which won for Gerald the Prince of Wales Scholarship in 1952, his first year at the RCA, his first real academic distinction. Legs like this came to be considered a sort of identity mark with the Festival of Britain 1951, in which much new British furniture featured outward-sloping legs with balls at the bottom. Tapered legs were featured by designers of almost everything shown on the South Bank, from big buildings and furniture down to small silver. The jug's surface texture is very subtle. The regularity and sensitivity of the hammer marks show that Gerald was already a master craftsman as well as an innovative designer. The complete teaset was made by Gerald in 1952 and is retained by him. Tom Boucher, the craft tutor, made another replica set also in 1952 for the Royal College of Art collection, where it now is

Two glass decanters blown by Gerald at Stourbridge, Britain's old centre of glass tableware production, where the technical college gave special facilities for making glass

Pieces made at the RCA were sometimes fantasies by immature young designers indulging their visual dreams; more often, they had a practical future as well, like Gerald's steel coffee percolator with vitreous enamel, intended for mass production

aluminium, fabric printing, as well as silver and jewels. The people he met were extraordinary, quite different from Brighton or the Army. They all sparked each other off, and he introduced everyone to big pre-war cars which they used to park in a line outside their studio/workshop, quite a spectacle.

His designer friends were extremely different one from another; but they all thought they were very elegant and smart. He never wore jeans; usually he chose beige cavalry twill trousers with a coat of pepper and salt pattern. David Mellor the silversmith preferred drain-pipe trousers and stiff, separate collars. Perhaps the main characteristic they all had in common was their energy. Together, they formed a fertile soil from which their diverse careers sprang almost like flowers in the greenhouse.

Gerald's best friend during these exciting years was perhaps the jeweller John Donald, who introduced Gerald to Janet, later to become his wife, and who developed an unsung second career for himself as a male model – he was and is very good-looking. When Gerald established his first workshop in Whitfield Place, it was John who shared it with Gerald for the first year. Later, John and Gerald's on-going friendship for each other was symbolised when John was best man at Gerald's wedding in 1957 to John's friend Janet.

John's aptitudes were different from Gerald's, so their activities fertilised each other: John moved more in the field of fashion than of the traditional craft workshops, led into it by his modelling and then by his secondary studies at the RCA, designing spectacle frames, fashion accessories and travel gear. It was John's friend and helper Ubbo Bakker, who helped John to establish his shop in Bahrein, and indirectly thereby stimulated Gerald to

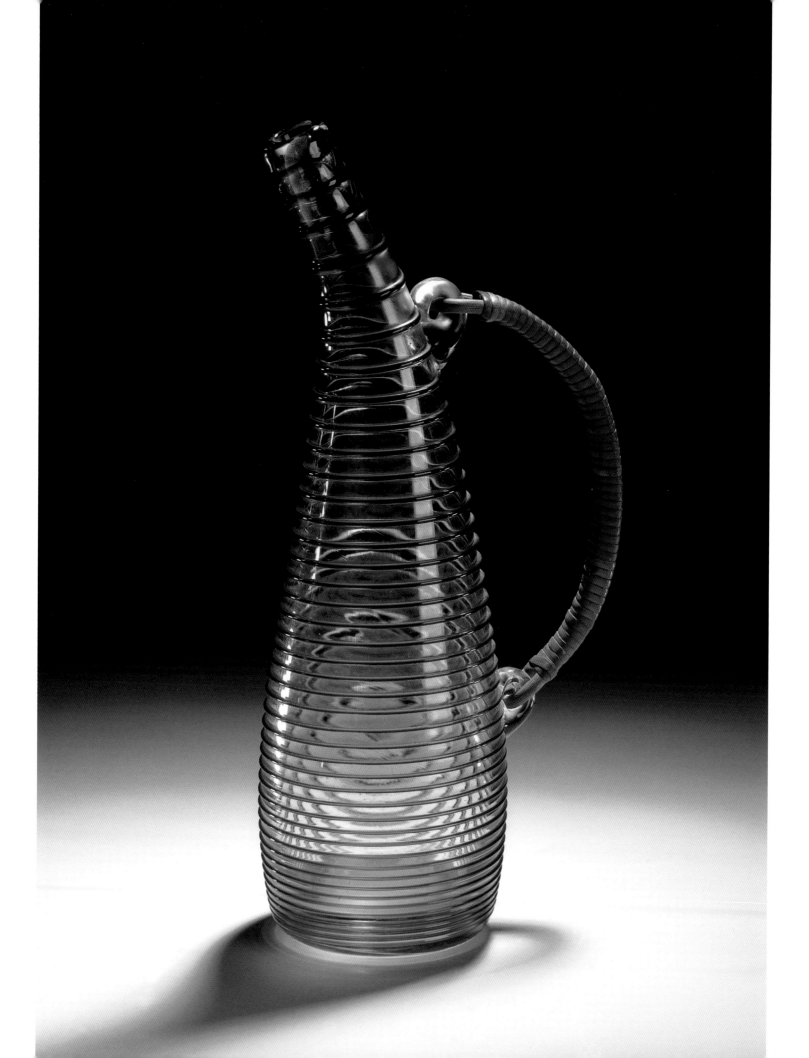

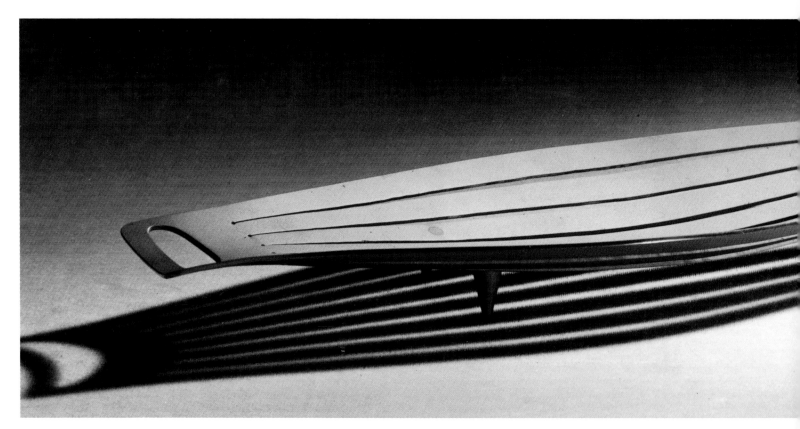

Pin tray with black oxidised surface and engraved pattern. Gerald has always been fascinated with variations in surfaces, and usually, as here, prefers an ornamented finish framed by a strong, muscular line

At the RCA, the wide scope of Gerald's interests was criticised by his teachers. He experimented successfully with several different skills and materials: here, an aluminium fruit or bread tray

take more interest in exports, which were promoted by the British government as a patriotic duty as much as a commercial necessity.

John's clients included Yardley of perfume fame, with their influential design chief Reco Capey, and a range of manufacturers of personal accessories such as suitcases. He was and is also an excellent natural athlete. I travelled with him once over the Atlantic in an aircraft to New York, where he participated in an export exhibition I had organised. I asked him how we could get some publicity in the cut-throat New York media world, and he rather shame-facedly produced from his pocket the Daily Telegraph for that morning, telling me that he was in that paper three times over in one day: once for winning a fashion prize, once for winning a golf competition, and once for a new jewel of his, hanging round a winsome neck. None of these distinctions would have been likely to come spontaneously into Gerald's life, so John's own personal interests helped to introduce Gerald to a big new world which he might not otherwise have penetrated: each of these designers broadened the horizons of all the others. John opened his exquisite small jewellery shop designed by another friend, the architect Alan Irvine, in Cheapside the old centre for goldsmiths, near Goldsmiths' Hall in the City, and it is still John's jewellery headquarters today.

Robert Welch, one of Gerald's silversmithing friends at the RCA, diversified into base metals, a sign of the wide interests of the RCA at that exciting time. Stainless steel was hitherto generally considered the preserve of the Scandinavian countries, specially Sweden, with their economical habits and pure taste. Wealthy Britain, by contrast, was the traditional home of sterling silver with its potential for luxurious showmanship and exquisite hand forming. John Grenville, the Suffolk painter, had already pioneered the production of hand-hammered stainless steel dishes, and sold them in sophisticated home furnishing stores like Heal's of Tottenham Court Road, London. But he found both the making and the marketing very hard work.

Robert realised that the new mass markets would absorb mass production as well as hand-made individual pieces. He worked with the enlightened factory J & J Wiggin of Walsall and, more recently, with Japanese firms who admired his grasp of simple forms suited to the hard, intractable metal. Robert also became the master of cast iron kitchen and table ware, whilst continuing to make his own silver in his workshop in Sheep Street, Chipping Campden, near Stratford on Avon. He still operates there today, now with his own smart retail shop in the High Street nearby. His income nowadays may mostly be in the form of industrial design fees from factories producing his designs, but he still makes silver for clients as diverse as the Royal Society of Arts and St. John's College, Cambridge.

Gerald inspired his friends with his love of vintage cars, then an unusual obsession. He went to Wales specially to buy this Lancia Lamda for his fellow silversmith Robert Welch. On the journey back from Wales, the Hardy Spicer needle bearings in the universal joint in the prop shaft attached at the engine end, not the differential drive end, broke loose. The great car ended this trip ignominiously on a transporter. Fortunately replacement parts could then be bought. Gerald's technical mechanics had been severely tested

David Mellor, another of Gerald's RCA silver friends, also developed wide interests unusual for the time. He was one of the first industrial designers to involve himself in street furniture, lamp-posts and traffic lights, with the happy result that almost every major road in Britain bears today traces of his practical, unassuming vision. He was brought up in Sheffield, the home of the British cutlery industry, went to Sheffield College of Art, then established his home and small factory in the beautiful Tudor mansion Broome Hall, his first essay at adapting an old building to a new use. Later, the architect Michael Hopkins and David himself built his new design studio, country workshop and dream home after 1996 in the nearby countryside at Hathersage. It was on the foundations of an old gas works, cleverly transforming a useless bit of industrial waste into a rural asset, and using the surviving buildings to help him to obtain planning permission to establish his small factory in the country there.

David was and is obsessed with cutlery design and manufacture. Stage by stage, he opened several retail shops, partly with the aim of creating a market for better products. Initially, he pioneered his austere, classic designs with Peter Inchbald the new head of Walker and Hall, the Sheffield cutlery manufacturers. David's "Pride" flatware pattern first appeared as a prototype at the RCA and is still a production favourite now in David's own factory, some 45 years later. "Pride" led to a government Ministry of Works scheme to commission him to make the "Embassy" pattern silver. This was to be used by British embassies overseas, as a sort of mute ambassador for new British silver and for British modern design generally.

By chance, I heard of the progress of "Embassy" from three directions at once. These were David himself who was naturally delighted with the important new opportunity, and with the prizes and honours which it won. This was a brave commission from the usually conservative British government. My second informant was Harold Glover, head of the Ministry of Works, later my chief at the Royal Mint, where I was Head of Design. Harold believed that the fine "Embassy" designs were certain to be popular because they were so good. The third opinion I heard on "Embassy" was perhaps the most important, because it came from an actual user rather than from a promoter. She was the first British Ambassador's wife who actually had to bring the new silver into use in her embassy, and she was, luckily, an enthusiast for new design. But she found her overseas friends reluctant to recognise the essence of Britain in these smooth surfaces. Architects and aesthetes might revere this cool restraint, but our overseas friends and customers understandably yearned for richness and ornament so soon after the destructive horrors of war. "Embassy" was much admired by artists, but was not specially successful in the market place, and eventually, in government offices, it yielded to old, traditional period replicas.

Art historians sometimes forget the social conditions which create the art, and so it has been with historians of this post-war RCA. Art students there of all sorts were not simply having fun and dreaming of beauty which they would help to create. Geoffrey Bellamy was typical of many of the older generation at the RCA, who have not received the notice they deserve. They were determined to create a better world and forget the carnage which had so nearly destroyed them all.

Geoffrey Bellamy was, like Robert Welch and David Mellor, Gerald's contemporary as a silversmith at the RCA, but he represented a different background. He was a symbol not so much of youthful hope as of mature courage. In his way he represented the experienced world outside, struggling to adjust into the tiny RCA silversmithing studio. He was a reminder of hard reality, a serious, sometimes sad part of the context in which the younger, perhaps more carefree Gerald was operating.

Geoffrey had survived terrible times. He had been an RAF bomber hero, joining up in 1940 when he was only 18, and staying on to the war's bitter end. He had flown Lancasters in 405 squadron, later moving to the Pathfinder force, winning the DFC and bar. He had the traumatic experience of losing two crews, one while he was on sick-leave recovering from a flak wound, one while he was seconded elsewhere. Eventually, he had 112 missions to his credit. He was one of many artists who at this time bravely tried to start a new peace-time life in what was to be a newly inspired country. After Birmingham College of Art, Geoffrey was a Royal Scholar at the Royal College of Art, winning first class honours. He and David Mellor were in fact the first two students to win "firsts" in the silver degree course. I mention Geoffrey because he was different from his younger colleagues, part of the sombre post-war back-drop. His grim memories and his quiet determination must have been a sobering influence against which the more showy young new stars could shine. With his awe-inspiring experiences behind him, so different from Gerald's, Geoffrey was admired by all, including Gerald.

Geoffrey started his own one-man workshop in a tiny basement beneath a dry-cleaners in Cadogan Street. After a long, hard spell making small repetition ashtrays and light household utensils there, sometimes for the retailers George Tarratt of Leicester, Geoffrey won a Design Centre Award in 1961 for his "Monte Carlo" cutlery, made by George Wolstenholm of Sheffield, where he soon went to work. Before 1964, he joined the staff of the Council of Industrial Design (CoID), as their liaison officer for the silver and allied industries, and there he rejoins our story after Gerald left the RCA. Geoffrey then taught at Sheffield, becoming Principal at Canterbury and Maidstone, until he died in 1997.

One war veteran from the Brigade of Guards who may stand for many at the RCA, was Aidron Duckworth, furniture designer. He created and introduced fibre glass chairs to Britain years before Charles Eames' ideas on the same theme crossed the Atlantic. He made them himself in his makeshift London backstreet workshop, then drove them in his old van to deliver them to his customers like Heal's the progressive department store. It was difficult for Aidron to compete with the lower prices of the big factories. But it was he, Geoffrey Bellamy and designers like him, who set a standard to inspire factories to employ good designers of the next generation. Aidron was not commercially successful, but his example did bear fruit in the present lively demand by factories to employ designers from the RCA.

Another fighter in the battle of styles was Geoffrey Webb, architect and glass designer. He hated what was then the pride of Bond Street shops, cut glass decanters and glasses: "death by a thousand cuts" he called them. He much preferred the simple experimental shapes like those then being created experimentally by Gerald in Stourbridge art school. These were some of the varied formative influences which helped to make the post-war RCA such an exciting place for its students.

British silversmiths who had established themselves before the war were still prominent. They helped to preserve the hand techniques built up since the Arts and Crafts revival at the beginning of the century, and it was their style which was the accepted norm, gradually blown away by the fresh air coming from the RCA. Leslie Durbin with his superb craftsmanship, taught at the RCA, Reginald Hill at the Central School of Arts and Crafts, R. G. Baxendale and Cyril Shiner at Birmingham, where Bernard Cuzner and Stanley Morris maintained their own workshops, while Boucher the master-chaser was at Sheffield, Leslie Auld in Glasgow and Alan Place in Edinburgh. Each had his own idiom, but all were influenced by the art of the past with its acanthus leaves, its bolection mouldings, its balusters and its garlands of fruit.

If these older masters were the Lutyens of silver, then Gerald was the Corbusier. The change in vision in post war British silver was acute. On a different scale and in a more intimate way, it was as dramatic a change as that of half a century before, when Diaghilev founded the Ballets Russes with its international, interdisciplinary artists, and astonished the world of art with individual dance expression and with stage designs by Picasso, after the anonymous group disciplines of the Bolshoi Ballet in Moscow and the Kirov in Leningrad.

I hope these glimpses into the careers of Gerald's talented friends will hint at the distinction of the clear-cut course which Gerald carved out for himself.

He did not emerge new-born onto a virgin field. He fought his way with strong conviction, knowing what he could and must do, in what was more a bog than a field, more soggy than fertile. To speak with a strong, unique personal voice as he did, needed courage as well as creative imagination. He had both. I cannot in a few lines define the process of education, but the attitudes of one's fellow students are certainly important to any impressionable young artist. Gerald enriched his life enormously simply by talking with other design students at the RCA. An unusual opportunity there, was the stimulating freedom which students were given to visit each others' workshops, so studies were not limited simply to one subject.

He introduced me to one of his fellow students from another department, the architect Alan Irvine, with a view to Alan designing exhibitions for us at Goldsmiths' Hall. I remember Gerald's words at the time: "there is one man who always seems to have ideas, and who knows exactly what he wants … Alan Irvine … " Before going to the RCA, Alan had already established a fine reputation and career for himself in the home of new European design, Italy, while he was training with the Milan architects BBPR. It was from Milan, that Alan brought to the RCA and to London, his valuable knowledge of Italian design practices. I already knew Gerald well enough to know that his recommendation, given in only a few words, was worth more than a morning's dissertation from a more normal aesthete, so I invited Alan to design some showcases for us. He proved a big success, winning world acclaim for some of the Goldsmiths' Hall exhibitions which he designed, and which usually featured Gerald's work. Alan went on to become a major designer of exhibitions and interiors, working frequently in Italy for Olivetti, Fiat and others, and in Britain for the Royal Academy and for many museums.

Fun was always a part of Gerald. With John Minton the painter, he helped to organise the annual Chelsea Arts Ball in the Albert Hall. Minton designed and made fantastic floral, mythological and human drapes with sound effects to match, all assembled with what then seemed to be magical high-tech gadgetry. The evening had a serious purpose, to raise money for charity, and to give students practice in carnival design, but by the early hours of the morning, any heavy thoughts about the philosophy of education were submerged beneath a froth of alcohol and dance. Gerald would share an upstair box with his brother Derek; paying the unwelcome corkage on wine bottles they brought in from outside, was avoided by the simple expedient of throwing the empty used bottles over the side of the box so that John's box next door had to pay. An economy to the inhabitants of the Benney box, but a shock to their neighbours. The score was evened when the Benneys went down to the floor: the Minton party quickly threw all the bottles back into the Benney box, plus their own.

Gerald bought this Crossley 1931 specially to impress the sculptor Elisabeth Frink. He parked it outside her favourite pub, Finch's in King's Road, Chelsea, hoping that she would notice it and him, but when she appeared she was leaning on the arm of her future first husband and did not spare a glance for Gerald. He did not meet her again until a garden party at Buckingham Palace twenty years later

Janet's cars were more graceful than monumental, like this Lancia Aurelia c.1972. Gerald always bought quickly, and usually brilliantly. But this big car proved to be a notable hiccup. The famous Lancia engine, which is what intoxicated Gerald, was great, the overall design was elegant, but there were holes in the floor. Possibly Lancia in Italy had not appreciated the vagaries of the English climate. Anyway, the Aurelia had rust underfoot and had to be returned to the penitent dealer

The little episode suggests the prevailing light hearted intoxication which created a brilliant party for all concerned. One of the high points of the all-night dream world created under the huge vault, was a procession of decorated floats drawn by Bacchus-like men, and bearing on top, semi-dressed girls. As the floats progressed across the floor, the girls' clothes became less and less apparent, until nudity became unavoidable. The students, female as well as male, loved it, but violence began over the years to spoil the aftermath, so the Ball was eventually discontinued.

One of the several brilliant, creative friends of those fertile student years was Helen Royce Jones. She was Gerald's constant companion or partner as we now say, for two years, and remains an intimate friend of his. He met her as an exceptional student in the Fashion School. She became a very successful designer, working for some of the most important names like Hardy Amies, Spectator Sports and Jaeger. She married a friend of Gerald's, the architect Patrick Guest, and together they shared a house in Carlyle Square with several of Gerald's student friends. She designed some lovely clothes for Gerald's future wife Janet including her wedding dress. Later, she married Paul Hamlyn, now Lord Hamlyn, the publisher and philanthropist. Paul has made fortunes out of international publishing, and then given them away. He helps crippled children in India, enables poor children in London to enrich their lives by seeing opera, and, in 1997, offered a big contribution of about £25 M towards the rehabilitation of the concert and exhibition halls at London's South Bank Centre, perhaps to be renamed after him if the works there proceed. Helen in 1997 endowed a study programme at the Royal College of Art for equipment to help the elderly to cope with the rigours of old age. An imaginative and generous couple. Helen still meets Gerald and Janet because they are old friends and have similar tastes. She has commissioned many of Gerald's pieces over the years; one of the most unusual and characteristic, is the silver Thermos flask to hold a half bottle of champagne for Paul to imbibe during his train journeys.

The Studio Club, on the corner of Swallow Street just off Piccadilly, often saw Gerald "holing out" or relaxing, to use the slang of the time. Dancing, drinking, eating there followed the long day's work at the RCA – the students all used to work very late, then got into their "limos" and "piled off" to the Club where they would stay till around midnight, then driving back to their flats which were quite cosy with coal fires and, sometimes, cats too.

Puccini's opera La Bohème is the classic portrayal of art students' life in Paris a century ago. Gerald's RCA with its industrial leanings and its world vision, represented a bigger dynamism than the dream world of Puccini.

What Gerald calls his best car ever, a "thumping great beautiful animal", a 6-cylinder in-line leather-bodied open four seater silver Crossley. It attracted the attention of Sir John Cockcroft at the Atomic Energy Research establishment at Harwell. Sir John then commissioned pieces of silver from Gerald. Gerald eventually auctioned the car. The buyer was the Beaulieu Motor Museum, where it now is still with the big wheels which Gerald fitted on the original Rudge Whitworth hubs. Gerald also earned a funny reputation for the car as having the earliest chrome plated radiator. In fact, Gerald had done the plating himself weeks before. Gerald bought a second similar Crossley in order to take from it its second gear, which was missing on the first, and sold it to his friend the painter and print maker the late Alistair Grant, who drove it through a window in King's Road, Chelsea

But human nature does not change, and opera lovers today could recognise something of Gerald in Puccini's Marcello.

Like Marcello, Rodolfo and most other art students throughout history, Gerald sometimes had to earn money by doing odd jobs outside his true vocation. For this purpose, he worked part time at the Old Vic making stage equipment, belts, swords, helmets and medieval equipment for Richard 11 and his like. Cash apart, though, there was another magnet luring him towards the stage, and she was called Claire Bloom. Richard Burton and John Neville were also there. Gerald remembers that at a party the first thing Burton would do was to "jump on a table and start to spout Shakespeare" which didn't impress Gerald at all, but which eventually won for Richard the favours of Claire.

Another early excitement for Gerald when he was about twenty, was the sculptor Elisabeth Frink, who became a life-long friend. Every night she seemed to go to Finch's in Brompton Road. He bought a huge open silver Crossley with a big angular hood, like a Bentley, specially in order to attract her attention, because he was still inwardly rather lacking in confidence. He parked the car outside, intending to offer to drive Elisabeth home when she emerged. Eventually she did come out, but with her future first husband who seemed to be about seven feet tall, and they brushed straight past the timid Gerald who did not dare even to speak. Romance did not always come easy in those days.

Interesting cars are one of the themes of his early life: he loved their appearance, their craftsmanship, their noises, their potential to attract attention, the way he could buy and sell them at a profit. He made for me a list of some of these heart throbs of his, some of the best and usually biggest cars he owned over a period of about ten years. This list shows an average of two different cars each year, an eloquent suggestion of Gerald's restless nature and his love of change. There were the early Chrysler with wooden wheels, the first car to have external contracting hydraulic brakes; two Silver Crossley Dropheads; Studebaker designed by Raymond Loewe; Citroen Light 12 1938, a rare collectors' specimen; Lancia Drophead; Rolls Royce 20/25 Drophead 1934; Bentley Corniche Drophead; Humber Super Snipe; Riley Monaco; Morris 10; three Austin 7s; Mini Cooper Special; Jeep; Range Rover; Land Rover; Ford Escort Drophead; Ford Station Wagon made in Australia; Renault; Jaguars 2.4, 3.6, 4.2, 5.3, XJS; Peugeot 205; Peugeot 504; Bentley 8. He still, nearly half a century later, remembers the registration number of his Morris 10, vintage 1928, AUF 415, sure evidence of his obsession with old cars. What an investment they represented in speed and in the joys of modern living!

Vintage cars became almost a talisman at the RCA. John Skeaping, Professor of Sculpture, owned perhaps the most flamboyant car of them all,

Trophy for the National Theatres of South Africa, made by the precocious Gerald whilst he was still at the RCA, showing comedy. Tragedy is on the reverse side. Both were inspired by a Mexican mask owned by John Skeaping

a huge bright green Rolls Royce of 1928. John Donald's was a Morris 10
also of 1928, while David Mellor was at home in a long wheel-base MG
*c.*1932 . They egged each other on to appreciate the design, the engine
sounds and the engineering of these early giants of motoring, and Gerald
was always in the lead.

His motor cycles were probably an earlier, more practical interest, more
a means of getting around than a breath of fresh air: they included a Francis
Barnett, Minerva in line 4, Harley Davidson, Enfield Bullet, Matchless,
Indian Twin, 250 A. J. S., B. S. A. 250, 500 Norton. All these mechanical
wonders were grist to Gerald's inventive mill: he could repair, improve,
cosset and love them, much as he later learned to do with some of his other
loves including girls, silver and jewels.

His Professor at the Royal College was Robert Goodden. Gerald
remembers gratefully how Robert left his pupils alone, how they looked
up to him and had great respect for him. He didn't interfere with them, was
a good guiding hand, a good helper with problems. The intimate
relationship seemed to mean that most of Gerald's talks with Robert were
not so much about Gerald's silver, more about how to replate the headlamp
reflectors of Robert's open Sunbeam car, vintage c. 1928.

Gerald always liked practical jobs more than theoretical exercises. His friend the sculptor John Skeaping asked him to make this ten feet long weather cock to surmount the spire of the City church of the Austin Friars, designed by Sir Christopher Wren. It is still there

For the final exam, students had to lay their work out in rooms in Prince Consort Road. A week before this exam, Robert had trapped himself by mistake in Gerald's innovative new deck chair, sitting in it uninvited before Gerald had inserted the pivots which hinged the two halves of the chair together. Robert was completely trapped for some time as in a clam shell. Gerald laughed a lot, but the Professor was not amused. He saw the hilarious joke as an embarrassment. Over 3 years, Gerald had made a huge number of products, but there was not much space so he chose only 5 pieces for his exam, the best masterpiece as he thought from each type. Full of excitement, he heard heavy footsteps along the corridor. It was the Rector Robin Darwin with Robert, doing their exam marking. He expected them to stop and talk, but they walked on, Darwin simply saying to Robert 'Bit thin, Robert, bit thin'.

Darwin wanted to give Gerald a third class pass degree, because he thought Gerald had not completed enough pieces, but Robert lifted the grading to a second. Gerald's silversmithing friends all got firsts. He did wonder if his poor exam result was connected with the trapping of his Professor in his deck chair, and he has his suspicions! Not too long later, in 1952, he drove Robert Goodden and Robin Darwin to Buckingham Palace in his rare, beautiful Citroen light 12, the only available car distinguished enough for the purpose, for them to present there the RCA Coronation present to the Queen. The artificial examination system may not have given fair recognition to Gerald, but this use of his car so soon after, showed there was already a spirit of partnership between him and the RCA.

The Royal College of Art story was by no means finished for him when he left not exactly overwhelmed with honours. Twenty years later, in 1973, Professor Robert Goodden was due for retirement. As Gerald says, Robert finally scraped the bottom of the barrel and asked Gerald if he would be interested in the post. He had recently undertaken some demanding commissions, chief among them the Institute of Chartered Accountants who were equipping their new London building with new silver paid for by member firms of accountants. So he did not have time to do much teaching, and felt he must refuse the flattering offer. Robert eventually made one of his rare forays outside his office in the RCA. He visited Gerald in his Bear Lane workshop to persuade him to relent, which he partially did, limiting his proposed appointment to a "2–day" Professorship. The compromise seemed satisfactory, subject to a final interview with the formidable-looking publisher Hans Juda, who was at that time influential at the RCA.

Gerald arrived for the interview at the RCA and found to his dismay, half a dozen well-known silversmiths also waiting there for interviews. Called in

for the unexpected ordeal, he found a dozen high-powered RCA aesthetes, amongst them David Mellor, seated along one side of a long table, with a small lone chair for him the other side. "Well, Gerald" asked Hans "what would you do if you were appointed?" Gerald pointed out that he hadn't the faintest idea, because he had left the RCA twenty years ago in 1953 and not been back there since. He said he could not spare five days a week for teaching, but just might manage to squeeze in two and a half days. It was rare for anyone to hesitate when offered a job at the then prestigious RCA, so he thought he had cooked his goose and went home disappointed. He had begun to dream privately with pleasure of being Professor.

To his delight and surprise, he got a letter two days later from the Registrar appointing him to the Chair. His honesty at the interview had paid off, as habitual honesty usually does. He enjoyed and helped his students, treating them as friends, sometimes inviting them to his last spacious workshop at Beenham to see the production there and to begin learning enamelling, with results that he calls breathtaking. These students of his discovered that "we are the industry".

There were in Britain at that time no exemplary modern silver and stainless steel factories like Jensen of Copenhagen, or Gense deep in the forests of Sweden at Eskilstuna. Gerald with his friends and students helped to create a forward-looking attitude in some old British firms and thus to bring new hope to a very old manufacturing base. His nine years teaching at the RCA were one of the best experiences of his life, brought to an end, he says, by "mismanagement at the top". His passion for efficiency was thwarted by sloth and timidity, two of his least favourite characteristics. He resigned from the RCA in 1982. David Queensberry, the international champion of glass and ceramic design, also resigned, and the Rector soon after. There was another big exodus of teachers when Jocelyn Stevens then took the driving seat. Gerald remains a great fan of Jocelyn, so admirable in so many ways, even if he does make the ladies cry and even if he does cause a lot of friction. Gerald would love to have still been at the College under Jocelyn's leadership.

Gerald still meets his ex-students – silversmithing in Britain retains some of its friendly aspect, almost like an extended family. His memorial at the RCA is a human one: the strength of many small silver workshops today is partly due to the ethos they learned from him. Dynamic efficiency is not usually associated with ancient crafts: more often, the word "crafts" is used to imply dreamy attitudes and late delivery. Gerald at the RCA was one of the young new brooms who swept away these musty sentimental cobwebs of the past.

He left another practical memorial at the RCA. When he was Chairman of the Senior Common Room, the handsome top-floor room where staff and visitors can eat, meet and talk together, he discovered that the RCA collection of art was far bigger and better than anyone had realised. The basis of this collection was the fruit of the RCA student passing out examinations: over the past century, staff had the duty of choosing one or more of the best pictures and craft products from each student exhibiting at these shows, a choice which was often amplified by gifts from grateful ex-students like Henry Moore.

Gerald took his job as Chairman seriously. The SCR before his time was losing money, which made him cross because he dislikes inefficiency. He realised the potential of these beautiful upper floor rooms to form a nucleus for the corporate life of the RCA, and tried successfully to breathe new life into them. A memorable evening there was his and Janet's 25th wedding anniversary dinner in 1982: with typical ingenuity, he had discovered that lobsters from Maine, owing to the strong pound, could be bought and airlifted over from the States less expensively than buying lobsters from Scotland and having them sent down by rail. The beneficiaries were the lucky guests, as well as his bank balance.

One day when he was inspecting the workshops, he heard a "drip … drip … drip" noise above him in the RCA annexe called the "Embassy", next to the main building. In a decaying attic with a leaky roof, he found stored most of the RCA painting collection, worth millions of pounds even then, uninsured and unguarded. Amongst them were pictures by David Hockney, probably in the 1960s the most famous young living graduate of the RCA. Gerald specially values these early Hockneys, with their sharp colours and jagged lines, often with numbers and words in all sorts of sizes and type faces. He remembers Hockney as a student being a "sort of batty reprobate". Mercifully, Hockney had always painted on board, which withstood the damp and the drips fairly well. When Gerald himself started to paint big oils, he remembered the lesson of the survival of these Hockneys, and always paints on board himself now. Gerald instituted a proper storage and hanging policy, the benefits of which may be seen today by any visitor to the SCR. At the time of writing, six big Hockney oils, mostly dated 1962, dominate the walls of the SCR, with his "Rakes Progress" series of prints giving distinction to the adjoining sitting room. These might none of them be there today but for Gerald. One result of this growing recognition for the RCA collections, was the superb Centenary show of RCA painters staged there in 1996. But the seeds of his initiative have not yet yielded their proper harvest; the RCA remains reluctant to acknowledge that its collections impose upon it museum-like obligations, in addition to its primary duties as the nation's senior post-graduate art teaching institution.

It will already be obvious that Gerald is an exceptional person. He has great creative vitality, whose corollary is an impatience with all forms of bureaucracy and organisational hypocrisy. Two years ago I was with him at the opening of what he calls a "naff" exhibition, meaning that the exhibits were trivial and the method of showing them was conventional and boring. Add to this dim impact, the necessity of listening to several self-congratulatory speeches, and you have the makings of a boring evening. I watched his sensitive nose begin to quiver with indignation and I watched his quick eye spotting the pretty girls. He eyed the nearest exit point in case he could stand it no longer. Luckily, his son Simon was with him and succeeded in calming him, but I realised how little of a team man he still is, and how clever the Royal College of Art was to retain him there for so long. The RCA set its seal on a happy relationship which was enabled by joint wisdom to survive some upsets along the road; in 1990 the RCA made him an Honorary Fellow. This is an association which he treasures all the more, remembering his faltering start and his uneven progress there .

All this was a far cry from his persuading his granny to melt plastic in the kitchen at home, so he could remake it into model cars. Gerald, the inventor, reflects today the weft and warp of his varied youth.

3 Early Commercial Ventures and Marriage

Early commercial ventures to finance hand made silver – S. W. Ide platers – Harwell
Atomic Energy – Fibreglass in Portslade – John Bloom – Glacier Metals – Westclox –
Geoffrey Bellamy and Co I D. Marries Janet in 1957 – at wedding is Charles Clee,
benefactor of London University, one of Gerald's first outside private patrons – children –
Janet helps Gerald.

He was a born craftsman, but he hid his true convictions behind an early composite mask. Even his close friends did not realise the speed, precision and love with which he could use his hands. He seemed to be the classic artist playboy, always changing his enthusiasms, always mastering complicated new skills, always dreaming up fun schemes which surprised everyone by their unusual blend of adventure and success. He was known for his motor bikes, big cars, big wall paintings – anything he could change from one function to another, responding to the magnetic appeal of pretty girls with a winning abandon, generally enjoying himself and playing the fool like any other creative adolescent. But underneath it was different.

I was lucky enough to share some of the parties given by him and his RCA friends, and I remember being amazed by their confidence in each other and their enthusiasm for the design work that each of them had in hand. Also, I was impressed by the way in which the girls and the boys sandwiched themselves on top of or underneath each other, a sort of laughing, screaming pile of human happiness. It must have been an uninhibited, delightful time for them at the RCA and during the years soon after while they were still in intimate touch with each other.

It was at this time that I, a normal ex-public school boy, came to know him. I had been for two years as navigating officer in a Royal Navy minesweeper based in Malta in the Mediterranean. That experience gave me a salutary shock. It made me realise how small was the social group I had been brought up in, how thrilling was the world outside. I also began to understand about hard work: we were nearly always sweeping mines, so we hardly ever got any leave, in contrast to my life at school where the British amateur tradition was paramount: a cult of leisured ease was adopted there as a fashionable facade to conceal any necessary effort.

In this context, it was perhaps the overall speed of Gerald's thoughts and reactions which first made me aware of his extraordinary gifts. I met him not so much as a happy-go-lucky student, but more as a serious beginner in what had always been, and still is, a tough and difficult calling, that of an independent silversmith. I was working at Goldsmiths' Hall, trying to find and help young craftsmen, and I noticed that Gerald, unlike some of his elders, was always eager to get more work. He never tried, as they sometimes did, to spin out the job in hand in case no further employment came along; he seemed to my admiring eye to be able to digest any silversmithing problem with dazzling ease, to make his pieces quicker than most craftsmen twice his age.

However, Gerald's first serious commercial ventures were hardly in the field of skilled hand-craft. They were shrewdly intended as a buttress to finance the silversmithing. Silver steadily became the dominant interest of

Gerald's mature years, but he knew it could prove at best a precarious occupation.

He won his growing commercial success through his love of cars. He bought and sold them often, partly to make money, partly because his impatient, restless nature would not allow him to stay still. He always needed fresh experience, and that meant new cars. He paid for his most significant early business venture by selling his car in order to enable him to buy the lease of a well-known trade gold and silver plating workshop, together with the services of its owner, its resident staff gilder, Mr. S. W. Ide.

Then he broadened out the Ide business to include specialised work like cadmium plating, which was extremely well paid. He found varied, specialised clients, like Hoover Ltd., who needed chromium-plating on their electric iron shells. Electro-plating car headlamps and reflectors with silver linings (known as re-silvering) seemed another good idea; they needed redoing every two years or so in order to keep bright. He would charge ten shillings for re-silvering a pair of Marshall reflectors including postage. But at the start the new scheme was losing five shillings a week, which a few years later had grown to about five pounds a week. He found he could not compete successfully with the myriad small family firms already in the headlamp business, many of whom operated on tiny profit margins using the whole family only one of whom was paid, not at all Gerald's scene.

The British government Atomic Energy Research establishment at Harwell presented him with one of those amazing, lucky co-incidences which have occasionally enlivened his career. He got the job to make cadmium-plated nuts and bolts and small parts for the new reactor there. Once, he was delivering these cadmium-plated nuts and bolts in his six-cylinder in-line leather-bodied open four seater silver Crossley, a massive, spectacular tourer. He went right in to the reactor bowl, and saw a little man coming towards him. He turned out to be Sir John Cockcroft the director, who was attracted by the sight of Gerald unloading sophisticated bits of modern technology from a beautiful vintage car. Sir John asked what he was doing; Gerald told him he was unloading absolutely marvellous cadmium-plated passivated nuts and bolts. Sir John's curiosity led him to look under the tonneau cover. He called over a friend who was Dr. Schonland, the director-designate. Gerald made a conquest.

It was a providential moment because Sir John had already been to Goldsmiths' Hall and asked me how to get a centre-piece for Harwell. He had come away with Gerald's name in mind. So now it was easy for him to commission a large silver centre piece for the establishment, one of Gerald's momentous first big jobs. Later, there were more pieces for the Cambridge college of which Sir John was Master 1960 – 1967, the newly

Silver centre piece for the British government's Atomic Energy Research establishment, Harwell, one of Gerald's first big commissions, which partly resulted from Sir John Cockroft seeing Gerald unloading cadmium-plated bolts from his spectacular Crossley car when he was making a delivery to the middle of the AERE

founded Churchill College. Thus, Gerald's love of old cars led to his attracting the notice of a leading patron; his keen business instinct undertaking the pedestrian activity of plating led to his receiving orders from Harwell, and gaining the entree there; and his lively social sense enabled him to make friends with some of Britain's foremost scientists, not always the easiest partners in conversation. His seemingly chaotic interests were melding into a powerful commercial instrument.

His next adventure, was when he joined with a partner Eric Mills – a good friend of his parents – to form "Fibreglass Developments Ltd." in Portslade near Shoreham, not far from Brighton. Fibre glass was a new invention of untried potential. He had the wit to imagine diverse uses for the intractable, unsympathetic material, so tensile, so hard, so cheap to produce. His father refused to provide any financial help, which annoyed him, but his brother Derek, by now head of Ipswich School of Art, was more generous and supportive. Anyway, a packet of fibre glass resin, and a few tins of fibre glass, were all the start capital needed. The Portslade company was tiny – it employed only some twenty people at its height – but his ideas, as usual, were large. The factory manufactured a bewildering range of mouldings: dispensers for Eldorado Ice Cream then one of the favourite

Aluminium ash tray for Parker Pipes Ltd., cast and anodised black. As a student, Gerald was already becoming fluent in glass and furnituremaking as well as in base metals

One of several clocks for Westclox, some of them still in production

Pram with a new type of undercarriage and folding handle, for Atkins Ltd.

Early Commercial Ventures and Marriage

brands for British children; seed propagating trays; and sailing boats.

Most interesting were the washing machine casings for the bold entrepreneur John Bloom of Rolls Razor fame. The old self-stropping razor business had been enlarged dramatically to make and sell a new invention, the washing machine, and it was sold by a revolutionary technique. A large team of salesmen would tour the country knocking on front doors, sometimes jamming the doors open by putting their foot in the opening, so the only way the householder could get rid of the unwelcome visitor was by buying something. Hence the term knocker-boy. Gerald says "We were quite good at turning these out quickly, but Rolls Razor were not quite so good at paying." Gerald had some difficulty in obtaining his due payments from Rolls. He already knew that in business, quick success could lead to total eclipse. So it was to prove with John Bloom's empire.

During a lunch party given at the Ionian Bank for Lord Longford, Gerald heard the other end of the table start discussing John Bloom. That morning a girl had been reported shot on his yacht, and the talk at the bank was to withdraw finance. Michael Behrens, head of the bank, said in his half funny, half caustic way "I don't think I would continue to finance a chap who is careless enough to get his girlfriend shot" … Gerald "shot off to Portslade with the news," and immediately put his company up for sale through advertising it in the Brighton evening paper, the Evening Argus. It was a successful company and sold well, just in time, because John Bloom went out of business three months later with catastrophic results.

At the RCA, Gerald and his friends used to make their own prototype models for industrial production, in metal, the only way they knew how to do it. His involvement in industrial design intensified after he left the RCA: his product designs were varied and successful. He designed prams and canopies, for instance. For Lord Wilkinson he evolved various innovations: at Glacier Metals there was the non-stick sheet from which came no-burn frying pans. In their Scottish Precision die-casting factory in Dumbarton, which he loved, he invented a cantilevered desk lamp which threw the light down onto your desk, instead of into your eyes. I know, because I still use one of them. Journal bearings, an all-purpose device, were made at Alperton. Fire alarms bearing Gerald's lettering on their face, were so successful that they are still in production. He and his friends designed mass-market clocks for Westclox in Scotland, some of them also still in production after nearly half a century.

But modern British industrial design was still groping towards a valid visual vocabulary of its own. Purity alone was not enough to sell the product, and it was here, as well as with hand-made silver, that Gerald's personal fantasy was admired. The Council of Industrial Design was founded by the government to promote British modern design at a time

Journal bearings before and after Gerald's re-design for Lord Wilkinson. Every big piece of machinery has one of these major bearings to support its main drives, but not every goldsmith has the all-round mechanical skill to design them

when we were chiefly known for our replicas of ancient classics. A typical instance was the Wedgwood china, a replica of the set designed for King George III two centuries before. It was chosen surprisingly by Robin Darwin, the Rector, for use at the RCA by the new wave of teachers recruited by him. Even after the new RCA had earned considerable momentum as the home of new British design, it was easier to look backwards and bask in the reflected glory of our prestigious past, than it was to dream up new visual symbols of our uncertain future.

Geoffrey Bellamy, Gerald's RCA friend, joined the Co I D as liaison officer for the silver and allied industries. His job was to encourage good designs, but he had a surprising, rather baleful influence there on Gerald's industrial reputation. It may be, and indeed it did seem to me, that Gerald's standing as a designer, as opposed to a flamboyant silversmith, was unfairly damaged by some of our prim aesthetes who ran the CoID committees of taste, and who presumed to judge what was good design and what was not. Too often, these committees rejected products which, like Gerald's, showed their designer's personality. Gerald simply cannot be so good at so many things, so the committee argument ran. He can obviously make luxury commissioned silver, but he cannot discipline his riotous imagination to make the sort of utility modern design favoured by the Co I D, simple shapes for the austere post-war world.

It was a bad argument because the best designs need not be the plainest, and furthermore, the plainest often sell the worst. Nevertheless, the Co I D under Geoffrey Bellamy soon rejected from its index and public displays, products designed by Gerald for no less than eight different companies, much to the dismay of the companies concerned. Gerald consoled himself by reflecting on the commercial success of products designed by him. Other designers' work might win more prizes, but the most important prize of all, financial security, went to Gerald.

Silver was beckoning him on, industry was providing him with some necessary cash stability, but the hammer-man of the age had still not yet found his true career.

Girls were always vital to Gerald's creative spark, and they still are. It would be impertinent of me to try to analyse their appeal. But I could perhaps advance the theory that Gerald's brain, and his consequent conversation, are as much feminine as they are masculine. He is a great lateral thinker: only thus could he have become during the war such a master of reusing old artefacts to make new. Turning scraps from crashed cars into saleable model aircraft, for instance, often causing a bewildering change of direction in the existence and nature of materials.

Such flashes of enlightenment may seldom occur to men, but are normal for women as they restructure the world in a moment's chat at their street corner. I could almost claim that men usually have a potential to be pompous, talking about infra-structure and doing nothing, whereas women prefer to cut the cackle and get on with the job in hand. If women are like this, then Gerald is mentally like a woman.

Women are not only an example to him because of their quick thinking. They appeal to him in many other ways too. He loves beauty in all its forms, so what more natural than that he should want to look at beautiful girls and to be with them.

Asked how his wife Janet had helped him, he said "Always", a good tribute to his devoted supporter over 42 years. He tells their story with characteristic openness. In 1955 he was teaching in his father's school at Brighton when John Donald, now a famous jeweller and still Gerald's great friend, phoned. He told Gerald he had found three rather interesting girls from the same ballet school in London, and needed Gerald's help to sort them out, because they were all going to arrive together for an evening out. Gerald immediately responded to John's invitation to meet in a pub in Oxford Street, London, dropped his tools, caught the next train to Victoria, and got there an hour before anyone else. After several drinks, he was what he calls "slightly going quite well". In came an amazingly attractive lady. She was Janet, and they got married very soon after this first meeting.

Gerald and Janet after their wedding at Sherborne St. John, near Basingstoke

The only other serious candidate for Gerald's hand seems to have been Molly Parkin. He loved to be with Molly, then known for her life-enhancing delight in men. Molly seems to have been friendly with several of the young blades who were bringing a new glamour to silversmithing as students at the Royal College Art. She probably played a part in waking them all up to the potential of life in the big city of London, as opposed to life in the tight, small, post-war organisations in which they had all been nurtured. Molly was very lively, called affectionately by some a crazy type. She was, like Janet, a journalist, but, unlike Janet, perhaps more involved with the world at large, less with her own intimate friends. Anyway, it was Janet who won Gerald, and the resulting partnership between them has been a pleasure and inspiration not only for each other, but for all their friends too.

Ideas on marriage have changed dramatically during the past century. In 1857 Charles Dickens wrote the novel "Little Dorrit", and in it he described the aspirations of an ageing unmarried lady, for whom marriage would have been the natural fulfilment of her life. Drawing and watercolour painting were then a common occupation for such unmarried women. Dickens suggests with subtlety and humour how the pencil and the paintbrush might lead to the altar. She was "a very decidedly grown up daughter indeed, which daughter went sketching about the universe in the expectation of ultimately toning herself off into the married state".

A century later, marriage was already beginning to seem to some women more like slavery than fulfilment, and it slowly became almost the norm to live with your man and evaluate him thoroughly, before marrying him. Now, a further half century on after Gerald and Janet's wedding, permanent relationships seem to be still rarer, and temporary links of convenience have often displaced the serious obligations of personal loyalty. All the more remarkable therefore, that she and Gerald came to suit each other so well for so long, and to help each other in the mercurial situations which they frequently created for themselves.

Janet was brought up on a farm at Ramsdell near the last Benney home at Beenham, where her father owned a building company. The marriage in 1957 was in the tiny medieval church at Sherborne St. John, where I remember finding myself next to a distinguished elderly man. I was moved when I discovered he was Charles Clee, probably Gerald's first devoted private client. He had just commissioned from Gerald, and given to London University, a pair of large round bowls with erratic, exciting pierced covers. Clee was in the forefront of a splendid new trend towards commissioning new silver, and he represented another equally welcome tendency, for Gerald's clients to become intimate friends as well.

Janet Edwards as she was before she married, was a writer on "Woman's Journal", one of the mass circulation magazines which transformed post-war Britain with their revelations about the new place of modern women in family life. She gave up regular journalism soon after their marriage,

Gerald invented this type of large bowl with fantastic pierced cover, and made more than fifty of them over four decades. Charles Clee commissioned a pair like this and gave them to London University

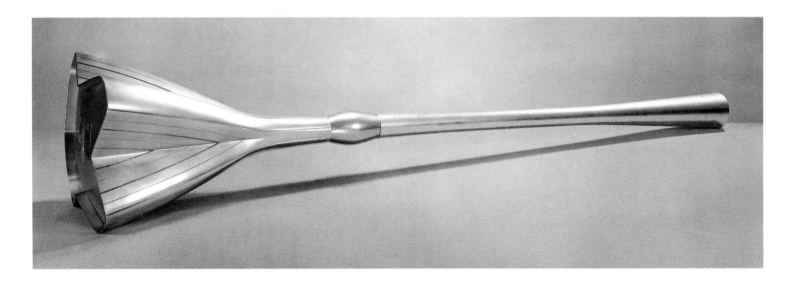

perhaps because Gerald did not want her to have independent work of her own – for many husbands, the proper place for a wife was still in those far-off days in the home. As he said in a later interview, he wanted his wife to be a mother. Perhaps, too, Gerald genuinely needed her practical help in his growing business.

She did his typing, worked out the complicated rates for Purchase Tax (later to become Value Added Tax or VAT), organised his publicity, and helped to look after his clients, as well as running their tiny first flat in Carlyle Square off the King's Road in Chelsea. In addition, she wrote children's stories and books, adventure stories, and stories for television, then in its infancy.

Gerald sometimes had problems with clients who did not understand the niceties of his provocative designs. Janet would make sure that his personality would convince his clients even if his designs were causing some hesitation. His patience was sometimes fully stretched, as when he was holding a red hot soldering iron in front of him, there was smoke everywhere, and he just wished that everyone would go away and leave him to continue his silversmithing in peace. On such occasions, Janet always seemed to be on hand.

She helped with her feminine insight: once, he complained he was having dreams. She said "don't complain, just remember them. They may contain useful messages". So it proved in at least one specific area: it seemed that, surprisingly, the more staff and equipment they enrolled, the larger their debts became. The dream, as recalled, entailed the sacking of everybody . Janet said "try it" and he did, paying off all the plating and polishing activity. Silver continued, a moderately profitable song without these over-ambitious accompanying descants. She continued to run the office, coming to London some two days a week, after they had moved to Berkshire.

Mace with details commissioned by Charles Clee and given by him to London University in 1957. The mace was carried in front of the Chancellor, then Lord Athlone, and is displayed on great occasions. Ancient British universities and public bodies often possess beautiful silver with which to embellish their ceremonies and corporate activity. In the '50s, the Worshipful Company of Goldsmiths led efforts throughout the country, to encourage private and public benefactors to commission new plate for presentation to newer institutions to enrich their corporate lives

During the six years after their marriage, they produced four children, partly looked after by an au pair girl. Paul, the oldest, is a successful and versatile painter, for the past six years sharing his time between living in a barge on the Thames near Kew, and in the family apartment in New York. He once showed me round the art galleries of the New York avant garde in Greenwich Village West, and the high quality of his artistic vision was obvious. He has exhibited his mysterious semi-abstract double-meaning compositions fairly often, in New York, Chicago, Boston, Barcelona and London. His parents own impressive portraits by Paul of them; he prefers not to be known as a portrait painter, but the exceptional quality of his latest commission from Jacob Rothschild (now Lord Rothschild) to paint some of the leaders of the Israeli nation in Jerusalem, makes it difficult for him to avoid that label. It was to celebrate Paul's birth that in 1961 Gerald, always very generous, gave to Janet the beautiful silver gilt and emu egg goblet, which she still uses for drinking all sorts of exotic concoctions at home.

Jonathan, the second child, began at Christie's and is now a skilled gilder and furniture restorer, currently working on antique furnishings at Lord Codrington's old house, the Palladian masterpiece Doddington Park not far away from Beenham, which will take him years to complete. His other clients include such varied names as Buckingham Palace, St. James's Palace, and MGM Studios.

Genevieve, after Downe House, was appointed to a secretarial job with the Prince of Wales. After five years, she tried Public Relations, then returned to Buckingham Palace where she became personal assistant to the Prince, during much of the time of the the sad separation of the Prince from the Princess of Wales. The Prince has been a client of Gerald for

Janet and Gerald painted by their oldest son Paul, 36 x 29 inches. The portraits were hung in the position of honour in the living room at Beenham

twenty six years at least, but that was through different links: Gerald says with a smile that Genevieve is so high-minded that the only royal benefit she has deigned to extend his way, is very occasional access to the royal car park in St James's Palace.

Simon is for our purpose the most important of the four children, because in 1994 he opened and organised the finance for Gerald's first retail shop, which now belongs to Simon. He manages this smart little shop, "Benney" at 73 Walton Street, London, near Harrods, and designs the jewels there, fine, convincing, unpretentious pieces which will last for ever. This all came after his jobs in Australia, Hong Kong and Japan, a good international apprenticeship. Simon is well qualified, having also worked at Christie's, and having passed the diploma of the US Gemological Institute in Santa Monica, California, a respected international institution. It is there that you can learn to differentiate between diamonds and paste in this age when a genuine stone is almost indistinguishable from a fake. Simon came

Gerald's son Simon who set up the Benney shop at 73 Walton Street, London, in 1994, and now manages it, transforming Gerald's sales

Through the sixties, the Worshipful Company organised many exhibitions overseas in order to encourage exports of new British silver and jewels, which were then little known, and very different from the simple unadorned pre-war Scandinavian designs. Gerald accompanied some of these missions and was a beneficiary from them. Here, the Worshipful Company's display designed by Alan Irvine and opened by the future President Nixon, at the British Exhibition, New York 1960, in the Coliseum in Columbus Circle, showing some of Gerald's silver in the showcase. Nearby are some of the old furniture and treasures sent from Goldsmiths' Hall in London. Above are some hall-marks as applied at Goldsmiths' Hall from 1400 to the present. Soon after this, Gerald and Janet were in New York helping the Worshipful Company's exhibitions. One was the first exhibition ever held in the new Lincoln Centre concert hall, the other was in Cartier, Fifth Avenue

top in his class of forty budding jewellers, mostly Europeans and Japanese, a distinction which he modestly shrugs off as the product not of talent but of hard work.

So the Benney family remain a united source of strength to Gerald and Janet, and certainly consumed much of Janet's energy in the early days. She was an excellent mother. She gave up full-time journalism, but managed somehow to make time to continue to write children's stories, and her experience with newspapers and magazines came into play in the increasingly professional world of public relations. She guided Gerald through the jungle of making press releases and press parties without which few free-lance workers could hope to survive. And she always seemed to be ready to help him with his letters and accounts.

Gerald and Janet organised their staff with strict discipline and regular working hours, leavened by good pay, a sense of humour and a close team relationship. None of these were normal in craft workshops at the time: devotion to the work in hand was, it is true, evident in any worth-while

Gerald designed and made a new collection for his one-man show at the Rutland Gallery in London in 1968, distinguished by a round circle of solid gold inlaid into each piece of silver. Each piece was numbered as part of a limited edition, as is usual with pictures and prints sold in series in a fine art gallery. Thus, the Rutland collection bridged the gap between craft and fine art, which normally determines that craft earns much lower prices than art. Art collectors prefer their purchases to be distinctive and part of a numbered unique series

workshop, but regularity of any sort was a rarity: most workshops showed a dreamy sentimentality to visitors such as myself, with erratic hours and probably uncertain pay too.

I was once with Janet when she was organising the annual staff treat for the craftsmen. It took the form of a dinner at the Playboy Club in Park Lane, a new concept of male pleasure where men came close to scantily clad gorgeous girls but were not expected to touch them. Janet suggested to me the nature of the titillations involved. Then I heard her making the necessary reservations by phone. She explained to the Playboy manager just how much exposure to modern glamour-girls her craftsmen could stand. I was impressed with her knowledge of the world.

She came to New York with a group of craftsmen invited by us at Goldsmiths' Hall. We had featured Gerald's work on our display designed by Alan Irvine and opened by Richard Nixon, later President of USA, at the British Exhibition in the Coliseum in 1960. Then in 1968 we staged the first exhibition ever held at the new Lincoln Centre, where Leonard Bernstein the conductor, and the New York Philharmonic Society members, seemed pleased by our glittering little cube showcases in the entrance foyer. At Cartier in Fifth Avenue, we presented new British silver and jewels for sale, including Gerald's latest work. It was a complex feat of organisation. It was then that I became aware for the first time of her extreme efficiency, which, allied with her undoubted charm, make her such a practical asset to Gerald.

Olivetti were, then as now, leaders of modern design, and therefore much admired by our team of young designer/craftsmen. The Olivetti Fifth

Small tree in 18 carat gold with pale carved Chinese emerald fruits on the branches, and nephrite jade base surmounted by cabochon rubics. When Alistair McAlpine first saw it, he said to Gerald it was "the only serious anti-art piece I ever commissioned". Nobody knew what he meant, but he certainly attracted attention to the charming, precious tree, which may have been his intention. Later Lord McAlpine gave it to his wife Sarah who has now lent it to the Victoria and Albert Museum

Emu egg-shell and silver gilt goblet made by Gerald for his wife on the birth of their first child, Paul

Watering can incorporating a
gold mouse set with ruby eyes
on a holly handle

Avenue showroom had as a publicity attraction on the pavement outside, one of the famous Olivetti 22 typewriters mounted on a pedestal and ready for use. She could not resist tapping the keys. The resulting speed and fluency were amazing to hardened New York passers-by, just as they were to us inexperienced Englishmen.

She is practical and logical, but she also has an understanding of the agonies and quirks and oddities of the creative process. Gerald was invited by Garrards to design wedding silver for the "wedding of the century", of the beautiful young Lady Diana Spencer and the heir to the throne, the Prince of Wales. It was a superb occasion. The glamour of the couple and the splendour of the pageantry caught the imagination of the whole nation, even of the whole world.

Gerald found himself over-awed, uncharacteristically devoid of appropriate ideas. He does not design royal platitudes such as were and are common on royal occasions, and he did not know how far his own personal art fantasies might be digested into such a context with the eyes of the world upon it. Janet came to his rescue. "Stay in bed all day" she exhorted him (normally he is a very early riser, so her idea was quite revolutionary for him to accept). She gave him his drawing pad and pencils, a copy of Debrett's Peerage, and the instruction "Now get on with it, using details from the coats of arms." He did, and the job was considered a triumph by all concerned.

Another temporary embarrassment for Gerald was when his friend and major patron Alistair McAlpine gave him some wonderful carved emerald pieces, some way removed from Gerald's usual artistic vocabulary. Janet brought him a succulent plant with weird leaf formations. "Look" she said "Make a tree like this using the emerald as the leaves" Alistair was enchanted with the invention, oriental and exquisite in feeling, yet also formed from the sinewy and direct lines which give Gerald's art its special identity. He said "Gerald, this is the only serious anti-art piece that I have ever commissioned". Nobody knew exactly what he meant, but the remark made an impact which it was no doubt intended to do. Probably Alistair was suggesting that the piece was unlike anything he had ever seen before, which is true.

One-man exhibitions are unusual for silversmiths and jewellers: the worry of security and insurance problems too often frightens off the latent enthusiasm of gallery owners and managers. It was therefore an occasion for Gerald to be offered a large show by Christopher Bibby in his Rutland Gallery off Bond Street, near London's fashionable church St George's, Hanover Square. Gerald wanted to differentiate all his exhibits from his routine products, making them into a limited edition which would give them an appeal to collectors. He had this promising idea in principle, which might help his art as well as his marketing, but he faltered at the moment of

execution and could not think of any way of marking the Rutland Collection more effective than numbering each piece as is done with artists' prints.

Janet sat him down in the Drawing Room, practically locking the door, and invited him to look around the room. "Somewhere in this room there's a shape or a shadow or a texture which will give you the theme for the exhibition." He found a Japanese box on a table, with the sun emblem. This germinated into a visual system to give unique status to the new Rutland silver collection. He inlaid a round gold circle into each piece of the Rutland collection, giving it all at once the indefinable lure of gold, an original and stylish art insignia somewhat reminiscent of the logo on the top of the bonnet of a great car, and a solid talking point to attract the journalists, always hungry for novelty. The collection sold well and introduced Gerald to new clients.

Steady support, such as Janet gives to Gerald, is lovely to behold. But perhaps more evident, even if less important, is her instinct for collecting. Sardine dishes and Goldsmiths' Hall china dinner plates, dresses, cheese

The stately rooms at Beenham made an exciting setting for big parties and for important discussions of new commissions for silver. Often one led to the other

The Georgian wrought iron staircase balustrade, one of the best features of the interior

covers, old spectacles, sewing machines, wash basins, silver fruit knives and jars, all these nudged against each other on shelves, and hung on the great walls round the big rooms at the old Benney home, Beenham House. They gazed at you as they lay in their open drawers and humanised the big spaces there. No doubt the new Benney home will similarly throb with these visual echoes of the couple's original taste.

These often amazing things may not be valuable, may not even be beautiful in any conventional sense, but they are curious and personal, and it is Janet who locates them and her magpie instincts which assemble them. Of course, Gerald with his gimlet eye stimulates and maybe sometimes regulates Janet's aesthetic appetite. But he generously attributes the love of small, personal treasures primarily to her.

Parties at Beenham were always memorable. Lunch for thirty friends was, as Gerald says, 'nothing'. When necessary there might be 200 guests, sitting eight at a table and using all three big rooms, 'a bit cramped' he says, but it was worth while to raise funds for charity.

Then there is her new life importing French horses, of which she often has as many as two dozen at a time in training. The art of horse eventing is a demanding one, with the stabling, breeding, training, travel, catering and finance which those skills involve. But my description of that, not to speak of her fund-raising for charities, has to wait until my narrative leaves these past excitements and arrives at the beckoning open horizons of the present and the future.

Beenham House, Berkshire. The Benney home for 34 years

4 The Workshops

The workshops – Whitfield Place and S. W. Ide – 19 Chester Street and Louis Osman –
Falcon Wharf, Bankside – Bear Lane, Southwark – 25% VAT imposed by Denis Healey –
Gerald pays off 22 staff making them redundant – 10 years of debt, disappointing times–
Beenham.

In Moscow I once felt tired and sat down on the floor of the studio of an eminent abstract painter. She looked queerly at me but said nothing, until my English friend and guide reminded me that an artist's studio is the place most intimate to him or her. "If you respect the art and the artist, you must respect the place, too", he said, so "please stand up". I stood, and all of us were able to smile again.

I had not till then realised how much of an artist's identity may be buried among the debris of stacked pictures, paint on the floor, tools on the tables, hammers and stakes or anvils in racks on the wall, metal sheets in the corners. I had somehow assumed that the private importance of an artist's studio diminished if the artist was not well known. But artists' studios are much more important to the artists concerned than the usual clutter in them might imply.

Gerald's several workshops, all of which I have been lucky enough to know, reflect his personality as truly as any photograph or portrait. But I can here only hint at the physical reality, not delve into the personal overtones beneath that reality.

For some artists, their home is sacrosanct, beautiful, and maybe unreal. Their workshop, by contrast, is a place of creative experiment, of drama and mess, of sketches and models and fragments. Not so Gerald. He seldom allows his surges of creative imagination to overflow into unharnessed chaos, and his mind is always ruminating on the next design opportunity. So he doesn't exile his silver away from his home, nor anaesthetise his home life so that you never see a drawing by him lying on the sitting room table. Specially in the early days, the discipline of work might be felt at home, and the graces of home, the light buffet or the civilised aperitifs, might stray into the workshop.

His first true workshop, in 1953, was in a large warehouse building, Suffolk House, Whitfield Place, Whitfield Street, off Tottenham Court Road. It had in fact once been a workhouse for the poor, which is how Gerald amusingly defines its practical function while he was there.

In his last term at the Royal College of Art, he heard that the electroplating and polishing company owned and managed by Mr. S. W. Ide was closing down. Gerald had used them for some time. One day, he cycled to the workshop to arrange for them to gold plate the inside of the first chalice he had made – they were the best gold-platers in London. There Mr. Ide told him this was the last job he would do, because he was determined to retire. Gerald cycled back to the RCA, and on the way realised that he had just seen exactly the sort of big empty workshop that he needed. He returned and discovered the lease was very cheap, conditional upon his repairing the bomb damage for which the tenant would eventually be responsible. Bombs had destroyed the floors, so you walked from bench to bench along builders' planks, through which you could see the cardboard box factory beneath, and the leather case-makers upstairs. Not safe, but cheap, in fact about the same price that he knew he could obtain from selling his current car, his rare and beloved Citroen Light 12, 1938 vintage.

He bought a thirty year lease without review, and persuaded Mr Ide to stay on to continue the gold-plating. For three years, Gerald continued the plating and polishing business there under the old name Ide, and Mr Ide showed him how to handle the plating vats. Resilvering car headlamp reflectors became the main activity. That helped his cash flow. And the workshop had a good London W. 1 address, useful to improve his business credibility.

It was there that he gave me the first of many lessons in practical economy: wood was cheap, conventional wall was expensive. He claimed to me that the cheapest, as well as the smartest form of internal walling, was simple tongue and groove planking. It needed no fitting and it looked clean, cheerful and modern, in fact it formed the ideal ambience for the little design studio into which he used to welcome me among his broken floor boards, his stinking vats and his murky windows. Eventually, after some fifteen years there, the whole block was bought for redevelopment by a property developer, Max Rayne of London Merchant Securities, and Gerald was bought out.

In 1960, soon after Paul was born, Gerald and Janet signed a sixty year lease of 19 Chester Street, Grosvenor Place, from the owners, Grosvenor Estates. The annual charge was only £250, ridiculously low, but there was dry rot on all six floors of the big Victorian terrace building in Belgravia, and the lease was conditional on Gerald commissioning the well-known architect Louis Osman to eliminate the decay. Gerald already knew Louis through the sculptor David Wynne: Louis had employed David in his visionary reconstruction of the Convent of the Holy Child in Cavendish Square. Gerald liked Louis and admired his work, so readily agreed to become his client. Janet's father was sympathetic to the project. He sent in a team from his construction company near Basingstoke who worked and slept on site during the following weeks. It was dangerous and difficult work, but the stage seemed set for a masterly creation.

What Gerald did not then know, was that Louis' extraordinary imagination habitually outstripped the mundane limitations of his budget, with dire effects on some of Louis' clients. Gerald's job turned out to be a much bigger operation than anyone had foreseen, involving an almost total rebuild, stripping out the five floors and taking down the back wall. After the demolition, before the rebuild had even begun, all the funds available to Gerald for the whole house had been used.

There followed a crippling blow. The door furniture for the whole house

The first family house was of spectacular modern quality, designed by Louis Osman at 19 Chester Street, Belgrave Square. Here, Gerald uses it for a lunch party in 1960 to launch the "Chelsea" pattern cutlery which he designed between 1958 and 1962 for Viners of Sheffield, and which was so successful that it transformed the British cutlery industry. He is talking to Viners' advertising agent

had been designed by Louis and cast in bronze by the Morrris Singer foundry. It arrived in two vans, an ominous sign. The invoice cost for this bronze was actually bigger than the first estimated cost of the whole rebuild. Gerald and Janet ended up with a beautiful house and no furniture other than doorknobs and hinges. It says much for Gerald's love of creative design, that he continued to admire Louis' work through all the builders' dust and rubble, through all the financial nightmares, and remained one of Louis' closest friends. Indeed, at Louis' funeral in remotest Wales in 1996, Gerald was the only one of Louis' many silversmithing friends, who was able to make the effort to be there.

As a friend and admirer of Louis, I used to try to protect him from the grosser charges of mis-management, and at about this time I found an unexpected ally, no less an authority than the British Prime Minister. No. 10 Downing Street had to be restored and partly rebuilt. The timing and the budget there had the attentions of British Ministries, of Treasury experts and of a very cautious architect. Nevertheless, the huge escalation of costs for the Downing Street job – a much bigger escalation than any of Louis – would have become a national scandal had it not been hushed up by some nifty political footwork at the top, such as was not available to the unfortunate Louis. The fact is that the new science of restoring buildings to an accurate budget, and indeed of architectural budgets generally, was hardly then born. Surprisingly, the situation had hardly improved three decades later when Goldsmiths' Hall in the City was restored. There, as in Downing Street, great reputations were deployed in the cause of financial control. As so often, the wood-worms had the last word.

The Chester Street saga had a happier end than it probably deserved. Gerald was soon able to sell the top floors to the chief executive of the Kellog oil company, whose family soon became close friends. Three children and an au pair girl later, expansion became imperative. Advertising of the ground floor and basement was by the new master of the property market, Roy Brooks, who had invented a new commercial idiom based on rather smart and funny jokes. His first day of advertising the Chester Street house won a cash sale. Perhaps this welcome success was because of the spectacular quality of Louis' interiors; they had been in colour on the front cover of "Ideal Home", and, amongst others, in "Architectural Review"and "Daily Telegraph". The unique character of Louis' work had after all paid off.

Meanwhile, Gerald's being forced to leave his workshop in Whitfield Place had proved to be a blessing in disguise. By then, his big client Alistair McAlpine had become a friend too, with whom Gerald could share his hopes. One day they were chatting and Gerald rather casually mentioned his workshop problem, wondering if Alistair had an idea. He had, and it was

An early press showing for an exhibition at Goldsmiths' Hall. L to R Frank Beck, master siversmith, Gerald, Robert Welch, Louis Osman who designed the Chester Street studio and home

characteristically big and generous. The McAlpine building firm came to Gerald's rescue, and built him a new workshop on his dream site. It was called The Falcon Deep Drawing Dock.

McAlpines owned derelict property on the South Bank of the River Thames opposite St. Paul's Cathedral. It was a whole dock with two cottages and a huge crane on it, a decaying survival from the days when the Thames with its boats and barges was the great traffic artery for the world's greatest city. Falcon Dock had been a big sailing ship repair dock in the 16th century.

Gerald obtained planning permission to build a new workshop there, and in 1969 took on the lease of Falcon Wharf, Bankside. Gordon Bowyer, friend and architect, designed a classic rectangular box of great style and beauty, made mostly of glass and steel. The Thames there is tidal, and therefore carries salt water. Gerald filled in the dock, but the tide still managed to come bubbling up the drains, polluting the bath with not-so-pure salt water on several occasions. Gerald wanted to humanise the area by planting some trees, which had to be tolerant of salt, a difficult botanical

Gerald's first purpose-built workshop, at Falcon Wharf, was on the bank of the River Thames opposite St. Paul's Cathedral. The chimney on the right was the South London Lighting Company; the low rectangular silhouette of Gerald's Falcon Wharf workshop (demolished after only two years) is just visible to the left of this chimney

The bomb-damage and industrial squalor around, made arrival inside the Bear Lane workshop a dramatic experience

requirement. The hole for the first tree was dug, and promptly filled up with salt water! Nothing daunted, Gerald planted there a huge 20 ft. Maple from Hilliers, which to everyone's delight grew like Jack's beanstalk in the fairy story. Nearly an overnight phenomenon like Jack's, the Maple soon came to dominate the car park.

These were big, sunny, workshops with a little apartment attached for overnight stays, an ideal setting for the creation of beauty. There was space for two hundred cars, and that forgotten stretch of the South Bank can seldom have witnessed such a sudden up-turn in its fortunes. Launch parties for new silver were followed in quick succession by fund-raising with the actor Sam Wanamaker, for his then seemingly unattainable vision of Shakespeare's Globe Theatre nearby, which opened in 1997 and is already a big success.

I remember with excitement and affection the sudden surprise when I used to come upon this clear modern visual statement in the middle of so much ruin, bomb damage, improvised light industry and general squalor which at that time surrounded noble old Southwark Cathedral. No wonder that Gerald again found his workshop home in "Architectural Review" and many other magazines.

Nemesis succeeded nirvana all too quickly. In 1971 Southwark rescinded its planning permission for the construction of the Falcon Wharf workshop, and offered inadequate compensation. Again, McAlpines came to the rescue. They paid slightly better compensation than Southwark had offered, and equipped the new place which Gerald found nearby in Bear Lane. There were four Victorian warehouses, with three small nondescript buildings between. The ceilings were twenty-five feet high with enormous beams seemingly four feet by three, and massive iron strapwork. The romantic, undulating row of craggy old buildings was rather quiet and in a secret position. It backed onto the Blackfriars railway line which had

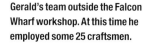

Gerald's team outside the Falcon Wharf workshop. At this time he employed some 25 craftsmen.

The view across the Thames to St. Paul's dome, from the workshop

A colourful and idealistic neighbour was the American actor Sam Wanamaker who eventually realised his dream of recreating Shakespeare's Globe Theatre nearby, opened in 1997. Gerald and Janet helped with several fund-raising parties and projects. Here is Gerald's beaker of 1984, made for sale in USA. Most of these were electro-types made by BJS Ltd

Boxes made in 1987, sold in aid of the Globe Theatre project

Inside the Falcon Wharf
workshop with its smart new
showcases designed by Gordon
Bowyer

minimum current traffic but maximum geographical romance with the
history of its old railway connections to cities as far afield as St. Petersburg
and Budapest.

In 1972 he bought three freeholds and some leaseholds there. With the
help of James Burford, the McAlpine company architect, he re-built the
disorganised pieces of masonry into an integrated model silversmiths'
workshop of some 12,500 square feet. It all seemed too good to be true, and
so it was.

He thought that Labour-controlled Southwark Council had behaved in a
thoughtless and immoral manner. They ought to have thought through
their plans before giving him planning permission, they ought to have
offered him good, not bad, compensation, after he had shown them the true
potential of his amazing site. He looked in vain for some moral sense in his
local authority.

But worse was to come, and it probably represented the low water mark
in Gerald's usually rather buoyant fortunes. Denis Healey, Chancellor of the

Often, a prototype piece will
follow the design. Assembly
involves concentration and
precision. If approved, the piece
will then be repeated into a
complete set of several dozens,
by the team of outworkers. This
is the sort of repeat job which
Gerald began to delegate to his
team of helpers, concentrating
his own efforts onto his creative
design. Alas, the team soon had
to be dispersed when high VAT
forced Gerald to leave Bear Lane
and move everything to
Beenham

Exchequer in the Labour government, had to remedy our national malaise. The "Regulator" he chose was an increase in VAT on luxury goods, from 8% to 25%. This was almost a killer for Gerald , and for many skilled producers like him. Various government schemes to soften the impact of the dreaded tax, were too complicated to have much effect.

He managed to survive for a year with nineteen staff working normally, but by 1974 he realised something had to give, and that something was him and his team of craftsmen. He stopped making stock – there were almost no sales by then – he paid redundancy to his staff, and moved everything to his huge new home at Beenham near Reading. He allowed his qualified craftsmen to retain their tools in the hope that when tax was reduced to more bearable levels, these craftsmen would return to him as self-employed outworkers. To some extent, when the tax came down to 10%, his scheme did work, but the wound had been deep and the damage to Gerald, as to British silversmithing generally, had gone too far.

He hoped that some of his craftsmen would come to Beenham with him. About half a dozen did respond, but family ties proved too strong for some of them. The team was destroyed, and he never saw most of them again.

Rates on the Southwark buildings went up over two years without warning, from some five hundred pounds to seven thousand. The property market slumped like the banks and the fine crafts. Only after six miserable months with a caretaker in residence, did Gerald manage to sell his precious Bear Lane building to another silversmith. This was Grant MacDonald, whose export business in the Middle East may have enabled him to survive

Bowl for the ruby wedding of Lord and Lady Astor of Hever. Knowing he had cancer, Gavin asked Gerald to complete the almost finished bowl in a fortnight, which Gerald managed to do, but sadly Gavin died the day before, after only thirteen days. The gold strawberries represent members of the Astor family

The Montagu Trophy, given by Lord Montagu of Beaulieu to English Heritage when he was its Chairman, then to the Historic Houses Association

Fruit bowl, silver with black oxidised silver lines, commissioned in 1988 by the world's leading engineer, Ove Arup, when his firm employed perhaps 20,000 people world wide. His first piece from Gerald, when he employed only six or eight people in his office in Fitzroy Street near Gerald, was a coffee pot, which had much use as Ove was a good cook. He was a frequent visitor to concerts and exhibitions at Goldsmiths' Hall which nourished his appetite for modern silver. Once, Ove's Finance Director told Gerald he was bringing an "old Arab" to commission some plate. Gerald had misheard the name Ove Arup and could not be sure that Ove was not an old Arab, until his austere taste became apparent

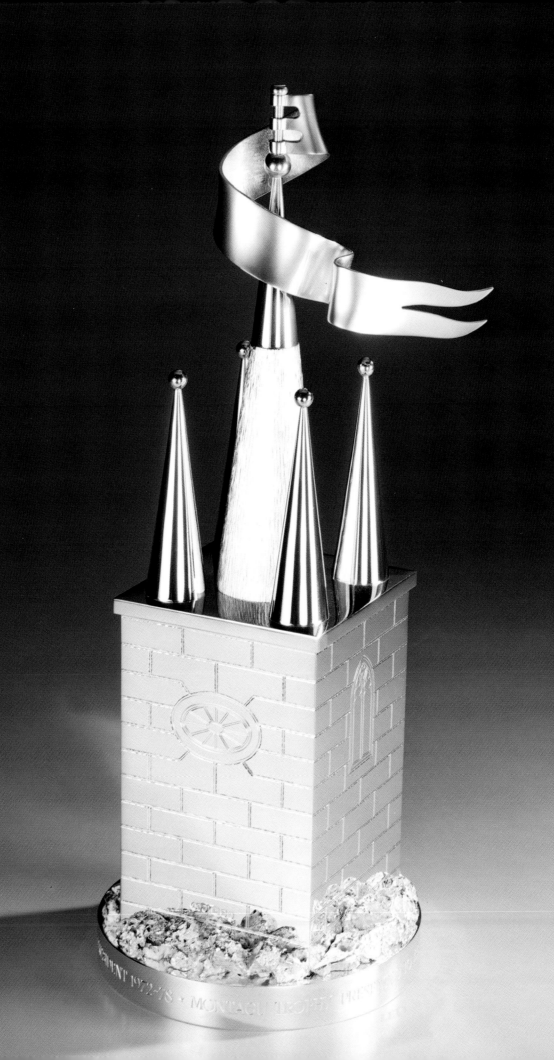

the crisis better than the home-based Gerald. It was a bitter time for Gerald. It is still reflected today by his dislike of the Old Labour Party which he blames for economic mismanagement and for our national malaise, and by his Chairmanship of his local Conservative Party.

He bought Beenham House with thirty acres, at auction in 1963, helped by Michael Behrens' bridging loan, and by Michael's advice to go to property auctions only on rainy days when there would be few serious buyers to brave the weather. There were several reasons for going there: Janet was born some eight miles away from Beenham, so Gerald's parents-in-law, always devoted supporters, were nearby. The Reading Corporation collection of his silver was already growing, and had become such an opportunity for him that it, too, was a temptation to move somewhere nearby. And the planned motorway would make London only an hour away. Initially the journey from Gerald's new home at Beenham to his workshops at Southwark, even with Gerald's high-speed driving, involved a hairy two and a half hours each way every day.

The difference between the sale price for his first home in Chester Street, and the purchase of Beenham, was almost enough to buy the furniture there, and equip the workshops. He immediately started rebuilding and redecorating.

This time, there was no big mistake, but simply a determination to purify what had become an architectural muddle. The big building had Roman bricks in its basement, but the present structure probably began about 1500. When Gerald found it, it was partly Georgian, partly Victorian, and its brick cladding gave it a somewhat gloomy overall impact. The huge roof area was

At Beenham, Gerald's love of mechanical equipment like tractors and lathes, found expression bringing the overgrown park under control. Legally, he had acquired the title of "Lord of the Manor" when he bought the house, and here he is acting the part convincingly

The new workshop at Rawlins Farm, near Beenham

leaking, so the damp made the parquet floors look like old sandwiches, curling up at the corners. Gerald's first painter was hired for an undefined period, and stayed there for sixteen years perfecting the essential works.

Slowly, Beenham became business headquarters as well as home, workshop as well as studio; in 1974, after the savage impact of higher VAT on the silver industries, Gerald moved everything to Beenham and closed his London workshops. The Beenham studios and workshops, the pictures and exhibits, the living rooms and halls and staircases, eventually presented an appearance of ordered vision of which any architect might be proud.

It was expensive, but Gerald sometimes achieved dazzling economies: for instance, he made his showroom out of almost nothing in just two days, of 4 inch cork boards stuck together with wooden meat skewers, linen scrim on top, "Florentine cement finish" everywhere. Economy of means sometimes lead to clarity of impact, and so it was here: this studio made a splendid front cover for Gerald's biggest and smartest silver catalogue in 1983. The revival of Beenham has taken nearly four decades, and it is an achievement almost to measure beside Gerald's superb silver.

It is sad that Gerald decided to sell this part of his life in 1998, and with characteristic speed he concluded the sale before most of us had realised he was even contemplating it. "There are 52 rooms here" he said "and only two of us in them". Nobody could argue with such logic, nobody could grudge Gerald the new creative outlet he has now earned, of building himself a new and manageable workshop in ideal surroundings nearby. His Beenham home was almost as memorable as his craft. I will return to them both as I contemplate the potential of his future.

The upstair showroom at Beenham, made in two days from corkboard impaled on wooden meat skewers coated with linen scrim, a brilliant and economical improvisation by Gerald

5 Private Patrons

The big personal patrons-the Worshipful Company of Goldsmiths and Graham Hughes –
Alistair McAlpine – Michael Behrens and Ionian Bank – Nigel Broackes and Trafalgar
House – the Royal family – the Princess of Wales.

The Worshipful Company of Goldsmiths at Goldsmiths' Hall in the City of London is a wealthy medieval guild, a sort of medieval trade union, called a City Livery Company. It is one of nearly a hundred, each representing a different craft or profession, each with its own character and scope. The Goldsmiths were first mentioned in 1180, and they still actively promote their crafts of gold and silver. I worked at Goldsmiths' Hall from 1950 until 1980, and those were exciting years for British silversmithing as well as for me. As Art Director I helped to organise exhibitions and competitions; to buy new pieces for the collections of old and new silver and jewellery, which are the biggest and the best in the world; to commission and give new silver to new institutions like universities with the intention of generating their appetite for starting a collection of their own; to help other companies and institutions to place their own commissions well – many of them chose to patronise the young Gerald; to help art schools with scholarships and commissions; to install treasuries in cathedrals.

Throughout these three decades, Gerald was constantly playing an intimate part in my life, and I in his. It was a fruitful relationship which helped the Goldsmiths' Company to achieve hitherto undreamed-of stature all over the world as the world's leading patron of new silver and jewels. Usually, the exhibitors bore the main costs, so with very little expenditure by the Company, I was able to stage as many as a dozen exhibitions a year in museums, galleries and stores in the wealthy countries. The Goldsmiths' collections were seen even more actively overseas than at home. America, Australia, South Africa and Japan became the main stages on which we performed, and young British craftsmen were our principal beneficiaries. Latterly, we were able to work with the Crafts Centre of Great Britain, of which I was Hon. Chairman, and we established permanent shows of British work, including Gerald's, in the Seibu store in Tokyo and at Gimbel's wholesale rooms in New York.

Gerald operated within, and contributed to, this framework where our cultural exhibitions often led to commercial results. We would sometimes begin with an exhibition in a museum, then next year we would follow up in a store. And there was always fresh new silver, just made, ready for us to borrow and exhibit. British industry in the 'fifties and 'sixties, was less prosperous and profitable then than it is now. But it attached more importance to prestige and honour, and less to the balance sheet. One of Gerald's patrons is now an ex-director of British Oxygen. He told me in 1998 that British Oxygen, one of the world's big companies, saw itself then rather as if it were the British Empire, with outposts to maintain in each dependent territory. As if to underline their high status, BO commissioned a complete set of dining room silver from Gerald, so that overseas visitors

The medieval City guild, the Worshipful Company of Goldsmiths, encourages its craft by patronising young craftsmen. Important pieces are commissioned and given to public bodies to help to form new collections of modern silver. Centrepiece given by the Worshipful Company in 1955 to Goldsmiths' College, London University

Another of the first large commissions. Their confident ornamental quality distinguishes them from other new silver both British and overseas, which was usually much simpler in concept. This bowl for Henley Administrative Staff College, with which the Worshipful Company was connected, was commissioned in 1956 by a thousand past students

Centrepiece bowl given by the Worshipful Company of Goldsmiths to the City of Birmingham in 1973, to celebrate the bicentenary of Birmingham Assay Office, which started to apply the Birmingham hall-mark in 1773. The bowl features the swirling lines of the motorway intersection system of Spaghetti Junction Birmingham, the centre of the British automobile industry

The first of more than fifty large bowls. Given to the new Leicester University in 1958 by Lord Adrian, its first Chancellor, for the use of succeeding Vice-Chancellors. Lord Adrian's son Richard Adrian was a Freeman of the Worshipful Company and advised his father on this adventurous commission. Later Richard was a liveryman, and eventually Prime Warden of the Worshipful Company

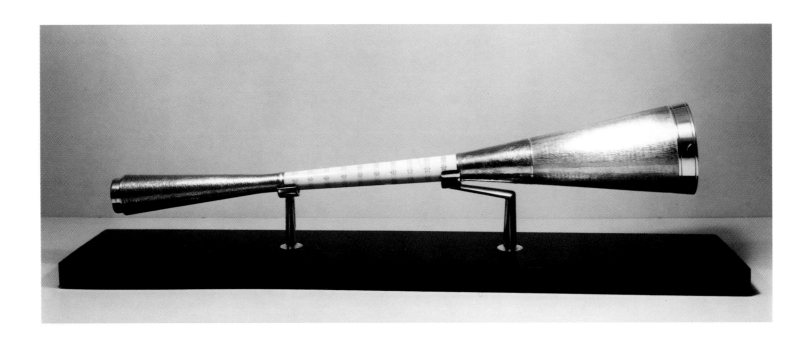

Mace, parcel gilt and ivory, length 40 ins., given by East and West Sussex County Councils, with advice from Goldsmiths' Hall, to Sussex University 1963

Water jugs, 2½ pint capacity, given by the Worshipful Company of Goldsmiths to the new University of Sussex at Brighton, 1963

An early disappointment. This condiment set, 3½" high, was made to order for Arthur Stewart Liberty, owner of the store in Regent Street, London, and a prominent figure on design committees, then refused by his buyer whose name Gerald still remembers, so sharp was the blow he inflicted on the young designer: Mr. Mahoney. Gerald survived what he viewed as this personal betrayal, put the set into batch production, and sold it successfully for years thereafter. It was one of his early pieces to be bought for the Goldsmiths' Hall collection in 1955

Beetle bowl inspired by an underwater microphotograph of bacteria, 22 carat gold eyes set with peridots, 20 ins across, 1962, Goldsmiths' Hall

The first of a big range of boxes in similar idiom, for Bill Shand Kydd. The patterns on the surface are tapped in with a chasing hammer, a new use for an old technique, but the continuous visual rhythm belies the extreme difficulties of the construction process. The yellow squares are solid 18 carat gold. Gold and silver behave differently under the heat of soldering them together, so the creation of a flat sheet made of the two metals demands skill and experience. Similar boxes are in several public collections, including those of 1965 at Goldsmiths' Hall

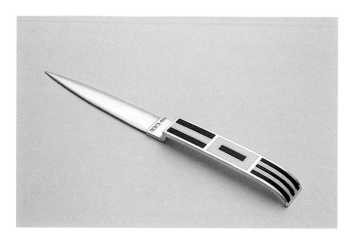

Enamelled paper knife, 1990. Gerald perfected his already skilled enamelling after 1968, bringing new colour and style to his rich designs. Goldsmiths' Hall

In 1987, Gerald won a limited competition for fifty place settings for use at Goldsmiths' Hall. The handles are engraved with the Company's crest, the touchstone and weighing machine used in the process of hall-marking at Goldsmiths' Hall, held up by an Elizabethan lady. The cutlery was made by the London specialist manufacturers C. J. Vander

One of the most recent purchases for the Goldsmiths' Hall collection, enamelled coffee pot 1997. A similar pot was commissioned for the Prime Minister's use at No 10 Downing Street

to BO would realise that Britain had magnificent craftsmen. Today, such powerful and imaginative patronage from British industry would be exceptional. Then, happily for Gerald, it was not rare, even if not exactly normal.

I was able to help the Goldsmiths to become Gerald's first major patron. They bought pieces from him in 1951 when he was still a student and his work was highly controversial, and they continued buying from him into the present day, a remarkable record of 47 years of continuous patronage. Their most recent purchase from him was the enamelled coffee pot, brother piece to that commissioned by the Silver Trust in 1997.

A welcome milestone was the limited competition in 1987 for new knives, spoons and forks, called flatware in the trade, for use on important occasions at Goldsmiths' Hall. The selected front-runners, each of whom made trial models, were Brian Asquith with his ball-ended heavy handles, Hector Miller with his linear grace, and Gerald with his flat textured handles, each hand-engraved with the Company arms. Gerald's submission was chosen, much to his delight, and is now regularly used at the Hall, an excellent ambassador for new British craftsmanship. The eminent visitors there can hardly overlook the message of this flatware, that old British institutions can enjoy new design. Sir Simon Hornby, one of the jury, told me the choice reflected the superior tactile and handling qualities of Gerald's pieces, no doubt the product of his long experience in this field.

The Goldsmiths' set follows a distinguished line of his cutlery, starting with the Ionian Bank, through the Christie's board dining room, ICI, British Oxygen, the Shand Kydd family cutlery, much of it made by the leading cutlery manufacturers of London and Sheffield, C. J. Vander Ltd., under the practical leadership of Richard Vander, Prime Warden of the Company in 1998.

This cutlery proved that he has not lost his inspiration with the passage of four decades: he won the commission in a limited competition against some of the brightest designers in the country, some of them only just out of their teens.

In one way or another, Gerald played a part in most of these innovative schemes. He often used to visit us in the City and became an intimate friend of mine as well as a valued professional associate. I cannot list all his contributions to the welfare of the craft, always eagerly offered and accepted. Typical of many, was his performance when he helped us to mount our big export exhibitions in some of the world's wealthiest markets like Tokyo, Stockholm and New York, demonstrating there his personal ability. Nothing was too small for him, nothing too difficult. He would dust the floor, clean the glass on the showcases, write labels for exhibits in his stylish manuscript calligraphy, unpack and repack our fragile, precious

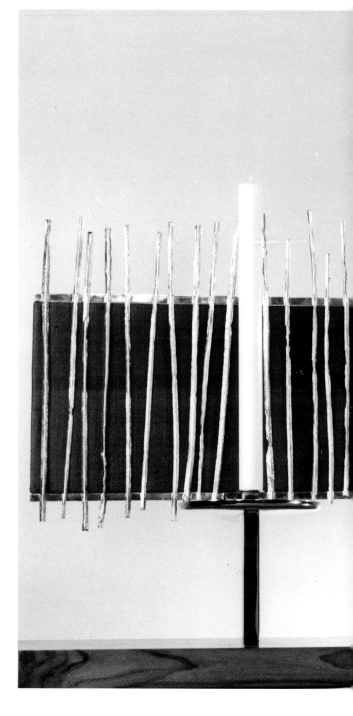

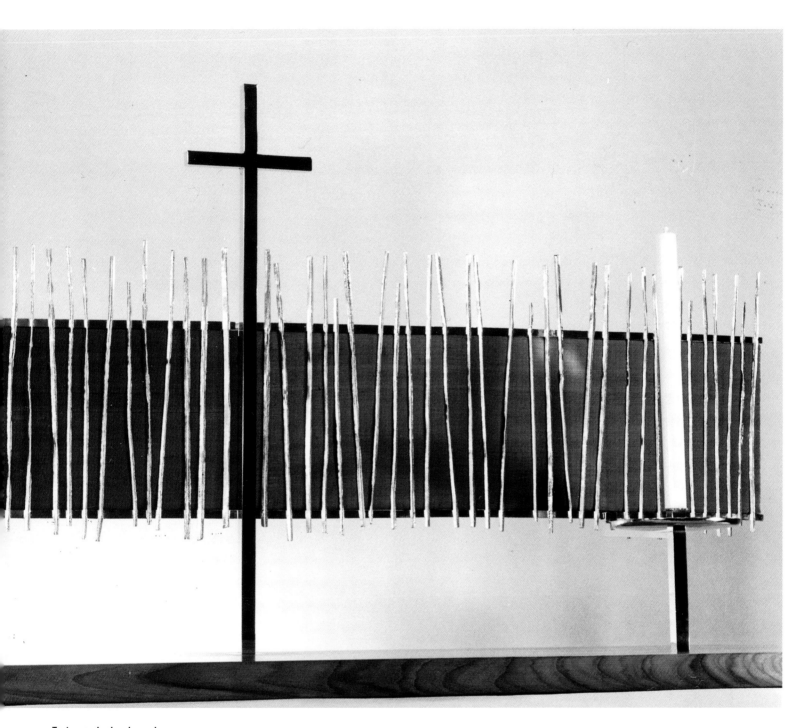

Texture and colour have always fascinated Gerald. This portable altar set with textured silver bars, and backing in Thai silk, was commissioned by the Worshipful Company of Goldsmiths and circulated through USA by the Smithsonian Institution with their exhibition of modern British artist craftsmen

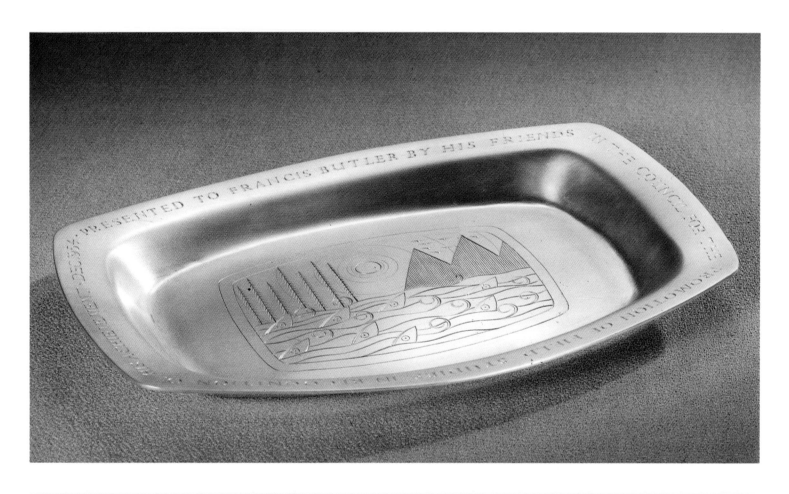

An early small table dish given to Francis Butler in 1954 by the Field Studies Council which he had built up with support from the Worshipful Company. Gerald's cheerful engraving suggests some of the Council's concerns: trees, mountains, lakes, air, sun, birds, fishes

Another early small table tray of 1954, also with engraving by Gerald. The Charrington family, who made the gift, were members of the Worshipful Company

Large bowl commissioned by Bristol City Art Gallery in 1955 to celebrate its 50th anniversary. The Worshipful Company had contact with the gallery because of a modern silver exhibition they organised there. They advised on this piece, one of Gerald's first big centrepieces. It is still on show today at the gallery entrance

**Silver gilt teapot with ivory
handle and blue enamel lid,
given by Bill McAlpine, now Sir
William, to his wife Jill**

The support of patrons is crucial to any craftsman. Alistair McAlpine, now Lord McAlpine of West Green, commissioned much of the best middle period work, as many as 450 pieces. He gave this teapot to his wife Sarah in 1970. After they were divorced, it was acquired by the Victoria and Albert Museum. The carved ivory handle looks like leather, a slow process first used five centuries ago

exhibits from the big laundry baskets in which they were flown round the world (we never lost, nor damaged any of them), entertain visitors and take orders from them, noting everything in our exhibition diary. He would get up earlier and go to bed later than any of us, altogether an example to us of efficiency allied to energy.

Alistair McAlpine, now Lord McAlpine, was one of the earliest admirers of Gerald to back his admiration with his bank balance, and is one of the most provocative people I have ever met. Likened by some to a wild boar because his physical good looks are not self-evident, by others to a genius because he holds such strong views and changes them so often, his public persona and achievements are well known.

He was an active member of the McAlpine family building firm. I once asked him when he, an enthusiast for modern design, would start building modern masterpieces: "Not a cat's hope in Hell" he told me with his usual devastating decisiveness. His firm worked for property developers and architect clients, and could not lay down effective style guide lines for them.

If he tried to dominate his clients' taste, he would lose his clients. He declared to me that there is only one decent new building in London, and that is already quite old: the Economist Building in St. James's.

I once visited him when he was Treasurer of the Tory party under Margaret Thatcher. He was driving a foreign car at the time, going through a period of disenchantment against British engineering. He had just been told he must "Drive British", but he does not respond easily to orders from above. The subject of our meeting was to have been silver, but he stunned me by the violence of his views on motor cars, then as now of only limited interest to both him and to me. Another conversation was more painful to me. He owned a luxury hotel in Perth, Australia, the Parmelia, and employed a friend of mine in it. I suggested to Alistair back in London that my friend deserved promotion, and thereby I caused a noisy storm. Alistair does not always like suggestions from other people.

I recall these trivial incidents only to suggest that Alistair has very independent judgment of his own, flavoured by a low threshold of boredom. What he likes now, he will probably find boring before you and I have even heard of it. His great speed of action is no faster than his changes of mental direction. A lynch pin of the Tory party, he turned away from the Tories in their hour of need, at the 1997 General Election, and became Chairman of the rival Referendum Party.

He is a lover of all the modern arts, a powerful socialite, an ideal patron if you can retain his interest. Probably his first astonishingly generous act of art patronage, was to launch the young sculptor David Wynne in a big way, buying perhaps fifty sculptures by him over a few years, then selling most of them. The same lavish unpredictable treatment was bestowed on Andrew Grima, the leading art jeweller, and, later, on Louis Osman with some of Louis' gold from his gold exhibition at Goldsmiths' Hall. Alistair bought many sculptures of the time by William Tucker and others, seemed to lose interest in them and generously gave many of them to the Tate Gallery. He started, then closed, a lovely bookshop together with a silver and showroom called Erasmus in Cork Street. Later he traded in fine antiquities in upstairs rooms nearby, but he soon closed those doors. Now he has become a lively and admired journalist.

One problem caused more smiles than tears: the glistening silver in the Erasmus shop kept turning into an alarming black. High research proved fruitless, but someone with vision said "it must be the Chinchilla". He had lined his showcases with exotic Chinchilla fur which unexpectedly gave off wafts of sulphur.

Gerald met him through David Wynne after a good lunch in Soho. The rapport was immediate, and continues to this day, even though Alistair's loss of some of the family fortune has dropped him off his high perch as art

18 carat gold table clock with blue and white enamel given by Alistair to his mother Mollie

Young designers usually have to start with small pieces, and Gerald was no exception, as with this wine mug of 1954, 5 ins high, for Professor Ward Perkins, Principal of the British School, Rome. A staff member at Goldsmiths' Hall was connected with the school and was able to suggest the commission

patron. They shared a similar explosive sense of humour, a directness of speech, a direct approach to the complications of life, cutting through problems like a hot knife through butter.

Alistair and his wife Sarah commissioned maybe four hundred and fifty pieces, which Gerald remembers as a colossal amount of his best work. When, sadly, Alistair divorced Sarah in 1978, he gave some of this Gerald treasure, including the jade tree, to the Victoria and Albert Museum, but sent most of it back for Gerald to sell on his behalf.

Alistair once told me his ideal holiday. It was to go all alone for ten days to the luxury Hotel Danieli in Venice, and sit in one of the medieval rooms there, writing poetry looking over the Riva degli Schiavoni. He is galvanic, cathartic and volcanic all in one, and we need more patrons like him.

Gerald's third big personal patron was Michael Behrens. After a chequered stockbroking career, he bought, revived, and became head of the then moribund Ionian Bank. He owned La Reserve restaurant, then a gourmet paradise, and enjoyed using it. He also owned the Hanover Gallery, under its manager Erika Brausen London's prime modern sculpture venue, and from it he enjoyed thrilling sculptures in his homes and at the bank. With his partner Jeremy Harris, he enjoyed having Aladdin's cave sessions, caressing some of their Rothschild inheritance of eighteenth century gold snuff boxes, and some of their newly created dream miniature fantasies in modern gold and silver .

The Ionian Bank led by Michael Behrens, became prosperous through North Sea oil and through property; they were energetic and imaginative patrons. This silver flatware of 1960 has gold ends engraved with the bank's crest. In those days, much business was transacted over protracted and enjoyable lunches in City banks. A guest at some of these meetings, was Sir Geoffrey Ely. He was so impressed with the Ionian bank silver, that he persuaded his colleagues at British Oxygen, a very much larger company than the Ionian, to commission from Gerald a magnificent spectacle, no less than fifty place settings in the early '70s when Gerald was still little known

Sauceboat for the Ionian Bank. Gerald's domestic designs like this are always full of movement, sometimes reminiscent of huge birds or animals dashing forwards

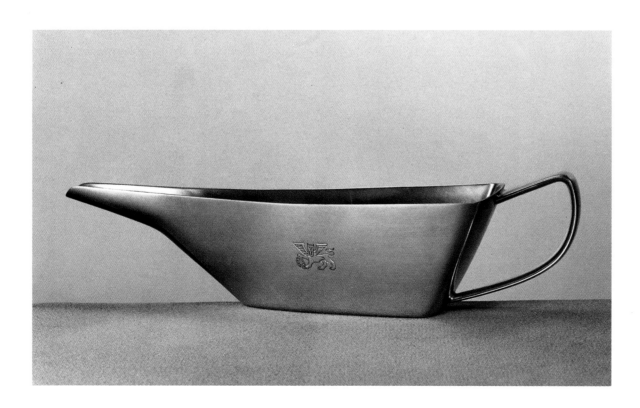

A brave investor in property, Michael once told Gerald never to offer more than half the asking price. Five times out of six, you would be laughed out of court, but the sixth time you might make a fortune. Michael did. One of the results was his paying anonymously for the cleaning of the exterior stonework of St. Paul's Cathedral, for generations a venerable black, now an ethereal white. Then he had the vision to be the first big backer of North Sea Oil, working on it with Phillips Petroleum.

It was at this point that, cheerful as always, he breezed into my office at Goldsmiths' Hall without an appointment. He had been in one of our exhibitions there, and asked me how to commission some new silver to use in his bank's new building in Coleman Street in the City. He took Gerald's name, and with Jeremy was soon inside Gerald's Tottenham Court Road workshop. Gerald remembers this visit well, because it was to change his life dramatically.

Michael and Jeremy looked very smart in their black City overcoats with astrakhan collars. They asked to see Gerald's stock, and Gerald, always disarmingly honest, said he had none. Luckily, however, he did have a pile of unfinished small boxes, and Michael loved fiddling with anything, especially if it was small and precious. The surfaces were getting scratched as one box damaged the next, then five boxes were piled on top of each other and, being only part-complete, fell over and fell apart.

Gerald noticed Michael lift his eyebrows rather sharply, a sign which Gerald later came to recognise and welcome. It meant that a large, quick sale was imminent. Michael asked how much all the boxes would cost. Gerald, stunned, retreated to work out the prices. Eventually the individual pricing proved too difficult for the short time available – already it was clear that Michael was a very quick and impetuous mover, and that this moment at boiling point, if not seized, might pass and cool for ever. Gerald decided to average the box prices and charge the same for them all. Michael asked if this was a mistake, and, on being reassured, flourished his smart personalised cheque book and bought the boxes there and then.

Even better, he then invited Gerald for ideas on silver for forty eight people in the directors' three dining rooms, "the whole works" as Gerald put it. These rooms were light years away from the usual heavy, bankers' bogus Georgian style with which so many bankers try to project an image of wisdom and respectability. They were light, bright and cheerful, with huge tables designed by Alan Irvine, chairs by Stefan Buzas and other leading designers, assertive sculptures by Lynne Chadwick and Elisabeth Frink, and outstanding food and wine to match. Gerald went round the rooms, was fired by all he saw, and was soon busy on the first big corporate commission for new silver since the war.

His main patrons each seem to have had a capacity for fun, despite the worries of running their alarmingly complex business enterprises. The best story Michael told me was about one of the sets of new dining room chairs at the bank. Designers, Gerald included, are usually thin as rakes because they worry so much. This chair designer, world famous for his skills, was no exception. He was very thin, and he had led a narrow aesthetic life. So he did not realise how banking, and the big lunches that used to go with banking, can make bankers fat. At Michael's celebration lunch inaugurating his new furniture, some of his banking guests got stuck in the narrow, elegant chairs and had to be physically hauled out of them. That meant an expensive repeat order for those chairs to be broadened to accommodate fat City of London frames, but Michael, instead of being angry, simply laughed in a Shakespearian way at the human frailty involved. His human understanding was as deep as his aesthetic enthusiasm.

Gerald produced drawings and prototype flatware with 18 carat gold tips on the handles, and he made half a dozen pages of financial estimates. Michael assumed that each page was independent of the others. He did not realise that the total on each page included the previous page. With his

Commissioned by the Ionian Bank and given by them to the Damson Oil Company. The top and bottom of the enamelled flower are open in order to expose an enamelled damson

Sir Nigel Broackes, head of Cunard, the Ritz Hotel, Trafalgar House, and now a Warden of the Worshipful Company of Goldsmiths, is unique among Gerald's patrons and friends, because he taught himself to be a silversmith. One of the four large candelabra which he commissioned for Trafalgar House to give to the Sultan of Oman in the Gulf

Ink wash drawing of Sir Nigel Broackes' yacht 'Mikado' in full sail by Gerald. The sails could be furled at the touch of a button

dazzling mathematical aptitude, he quickly added the totals on each page together, instead of simply looking at the cumulative total at the end. Michael reached a total about twice too big, tens of thousands of pounds higher than Gerald intended, smiled delightedly and said "Fine, that's about right". Gerald pointed out the mistake, Michael overcame his surprise and humiliation, and they became friends for life. The flatware sets were finished about 1960.

Gerald now says nostalgically "those were the days" and so indeed they were. The youthful optimism, the easy attitudes to money, were rare then, probably non-existent today. Gerald sometimes stayed at Culham Court, Michael's beautiful 18th century country home near Henley, where Cecil King had previously lived, and there learned from Michael some of the technique for running a large country house. In Burgundy, Gerald would visit Michael's partner Johnny Trusted, and there absorb at leisure some of the bank's financial wizardry. Michael introduced Gerald to the Eden Rock Hotel at Juin les Pins, perhaps the first time a working silversmith had ever been touched by its interior glamour. It was altogether a fruitful relationship, and the silver commissions for the bank's gifts and celebrations continued almost until Michael's sad death in 1989.

Nigel Broackes, now Sir Nigel, was the fourth giant among Gerald's patrons. They met at Alistair's party on Election night in 1979, and stayed up very late celebrating the Tory victory, a good basis for the friendship which followed. Nigel was already building up Trafalgar House to be a leading conglomerate company, which later counted amongst its more colourful assets the Cunard shipping line, with the enormous QE 2 cruise liner, and the Ritz Hotel. There he accommodated Elisabeth Frink and her husband Alex Czaky when Elisabeth had her solo show at the nearby Royal Academy, sponsored by Trafalgar. Every day as she walked to her exhibition, she used to walk past her bronze horse which Nigel had bought from her and placed in a Piccadilly forecourt which he owned. So he was generous in private as well as conducting his public business with an attractive flourish.

He commissioned Gerald to make a set of silver gilt flatware and dinner plates for the VIP dining room at the Bristol Hotel in London which he owned, and continued for years to present pieces of Gerald's to his business associates. But Nigel had a big surprise for Gerald. At Saturday lunch one day at Beenham, he said he would like to be able to make silver. Gerald finds this is quite a standard conversational gambit, leading nowhere, so was non-plussed when the busy Nigel asked to come over to Beenham the next week, to make a beaker! "Ha!" Gerald thought, "that will slow him down". Gerald showed him how to cut a circle out of a sheet of silver and how to block the edges with a hammer, and went out to catch up on his gardening.

But not for long. Gerald told me: "Bless me if Nigel didn't advance across the lawn in a very short while with a formed bowl, and soon he had made a beaker sufficiently well to be able to drink wine from it at lunch".

Gerald's new pupil came on fast, and presented a unique threat: the better Nigel learned, the less he would buy from Gerald. Nigel's production grew until he was not only making belt buckles to give to his business associates, but candelabra and tableware for his own use at home. Gerald and Janet stayed with the Broackes regularly in the South of France, where Nigel's hospitality raised another problem. It was pointless for Gerald to give a small piece of silver to Nigel to show gratitude; Nigel was now making all his own small pieces. So instead, Gerald drew Nigel's yacht, called Mikado, his house, and numerous young girls who used to decorate the swimming pool there. Fresh air for all concerned.

Nigel told me that, at the height of his business involvement as head of a big international conglomerate company, he made a point of spending at least five hours a week silversmithing. This was quiet, sober craft devotion indeed, another manifestation being his recent Chairmanship of the Craft Council. But I like to think of him spending £1 M enlarging the stern deck of his yacht, which became the longest of its type in the world. Good patrons of art sometimes hide their light under a bushel; they live poorly so their art can have all the cash available. I prefer them to look as confident as the art they buy. President Reagan used to say that good Americans should walk tall, and in the select company of the patrons, Nigel is indeed among the tall ones.

The words "The Establishment" were minted by the journalist Henry Fairlie about this time to describe the narrow group of friends who together helped each other to run the nation. The Royal Family, if not part of it, might seem to have been the umbrella under which the Establishment sheltered. Prying journalists, jealous egalitarians and greedy tax-gatherers have long since spread far and wide the butter of the Establishment, but this intimate, secretive coterie of power-brokers was cosy while it lasted.

The extraordinary thing was that none of Gerald's first three big private patrons, McAlpine, Behrens and Broackes could be called Establishment figures, because they were each radical, original thinkers. At the time when these adventurous spirits were commissioning imaginative new art statements from Gerald, pillars of the Establishment were propping up their decaying institutional structures by buying ready-made replicas of antique silver from the stock of famous retailers.

I hope I have not given the impression that these great patrons were easy to satisfy, or that Gerald's times with them were pure relaxation and pleasure. Good patrons are usually exacting, moody and erratic, and creating for them is anxious and sometimes bewildering. Ted Heath was not

When Ted Heath became Prime Minister, his constituents offered him a present. He said he would like a cheque, but the Town Clerk demurred, so the Prime Minister asked for a big bowl instead. He was very pleased with this cream coloured enamel bowl, and years later, brought it in to Gerald for repair: it had two pock-mark holes in the enamel. Gerald said it was impossible to repair this flawless surface. The only possible remedy was a complete remake. Then he was told the holes were the result of an assassination attempt when a bomb was thrown into the Prime Minister's room. Gerald immediately realised that, even if a repair had been possible, it would have been wrong. The holes must be preserved as a part of British history. The Prime Minister had not looked upon the holes quite in this light, but he readily appreciated Gerald's sympathy with his lucky escape from the threat of death, which was kept secret. The holes remain as a vivid memorial to a squalid incident

18 carat gold decanter, a tour de force of the technique of chasing by Christopher Lawrence, and another superb piece with a picturesque story. Gerald sold the decanter to Ken Whitaker, head of Gerard and National Discount Company and a good patron. Ted Heath who had seen the decanter in Gerald's showroom some weeks before rang up to see if the decanter was available. On hearing that Ken Whitaker had just bought it that very week, he sent a motorcycle detachment to the Whitaker office. The decanter was duly released and Gerald was insructed to engrave GIVEN BY THE RT HON EDWARD HEATH TO M. POMPIDOU ON THE OCCASION OF BRITAINS ENTRY INTO THE EUROPEAN COMMON MARKET. This had to be done overnight as we had heard over the bush telegraph that the French were preparing a gift of 180 pieces of priceless antique Sevres porcelain. At that point the British Government had been minded to give only a rather handsome 19th century British sporting print of fox hunting

untypical. When he became Prime Minister, his Parliamentary constituents offered him a present. He said he would like a cheque, but the Town Clerk demurred, saying a mere cheque would be an inadequate symbol of a great event. Mr. Heath then chose a Benney bowl, but by then time was running out before the date of the presentation. Gerald had to work on it for fourteen hours non-stop in order to be punctual. Many makers would have invited their patron to have more foresight, and refused such a demanding opportunity.

The Royal Family

This family have had an amazing publicity bonanza recently, perhaps more to their detriment than to their advantage. I happened to be in Italy in September 1997 and was able to share at first hand the enormous wave of grief which swept the whole Italian nation, rich and poor alike, when the Princess of Wales was killed in a motor smash. We were offered genuine sympathy dozens of times in two or three days, usually by total strangers, and all we could say, which was true, was that we were very sad, she was so young, so beautiful, might have done so much. "A loss for the whole world, not just for England" was the universal feeling.

Many tears were shed, "Addio, Lady Di" was the mourning front page banner headline in several big daily papers, a leading fashion magazine gave no less than 50 excellent colour pages to a review of her short life, our Italian questioners and friends began to ask us seriously "Will there be a revolution in England against the Royal Family, there is so much rage?" The prosaic Swiss national television programme gave three continuous hours to cover the Princess's funeral.

At home in Britain, there was a traffic jam for a whole week night and day along Kensington High Street, the London highway leading to Kensington Palace, the Princess's home, so that normal activities in the region were paralysed. The traffic was caused not by roadworks nor by exhibition crowds. The cause was myriads of ordinary people walking to the front of Kensington Palace there to leave on the lawns thousands of mourning bouquets of flowers, to build humble shrines of Christian crosses or candles, or simply to stand for hours, even days on end, praying or crying.

What has all this to do with Gerald the devoted craftsman, the last person imaginable to want to drop names? He is the man who has climbed more technical ladders than most, but the social ladder does not interest him. He is the least snobbish person imaginable. Perhaps it is his inherent modesty which partly explains why the Royal Family have become one of his loyal patrons. He finds it difficult to be boastful.

Prince Philip led the way with Gerald, by buying one of his silver boxes

Blue and black enamel box given to the Princess of Wales by the Royal College of Obstetricians and Gynaecologists 1989

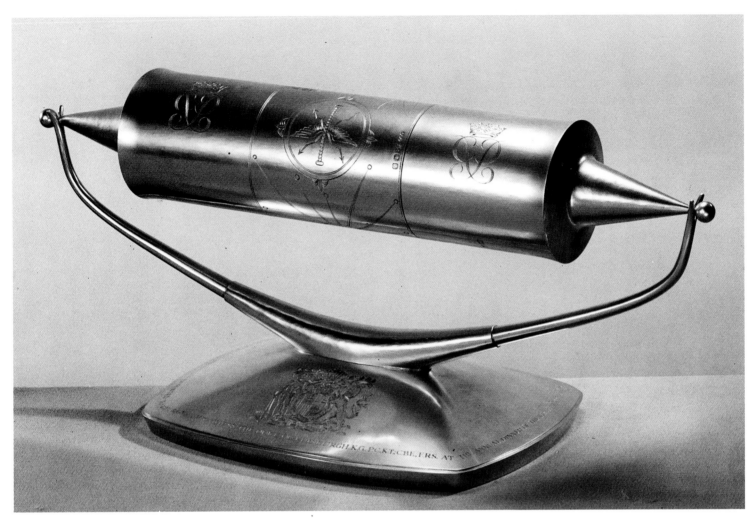

Scrollholder, 17 ins long, a new type of container invented by Gerald for old-fashioned parchment certificates, commissioned by the Institution of Electrical Engineers to give to Prince Philip when he became an Honorary Member 1956. The engraving, designed by Gerald and executed by T. C. F. Wise, symbolises electricity in a typically light-hearted manner

from the Crafts Centre of Great Britain. This was the artist-craftsmen's national co-operative of which he was patron, I was Hon Chairman, and with which Gerald was closely connected, so we all helped each other in quite a constructive way. Sometimes in those days in the '50s, a royal purchase would lead to further royal favours, sometimes not. Whichever way the omens developed, the supplier was not expected to show any commercial initiative: commerce was still considered vulgar, and art was considered part of commerce. Equally sad for the Royal suppliers was the Royal provision that publicity was unwelcome. Gerald's work for the Royal family flourished, but he was not expected to talk about it, still less to put it in the newspapers. So he was tantalised; he enjoyed good royal family patronage, but he could not tell the world at large.

Prince Philip continued to support Gerald. On one occasion, there were happy coincidences which strewed metaphorical roses in Gerald's path. I was consulted at Goldsmiths' Hall by the Institute of Electrical Engineers. They were making Prince Philip an Honorary Member, wanted to give him

A later, more sophisticated scrollholder given by the Borough of Aldershot to the Parachute Regiment with the Freedom of the Borough. The base is teakwood inlaid with silver

Small wine mug in the form of a thistle, gold with green and violet enamel, one of two given to the Queen by the Weir Group when she opened a water desalination plant in Saudi Arabia

Bracelet commissioned occasionally for the Queen to give to visiting VIP's - eminent people who are known colloquially at Buckingham Palace as "Firemen"

a present, and asked me how to do it. They made a brave and unusual decision. The present would be an extraordinary object, a silver container to hold what is normally a useless sheet of paper with no function and no home. And the austere piece of paper would become an object of interest and beauty to its royal owner. It would be rolled not into the normal pompous baroque casket, but into an elegant circular "scroll-holder", an invention of Gerald's, the first of its type ever made.

It is interesting to contemplate how important commissions like this arise. They are usually the result of personal conviction by a few enthusiasts who impregnate each other with the rare, almost electric charge called patronage. There was an illustrious bridge between the progenitors of the new scroll-holder, and his name was Sir Harold Hartley. Sir Harold was probably a fair representative of the Establishment. Certainly he threw his personal bridge over many chasms among the eminent people who ruled Britain. He was on the governing body or Court at Goldsmiths' Hall, and took a keen interest in our patronage activities. He wrote some of Prince Philip's speeches and was a frequent visitor to Buckingham Palace. And he was an Electrical Engineer. So I detected some influence from Sir Harold in this splendid commission for Gerald.

The Queen followed her husband. She bought another box of Gerald's. This was on display in the visionary new shop of jeweller Andrew Grima in London's Jermyn Street. Andrew is an innovative, creative jeweller, who commissioned several of Gerald's friends from the Royal College of Art, including Brian Kneale and Geoffrey Clarke. They designed the shop, with Andrew's brother Frank Grima. The whole corner site became a startling modern sculpture, and it looked like an exotic jewel box. It was a bold move, and it paid off, becoming London's prime centre for the display and sale of modern precious metalwork, and attracting many modern patrons including the Royal Family.

Andrew used to mount important exhibitions in the basement, accompanied by lavish parties. Perhaps more international than Gerald, both by inclination and by upbringing, he soon opened branches in Zürich, Sydney, Tokyo and New York. It was a big loss to London, and to Gerald, when a downturn in business caused Andrew to move to Gstaad, Switzerland. There, in the exclusive old town, he continues to create his personal idiom of theatrical fantasy in gold.

The Queen continued to acquire Gerald's work. Her purchases and commissions gradually became bigger and more personal. Then she started to come to Gerald to satisfy more routine Royal needs, with many orders every year. Gerald remembers how he wanted to up-date the poor quality traditional lettering on one of the highest Royal awards, the Garter, and how he was not allowed to make such a sharp break with tradition.

Coffee set given by the Queen to the Grand Duke and Duchess of Luxembourg during their state visit to Britain in 1972

The Queen's Anniversary Prizes for Higher and Further Education. She presents about twenty annually

The Royal Household's gift to the
Queen and Prince Philip for their
Silver Wedding 1972

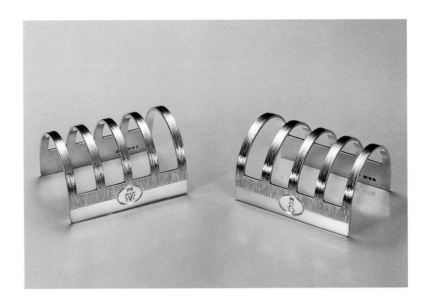

Prince Philip's gift to the Queen
to celebrate their Silver Wedding
1972

Bowl commissioned by the Prince of Wales to give to the Queen for the Silver Jubilee 1977

The gift by Coutts Bank to the Queen and Prince Philip for their Silver Wedding 1972

Decanter stands given by members of the Cabinet to the Queen and Prince Philip, for the Silver Wedding 1972

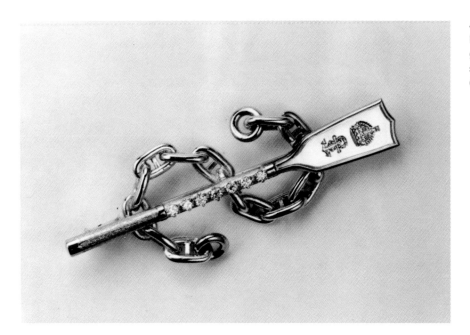

Jewelled oar and anchor chain brooch in gold and diamonds, given to the Queen Mother when she became Lord Warden of the Cinque Ports

He also remembers some amusing meals shared with the Royal family at Buckingham Palace, notably a small dinner party with Lord Plunkett. The Palace, huge and daunting at first, could become a very friendly place.

Next in Gerald's Royal succession, came the Queen Mother, who purchased from Gerald some of what was then his latest idea: his enamels, and used them in her home. She would also sometimes commission larger pieces for her to present to official friends such as the Shah of Persia. A brother medieval City Livery Company to the Goldsmiths, the Fishmongers, reversed the presentation process by giving to her an elegant pink gold salmon in an engraved yellow gold box, the surface chiselled, an early precursor of Gerald's growing interest in textures on metal.

Once, Gerald's great achievements for the Queen Mother took an unexpected knock: affectionately, she stroked with the back of her hand the enamelled lid of a new enamelled box he had made for her. "Oh, how beautiful" she said. Stroke, stroke. Unfortunately, she was wearing a large diamond solitaire ring, and the effect on the enamel was just like the marks made by the first skater on a new ice rink, plus a zipping noise and showers of powdered glass. "Oh, dear!" she said, "This enamel appears to be scratched". We will never know if she realised that it was she who had scratched the enamel, and that there was no fault by the maker. Anyway, Gerald knew the old business adage that the customer is always right, so he did not attempt to clarify the delicate situation. The Queen Mother's admiration for Gerald's art fortunately survived intact.

The energetic, idealistic young Prince of Wales occasionally visited the Crafts Centre of Great Britain. I showed him the work of young designers

Smoking set given to the Queen Mother by the Institute of Chartered Accountants

Private Patrons

Big silver oar given to the Queen
Mother on becoming Lord
Warden of the Cinque Ports

Large standing salt given
by the Queen Mother to the ship
S.S. Northern Star which she
launched

Coloured gold jewel box given to the Queen Mother when she became a member of the Worshipful Company of Fishmongers in 1970. The treatment of the Merman and Mermaid supporters of the Fishmongers' arms, and the salmon on its platter inside, comprise one of Gerald's delightful fantasies. The engraver T. C. F. Wise cut a replica for the Fishmongers' Company to retain in their collection; the engraving was so deep and concentrated that he ended up with a blue thumb

Gold, silver gilt and red enamel box with opal at centre, given by the Queen Mother to the Shah of Iran in 1974. It was the enamelled cover of this box which the Queen stroked appreciatively with the back of her hand when Gerald delivered it to her. She was wearing a big diamond ring, and the sharp point on the stone scratched the enamel, an embarrassment which they both noticed. She said "Oh, dear, the enamel is scratched". Gerald had by then discovered that the customer is always right. Nothing more was said, Gerald re-enamelled the cover, and the Queen Mother remained one of his most charming patrons

Big cigar box, the enamelled lid edged with 76 emerald-cut diamonds . This was the trophy for the 25th anniversary race for the King George V1 and Queen Elizabeth Diamond Stakes at Ascot on Diamond Day 1975, sponsored by De Beers. De Beers also gave a slightly smaller box to the Queen Mother, also bearing the Queen Mother's arms and those of her late husband King George V1

which we had on display, and I think these informal visits struck a sympathetic chord. Anyway, Prince Charles began to commission from Gerald a long series of smaller pieces which he gave away on his frequent visits overseas. There were more ambitious ideas, too, like the Mountbatten Memorial Polo Trophy for the Prince to give in memory of his uncle, Lord Louis Mountbatten, who had been murdered by the IRA.

Gerald first met Lady Diana Spencer before her marriage to the Prince of Wales. At Buckingham Palace, Gerald had dropped into the Prince of Wales' office to make sure that all the Prince of Wales' and the Queen's gifts were accounted for. He was amazed to see Lady Diana sitting at a desk right opposite him. Michael Colborne, then the Prince's personal assistant, introduced them. Gerald's opening words were "Which is the out tray?" pointing to one which was empty and the other which was full. Those marvellous eyes flashed from side to side and, putting her hand over her mouth, she began to giggle. He was enchanted, and the enchantment continued as he went on to make things for her after her marriage, right up until after the divorce.

On the night before the wedding, Gerald was at Buckingham Palace to give them the wedding present which he and Janet had dreamed up. It was a small silver box with, inlaid into the lid, an Indian watercolour painted on ivory of Gulab Singh, grandfather of Kuran Singh, the Prince's polo playing friend.

The connection was rather lost on Lady Diana. To hide her embarrassment she started to rearrange the surrounding hordes of flowers while wearing a very large ten-gallon hat. She picked up a vase of flowers saying "there are far too many flowers in here" and began to walk out of the room with them. Unfortunately, the vase was full to the brim with water. Not surprisingly, she sloshed it everywhere, soaking her dress, the floor beneath and the furniture on which the vase had been standing. She turned the presentation scene into a cheerful farce.

He was honoured with an invitation to the wedding of the young Royal couple in St. Paul's Cathedral. He found to his consternation that he had been seated right behind the great bulk of the King and Queen of Tonga, who completely blotted out the proceedings taking place in front of him. He had to view the entire ceremony on one of the television screens which had thoughtfully been provided on several of the cathedral columns. Royal events can be impressive, amusing, or monotonous, but they can be agreeably unexpected too.

A pleasant, informal by-product of Gerald's Royal connections, was that he was allowed to rent a cottage on the Balmoral estate in Scotland. There, in the tranquil mountain surroundings, he and Janet used often to spend a

Small box, one of a few similar boxes commissioned by the Prince of Wales to give to friends and to state visitors

Small box, shell with gold mounts. The shell was given to the Prince of Wales on a beach in Australia, by an unknown pretty girl when she suddenly ran up to him and kissed him on the lips. They never met again

Balmoral Castle, ink wash
by Gerald

Menu holder given to the Prince
and Princess of Wales by their
staff and all those who helped
with the preparations for their
wedding, 29 July 1981

fortnight of their spring holidays. He looks forward eagerly each year to this fortnight of country peace, with its beautiful Scottish light, its long walks, two or three old friends to meet, and endless time for rest and contemplation. He started to make watercolour sketches there to give to Prince Charles, the beginning of his later painting career. It is possible, too, that the proximity of the Royal family did no damage to his business interests with them.

Lord Snowdon the distinguished photographer, accompanied by his then wife Princess Margaret, complimented Gerald by opening two of his exhibitions. Events went smoothly in the Rutland Gallery in London, but in the Springael Gallery in Brussels, unforeseen snags had to be overcome. The freeway through the city centre made it difficult to penetrate to the gallery from a parallel boulevard. Gerald was waiting for the Royal party, politely standing outside the gallery, when he saw the Royal car whizzing past on the freeway and then vanishing into one of the numerous tunnels. Minutes later, the car returned in the opposite direction; everyone waved, but it couldn't stop. Back it came again for another approach, this time more slowly, but still it hadn't managed to get off the freeway. Suddenly it did stop, causing an alarming screech of brakes from the following cars which had been going too fast. The doors opened and the Earl and Countess of Snowdon stepped coolly out, vaulted over the barrier off the freeway and onto the boulevard, and, neatly avoiding the oncoming traffic, walked into the gallery without turning a hair. Sometimes the Royal prerogative can save embarrassment as well as cause it.

Gerald is proud now to be able to display all four royal warrants, from the Queen, Prince Philip, the Queen Mother and the Prince of Wales. They are a rare distinction anyway, but in this case they are unique: Gerald is the first person to be awarded all the warrants in one trade, and the first living craftsman ever to be so honoured. The emblazoned certificates make a brave show today on the walls of 73 Walton Street.

Any supplier of goods to the Royal Family may apply for a royal warrant after working for the royal person concerned over a period of three or more years. If granted, the supplier then has to behave discreetly and not use the warrant for advertising or commercial promotion. To be allowed to display the words "By appointment" in one's shop or gallery, or on one's notepaper, is a great privilege, but its benefits to one's business, if any, are long-term and indirect. Gerald's Royal connections may therefore have done more for his self-confidence than for his bank balance.

Given to the Queen for her Silver Wedding, 20 Nov 1972, by Princess Alexandra and Angus Ogilvy. Gerald made this silver bar paper-weight featuring his personal virtuoso texturing, and big hall-marks deeply stamped in, suggesting the richness of the metal's substance

Princess Alexandra encourages exports by opening the British Exhibition, Stockholm in 1962; she is admiring Gerald's pieces in the display of the Worshipful Company of Goldsmiths

6 Public Patrons

Public patrons – Reading Corporation – Law Society – Chartered Accountants– Coventry
Cathedral with Basil Spence.

At Goldsmiths' Hall, one of several travelling exhibitions we mounted was called "Public patronage". Private individuals, the traditional patrons of silversmiths, were beginning to suffer from high taxation. We hoped that institutions might inherit the mantle of ancient Renaissance patrons like the Medici, and keep the arts flourishing to mutual advantage. We wanted to encourage a sort of benevolent self-advertisement, so that the merit of institutions might again be assessed, as it had been in Renaissance times, by the splendour of the plate they could put on display.

We encouraged public bodies to enhance their image and bring some colour into their functions, by commissioning a collection of new silver. We did this in several ways, by presenting an important new piece to start a new silver collection in new institutions who possessed nothing, like the new universities; by personal persuasion through friends, many of them members of the Worshipful Company of Goldsmiths; by publicising what already existed in comparable ancient institutions like the Oxford and

Large bowl given in 1986 by Peat Marwick Mitchell to the Institute of Chartered Accountants for whom Gerald made an entire collection. Big pieces like this often contain mysterious hidden symbols to give private pleasure to the owner: here, the aquamarines and peridots show Chartered Accountants encircling their customers, and spitting out any indigestible pips they find

Cambridge colleges, so that newcomers to the field would feel inferior unless they emulated their elders and betters; those bodies who possessed nothing would want to remedy the omission. We tried to draw attention to the vitality of modern British silver by publishing books and leaflets, and by exhibition publicity generally. And Gerald, being by now much the most successful independent producer of his type, was the biggest beneficiary of our substantial efforts.

For a few decades, this system worked admirably, until in the late '70s the change of pace both in local government and in the structure of trade, made this sort of show of altruistic loyalty seem anachronistic. A new short-term commercial greed often replaced the old family and local allegiances, so the commissions for silver from public bodies sadly began to diminish.

During the boom times of the '50s '60s and early '70s, there was one early patron of such impressive generosity and loyalty, that it deserves special discussion. It was Reading Corporation, and it set an example which was widely followed. Reading was a small town earmarked by the government for development into a model residential and industrial centre within easy reach of London, a sort of ideal dormitory suburb.

The Town Clerk, the quiet and self-effacing George Darlow visited us at Goldsmiths' Hall several times with members of his Council and with heads of local industry. He was determined to prove that Reading was big in spirit, even if not in size, and he chose modern silver to spread his message. His idea was that the Corporation should set the ball of civic pride rolling with some initial commissions, and that local commercial companies should then take up the challenge and each commission a piece according to the size of the company and the nature of its civic committment.

One brave and unusual aspect of the scheme was its artistic unity. In order to give the new collection the character of all being part of one family, it was all to be made by one artist, and the artist chosen by Reading was, sensibly, the young Gerald. The commissions for Reading appeared at the right time for him.

In 1966, the pieces by then made for Reading by Gerald, who was still only 36, were exhibited there. I wrote in the catalogue my hope that "the example of Reading will inspire other towns to embellish their official life and to put their faith in youth". We had already since 1962 shown the growing Reading collection in Stockholm, Dallas, Sydney, Düsseldorf, Norwich, Tokyo, as well as in London at the Ideal Home Exhibition and at the Royal Academy's Treasures of the Commonwealth. Seldom can a growing public art collection have earned its patrons more affection and admiration than this.

The visionary scheme started with a big dish for the Chamber of Commerce, then another for the Junior Chamber of Commerce, then other

Local firms comissioned over 150 pieces from Gerald and gave them to the civic collection of Reading, Berkshire. Other towns have collections, but not all by one designer, very few collections are as large, and probably none is as distinguished. One of the first gifts was this dish from the Junior Chamber of Commerce, with fine, crisp engraving designed by Gerald. His designs for Reading are all unusually restrained, he says because he wanted them to create an aura of splendour, not of ostentation

Given to Reading by Huntley and Palmer, whose arms feature four biscuit barrels

Cigar box given to Reading by Simonds Brewery

Detail from the big rosebowl with pierced cover including sapphires in square settings, given to Reading by Mr Taylor

Part of the Benney collection of silver for the Institute of Chartered Accountants

pieces great and small commissioned by local shops and supermarkets, parking areas and accountants and solicitors. Gerald made over 150 pieces for Reading, thereby winning local celebrity. One pleasant result was his being made a Freeman of Reading.

His Reading collection was used frequently for civic functions, giving personal delight and artistic interest. Now, changes in political emphasis have quietened these public pleasures, and the range of modern masterworks are used simply to give lustre where they are displayed in the Town Hall.

The Reading example continued for years. It provided a great outlet for Gerald's art, and it proved to be an inspiration for others. The Institute of Chartered Accountants is another of those corporate bodies, quite unlike Reading but with one crucial common interest. They both commissioned big, distinguished collections of new silver from Gerald. Public bodies did not, and they still usually do not today, appreciate their potential either for good or for bad. They are composed of dozens, maybe hundreds of members, each of whom may be a reluctant member who resents his annual subscription, each of whose private ambitions may be limited to how soon he or she can extricate himself or herself from the office chores to the liberation represented by an early round on the golf course or an early plunge in the pool. But place them together and, given a cathartic influence at the centre, they may unexpectedly realise that they are bigger than they knew. New collections of modern silver specially commissioned by local businesses, could provide just that catharsis. So it had been with Reading, and so it soon became with the Chartered Accountants.

The Chartered Accountants' headquarters is nearly a century old, not far from Liverpool Street Station in the City of London. Not a very special pedigree, you may think. But they retained an architect of enterprise and vision, William Whitfield, now in charge of the City's Paternoster scheme by St. Paul's Cathedral. He interested himself in the corporate reputation of his clients. The results, after a few visits to Goldsmiths' Hall, were lots of modern silver commissions, maybe the City's biggest single collection outside Goldsmiths' Hall itself. Gerald made most of the set of some 600 pieces, finished in 1970. Each member firm made its own choice, and Gerald, as usual, did well, as did some of his friends like the silversmith David Mellor who made the cutlery.

These were decades, now alas past, when a public institution's honour seemed to mean more than money, and silver represented a valid statement of honour. There were some exceptionally imaginative ideas: one was the set of four 5 ft high four light candelabra for the Law Society, the prestigious solicitors' pressure group. Another, the dish for the Gestetner

Part of the table plate commissioned in 1969 by what was then Britain's biggest company, ICI, for their three Directors' dining rooms, still in use today. Gerald had advertised in the Country Gentlemen's Association magazine for a Dinner Jacket and Morning Dress. He finally bought them from an ex-Director of ICI, who remembered using Gerald's beautiful plate in the ICI dining rooms. He said he had got thinner since leaving ICI, and missed the fine plate as much as the fine meals. At that time, meals were a normal method of attracting the sympathy of customers, and the quality of Gerald's table plate was an important part of the impact made by the commercial companies who had commissioned it from him. Now, sadly, the sort of personal bond created by business lunches has receded in favour of impersonal scrutiny of balance sheets, much to the detriment of modern silver tableware

Large bowl commissioned in 1985 by Jesus College, Oxford, to celebrate the memory of their principal benefactor, Sir Leoline Jenkins on the third centenary of his death in 1685. He was Principal of the College 1661 to 1675. He gave to the college vast benefactions of land, including some in Glamorgan, Wales, from which the Welsh association and the Prince of Wales feathers originate. These tremble when you breathe, or when the bowl vibrates. The present Prince of Wales has visited the college

Symbolism and stories often spoil the direct appeal of a powerful shape. Unusually, this 14 inch high sculpture commissioned in 1979 by the Airborne and Commando Royal Engineers Officers Association has a high emotional content of poignancy and threat

company with food compartments big enough to feed the ancient gods of Greece. Not one but three dishes were considered an appropriate ration for the British and French Bank, run by Sir Patrick Reilly, brother of the design leader Paul. The red enamelled strawberries bowl, each gold berry representing a member of the family, was made for Lord Astor of Hever. Gavin Astor said to Gerald "Please try to deliver it within a fortnight" . He did just that, but Gavin tragically died from cancer after 13 days. His widow retains the bowl as a beautiful memory of their ruby wedding.

The list of Gerald's patrons is long and impressive. It is perhaps best enjoyed through colourful photographs of the work rather than through arid names of the people. But some of the commissions did generate strange stories. Last but not least of Gerald's public patrons up to the 'nineties, which I have selected for discussion, is Coventry Cathedral. It is distinguished, and its story is strange. Basil Spence, the Cathedral architect, before he was knighted, had commissioned from Gerald various crosses and chalices for churches he was restoring, but Coventry was, as Gerald says, ecclesiastically the big commission of the century.

The Provost had visited me at Goldsmiths' Hall, and discussed possibilities for the new cathedral plate, but I did not know if funds were available, nor did I hear of any decision. Spence's office was near to Gerald's in Fitzroy Square, and Gerald had been at school with his son-in-law, Anthony Blee. The omens seemed fair, but four weeks before the opening of the new cathedral, no new plate seemed to have been initiated.

...ING · BY · PROFESSOR · GERALD · BENNEY · 1979 · COMMI...

Commissions often arose through personal friendships. In 1989 Christie's commissioned the dining room service of which this is a part, because of Christie's experts' frequent visits to Goldsmiths' Hall, often in connection with studying the hall-marks on the antique silver which Christie's sell at their auctions

Pair of jugs 10 inches high, commissioned by Winchester College to celebrate the sixth centenary of their foundation by William of Wykeham, 1382 to 1982

Bowl given by W. H. Smith to Swindon, where the stationers had just built a depot. The rim was textured, then soldered on

One of a set of four large
candelabra for the Law Society,
1982, measuring five ft. high
including candles.
Commissioned on the initiative
of Mark Sheldon, Treasurer and
later President of the Society,
now partner at Linklaters and
Paine

Verger's staff four ft. high with ebony stem, given to Coventry Cathedral by the Diocese of Toronto, Canada, and finished in May 1962 in time for the consecration service on May 25 1962. The maple leaf for Canada is textured with Gerald's "tortoise neck" surface, surmounted by the cross of nails. Gerald's ciborium of three years earlier, was the first time that the cross of nails, found in burnt timber from the bombed medieval cathedral roof, was used by any artist in the cathedral interior. This cross soon became the symbol for the cathedral. The cathedral architect, Sir Basil Spence, chatting about his design for the cathedral, told Gerald "The vision has come from God". Gerald also made for use at the High Altar, two chalices with patens, a flagon and a salver

Crozier for the Archbishop of Philadelphia. Church work tends to receive less publicity than secular, because of its quiet settings or its intimate use where the public often cannot approach the silver closely

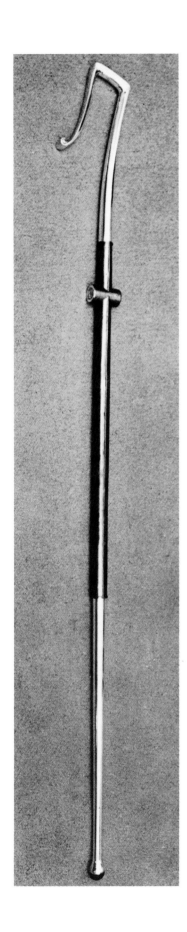

Suddenly Gerald got a panic call from the Provost via the Precentor. Would he consider making plate for this fabulous new building, the great symbol of Britain's spiritual regeneration, risen from the war's bomb-damage, created by the greatest artists of the age. Gerald was in Coventry immediately, and was told, to his bewildered delight, that this was to be "the works", as fast as possible, two of everything. The designs were soon approved with enthusiasm, the pieces were being made so quickly there was not even time to get them hall-marked.

Then the drama heightened. Spence phoned and asked Gerald round immediately. He sensed big trouble, rushed round the corner, and there was Spence looking out of his office window with his hands behind his back, always a bad sign with him. As Gerald says, it was just like the behaviour of some of his headmasters. "How could you do this to me, going behind my back?" Spence asked. "The Provost never asked me who I wanted. I'd like you to step down." Gerald said "No, Sir. I've been commissioned. In any case, I assumed that all designs were passed by you. I'm three quarters of the way through. I can't step down". Spence said "Well, that is the end of our relationship" and he never spoke to Gerald again, nor offered him any more commissions. I never dreamed that a great architect under stress could in a fit of pique damage a friend in this way.

Then Geoffrey Clarke, that brilliantly original stained glass artist credited with the revival of that art in Britain, whose medals and metalwork are in the collection at Goldsmiths' Hall, told me another damaging tale. Sir Robin Darwin, Rector of the Royal College of Art, and Sir Basil Spence were both eventually knighted. They both separately recommended Geoffrey for the Coventry windows, which with his friends at the Royal College of Art he executed triumphantly.

But, because Darwin and Spence had not consulted with each other about their recommendation before they spoke to their committee, they felt in some way humiliated to be deprived of the exclusive honour of having been the first to recognise Geoffrey, then an unknown talent. These two great arbiters of taste behaved in a surprisingly small minded way – they neither of them ever spoke to Geoffrey again, although he had behaved impeccably and had had absolutely nothing to do with the meeting. The results for the new knights may not have mattered, but for Geoffrey they were dire. He received no more commissions from these two specially influential patrons, who had both been big supporters of his. Artists remain very vulnerable despite all the support which fame may temporarily give them. Gerald's Coventry experience was better than some.

Walter Hussey, Dean of Chichester, commissioned Henry Moore, Graham Sutherland and Benjamin Britten when he was at St Matthew's church in Northampton and continued his fearless patronage of new designs in Chichester. The altar set of 1957 for Bishop Otter College with gilt inside the cross, was one of Gerald's first church successes. A technical and artistic contrast is the very simple cross in the chapel of the Mary Queen of Scots Memorial Society in Westminster Abbey: because of cash shortage, Gerald sawed it out of half inch thick brass plate and fixed a ring round the outside, creating a strong design with minimum handwork

Cross, three ft high, and candlesticks for Caius College Chapel, Cambridge 1960. The silver gilt tapered stem has Gerald's "shrunk gold" tortoise neck texture, giving it depth and contrast with the gold-lined silver sheath. One of Gerald's first truly modern concepts, the beginning of his taste for spikes

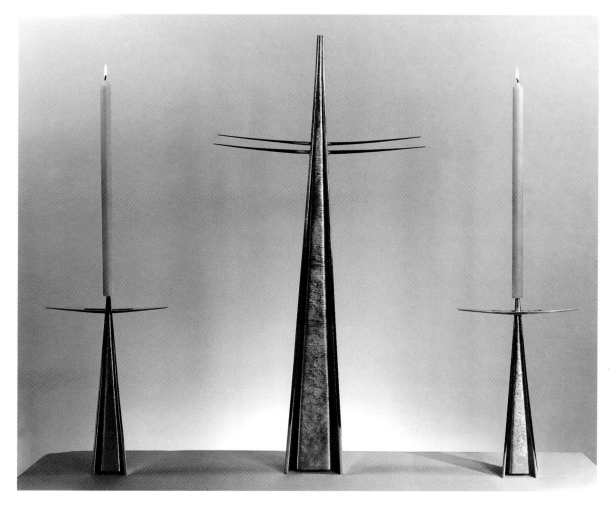

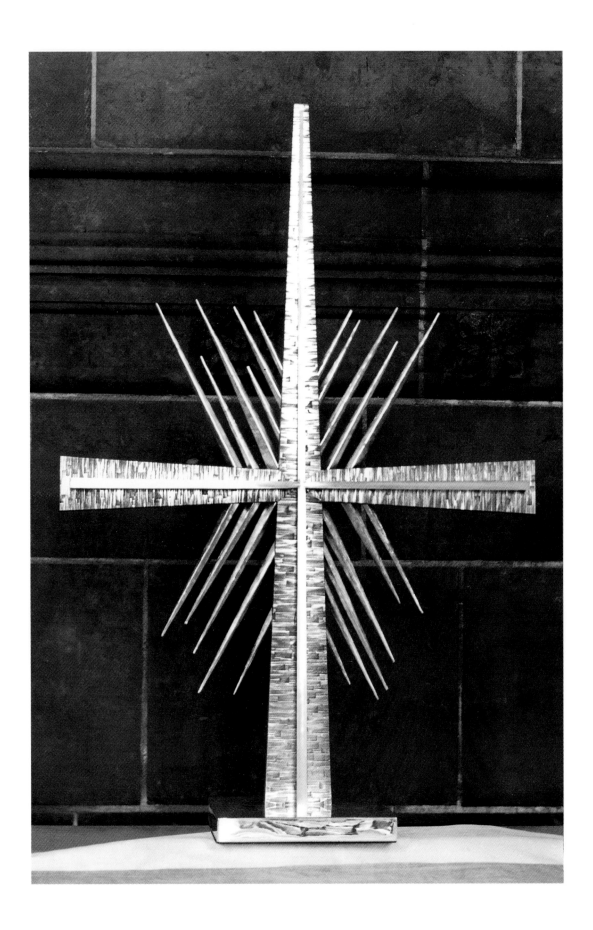

Cross with candlesticks to match, for the High Altar at Charterhouse School Chapel 1963

Altar set given in 1990 by the Worshipful Company of Goldsmiths to St Dunstan's chapel, the mourning chapel in St. Paul's Cathedral, London. St Dunstan, the patron saint of Goldsmiths, was Archbishop of Canterbury a thousand years ago, and himself a working goldsmith

The benefits to artists of gifts made in a commercial context can be marvellous. The Metal Box Company, led by Brian Smith (right) gave this great Christian cross to a Nigerian cathedral. The Archbishop (left) looks impressed

Celtic cross for the Celtic chapel on the McGill family estate in Ireland.

SURSUM CORDA

7 Overseas Adventures

Overseas adventures – the Worshipful Company of Goldsmiths export exhibitions – Vernon Pick in Arizona and Las Vegas – Gerald in Moradabad, India – Indian hall-marking – Royal Selangor Pewter in Kuala Lumpur, Malaysia – Dubai – Viners of Sheffield world-wide exports.

At the opening of the British
exhibition in Sydney in 1964, on
the display of the Worshipful
Company of Goldsmiths: Sir
Robert Menzies, Prime Minister
of Australia (right), Lord Boyd,
Prime Warden of the Worshipful
Company (centre), and Sir Peter
Runge, head of the Federation of
British Industry (left). Gerald is
in a confident mood because he
had just bought a new suit
whose style he thought was a
joke. Usually when he is faced
with ceremonials, he feels ill at
ease

Exports

"Exporting is fun". This portentous government pronouncement became a sour joke. A Cabinet Minister who did not realise that exporting is hard work, tried to stimulate the British economy, and encourage manufacturers to undertake more foreign travel by these silly words of false encouragement. Exporting was and is arduous and difficult. Gerald's principal exhibitions 1956–95 are listed at the end of this book. The list is not comprehensive, but of the 57 exhibitions considered, 26 were overseas, a fair tribute to Gerald's energy, especially as he does not specially enjoy foreign travel. Some of these shows made good sales openings, some won good newspaper publicity for Gerald both at home and abroad, some achieved nothing for him except valuable experience. All of them were hard work, but it would be tedious to elaborate further on that.

Statistics tell their own tale of endeavour. In one year Gerald went round the world not once but twice. He travelled 72,000 miles, enough to keep most of us happy for a lifetime. He had by then established boutiques, or small shops bearing his own name, in at least six powerful stores, a great coup for him. The main purpose of his trips was to service these boutiques, to replenish their stocks of his silver, to discover what type of Benney work the stores liked best, to nourish confidence generally. The stores he visited were Jensen of New York, Warren of Detroit, Meister of Zürich, Bolin of Stockholm, David Jones of Sydney, and Wako of Tokyo. But his sales were small, his profit margins were non-existent, and the whole idea of exports was beginning, he says, to drive him mad. He had to retrench.

Let us participate in a few of Gerald's most colourful exploits. They were not typical, but they suggest some of the zest and verve which he brought to his work. Gerald travelled both on his own and with Goldsmiths' Company missions which I organised: an early project was in 1958 when he helped our exhibition on the Grand' Place, Brussels, in the medieval vaulted chambers beneath the superb City Hall. Owing to the unique status of the Worshipful Company, we were often able to exhibit in amazing places which would be denied to more overtly commercial bodies. Gerald helped us to unpack our masterworks of gold and silver, both old and new, from the old laundry baskets in which we packed them.

A combination of these springy, discoloured baskets with their tough old locks, torn tissue paper wrapping and rough straw padding made a shock proof container which served us well all over the world, avoiding all damage to many hundreds of fragile treasures over three decades. The baskets were very light, so saved a fortune in air freight costs. And they had another less evident advantage: they looked so shabby that no burglar ever, so far as I know, showed any interest in them even when they lay unobtrusively in

Three large centrepiece bowls with sculptural pierced covers, made for private French clients. It is probable that no French goldsmith could make this sort of uninhibited work. The more personal the expression, the more possible it is to export it

Another centrepiece bowl for a private French client. Gerald's "rosebowls" to use the traditional name for a centrepiece with pierced cover to contain rose petals, are unique to him and give him an outlet for his exuberant imagination. If the name of individual craftsmen could become as famous as that of some painters or sculptors, these craftsmen would be able to export their work to galleries on the strength of the artists' names

Overseas Adventures

Sold to the courtly retailer
Meister of Zürich after the
Worshipful Company of
Goldsmiths' show in the British
Week there in 1963. Meister in
his turn was pleased to sell it to a
Japanese client but the order
was not repeated. Craftsmen
selling through retailers or
galleries have no control over
the commercial activity
generated by the gallery

Exports of exuberant silver with great personality are never easy; often they result from an international business association. This big cigar box, 13 inches long, was given to the Frankfurt firm Metallgesellschaft to celebrate its 75th birthday in 1956, by its British associate company, at the time of the Worshipful Company of Goldsmiths' exhibitions in the British Week, Düsseldorf

American private collectors can be even more useful allies to an artist than British, simply because they are richer. This coffee pot went to Chicago to a private collector

Lavabo for Princeton University, New Jersey. Part of a set including cross, candlesticks, chalice and paten. In one year, Gerald had boutiques under his own name in at least six big stores: Jensen of New York, Warren of Detroit, Meister of Zürich, Bolin of Stockholm, David Jones of Sydney, Wako of Tokyo. To keep up with them all, he traveled 72,000 miles in the year, twice round the world. His profit margins were nil, and he discovered that exporting was driving him mad

American women like to carry a jewelled "clutch bag" like this textured bag with yellow sapphire knob, for a private American client

Cigar box for Kerry Packer, the Australian who revolutionised cricket and transformed the ancient sport into a modern industry. Energetic new visionaries like Kerry often become better patrons of modern designers, than conservative old families with inherited collections of antiquities

Bowl given by the British government in 1966 to Botswana to celebrate independence

Gavel given by the Institute of Chartered Accountants of Great Britain to the Accountants of Australia, c1990

Large bowl with black enamel base given by Willis Faber and Dumas to Tokyo Marine and Fire Insurance. Japanese people prefer to receive new art from famous artists rather than from unknown beginners

Badge of office for the College of Obstetricians of Hong Kong, enamelled by Alan Mudd. A similar badge is now being made for the Physicians. Institutions have conferences and parties at which it helps if the President can wear a badge so that everyone knows who he or she is

Mace for the Royal College of Obstetricians and Gynaecologists of Australia

Given in 1983 by the Royal College of Obstetricians and Gynaecologists, to the Royal New Zealand College. This and the related mace for Australia show how a skilled designer can establish a family likeness without monotony

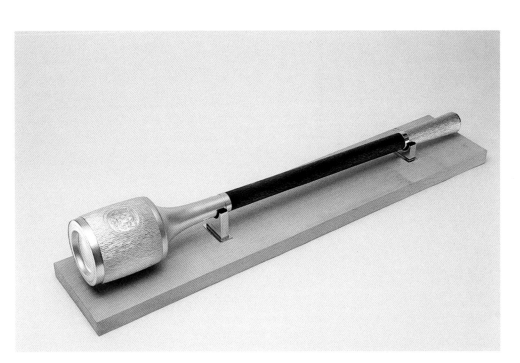

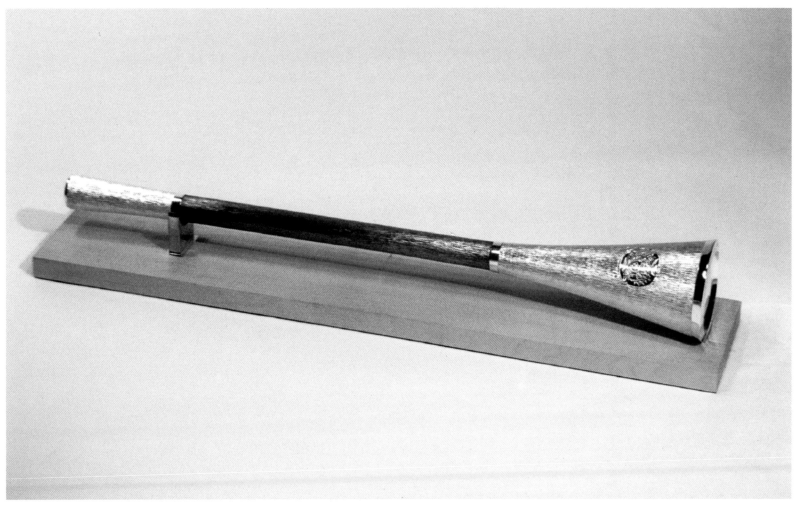

some far distant insecure airport warehouse waiting for customs clearance.

There was some amusement in Brussels that the grand, ancient Worshipful Company, a prime exhibitor in the British exhibition there, surrounded itself in this way with dust and young craftsmen, instead of the wooden crates and leather cases and pin-striped suited salesmen of the conventional British exporting companies. The surprise turned to envy as it transpired that our display was beautiful and professional, that we dominated the publicity of the group exhibition, and sold well to local firms who had never bought British since before the 1939 war. One such firm was the crown jewellers, Wolfers.

Another memorable British exhibition was in Stockholm in 1962, in an industrial fairground. There, Gerald's new silver dominated our show stand, just as the stand itself, designed by Alan Irvine, was pre-eminent among the more mundane British industrial products nearby. We gave a dinner party for our friends and for the Swedish retail shops who had staged small exhibitions of British silver and jewels with us. The young Swedish Crown jeweller, Hans Bolin, suddenly started what sounded to us like a weird atonal shout, during which Gerald and I became embarrassed. Hans' pagan cries soon became a Viking drinking song in which we all had to join at the top of our voices. With no training or warning, we sounded more like squeaking mice than marauding Norsemen, but a few more glasses of Schnapps soon put that right, and Hans became a good customer, inviting Gerald to stay for family holidays on his farm in South Sweden.

Vernon Pick

A most unusual client was Vernon Pick. He turned up in my office at Goldsmiths' Hall, saying he wanted to become the Benvenuto Cellini of the twentieth century, and could I please fix it for him. He had mining interests in Texas, his home state, and Colorado, he spoke with a slow Texas drawl and I thought I could detect a streak of irony and humour somewhere beneath the rather naif dreams he shared with me. He looked very old, about 75, and said he was very rich having discovered uranium deposits. I thought he could not become a Cellini unless he surrounded himself with modern silver and jewels to get his eye in; at least, I hoped I was talking to a big American buyer, if only he was handled sensitively and coaxed into buying from others, rather than trying to make himself into a master craftsman. There was only one man who might make this hesitant old man into a glistening cornucopia, and that was Gerald, to whom I introduced Vernon.

They met at Goldsmiths' Hall about 1970, and the personal vibrations seemed promising. Soon, Gerald visited Vernon in his ranch in California to help him set up a workshop. Then there was a second visit with Andrew

Commissioned in 1988 by Harry Oppenheimer of De Beers in South Africa and the Anglo American Corporation, with green enamel and ivory, now bequeathed to his son Nicky

The "Classic" pattern teaset, small and inexpensive, almost an industrial design intended for batch production for the Japanese market. It sold well for several years in the grand Mitsukoshi store in Tokyo and elsewhere, but eventually the market faded. Exports of tableware are as vulnerable to variations in fashion, as they are to currency and political fluctuations

Grima the jeweller. Vernon got into his stride with tricks and jokes, and announced on the first evening that he had a surprise ready. He had arranged an evening party not in his rambling ranch, but in a large wooden shack which he had built much further up the mountain. Vernon and his wife set off up towards the shack; Andrew and Gerald stayed behind with lots of drink and an Alsatian dog for company, waiting to be called by phone when the guests had all got to the shack. As the guests began to arrive, Gerald noticed through the window several silver-grey Rolls Royce cars winding up the road towards the shack. Later, he realised that not some, but all the guests possessed silver-grey Rolls Royces. There were about 40 of them.

The phone did not ring to call the Englishmen to the banquet. Although the approach road to the shack was long and winding, the shack was quite close as measured by straight line. Gerald and Andrew could smell the barbecue and were tempted as they were very hungry, but the Alsatian, a ferocious German Shepherd, would not let them out. They only got to the party four hours later and Vernon thought this amusing. This sort of one-up-manship was exceptional, but it does suggest the adventures, hardships and hazards of exporting. The customer is always right, even if you, the exporter, do not always see the joke and feel like punching him on the nose.

Vernon had, amongst other exploits, flown solo to the North Pole to do some prospecting. He now suggested that Gerald and Janet should accompany him to Las Vegas in his old single engined De Havilland Otter seaplane. On the way, he dropped off at Los Angeles to pick up the Commandant of the Californian Marines with his entourage of six film starlets without whom it seemed he could not function fully. They gambled in Las Vegas for a few days and nights; Gerald was surprised to have to pay the hotel bill, even more surprised when Vernon paid him back a few days later.

When they departed to fly back to Los Angeles, they intended to leave at dawn when the air is cool. But the commandant and his film starlets were late, so departure was delayed until the sun was already high and hot, and the air thin. The little Otter tried to climb above the mountain range which surrounds the desert resort, but began to boil, so down they came to cool off the engine. They repeated this alarming exercise half a dozen times and eventually succeeded in scraping over the top, just clear of the high peaks. The other side was a jagged gorge. The journey had overrun by hours, it was late, dusk was falling, and as they flew up the gorge, Gerald saw a red light flashing on the instrument panel. Vernon noticed too and tapped the glass, which caused the light to come on in earnest. They were running out of fuel. Vernon groaned that he was lost.

He pulled the stick back to bring the fuel to the rear of the tank, the plane climbed till it was level with the mountain tops enclosing the gorge. The

Large ice-bucket with thin-wall cast body requiring no carving. The more efficient the Indian production became, the smaller the number of workers were needed. But the old designs were very labour intensive and therefore remained socially valuable in an area where more unemployment might be unbearable

engine stuttered and failed, and all that could be heard was the rushing of air past the wings. Vernon got busy, almost panicky, on the radio, as the long glide missed the mountains by inches and Gerald thought he could see in the bright moonlight the vultures which he imagined were on the ground below, waiting for some succulent corpses, the usual outcome of a remote air crash. Then, out of the blackness ahead emerged some lights spelling the word BAKERSFIELD. It was a military airbase shut down for the night, but specially opened for the waif Otter in its emergency. A tanker bustled out to refill Vernon's tanks, and the airmen clustered round the Otter in amazement; was this a medieval craft, they asked, could it really fly? When Vernon and Gerald finally did succeed in returning to San Jose Airport, Gerald discovered he had lost the car keys, but that's another story.

Vernon never became a Cellini because he tackled all his problems as an engineer or inventor, not as a craftsman. But he really was a big star, not a starlet. He discovered the biggest uranium deposit in USA, using a sort of Geiger counter invented by himself; he mined it, then sold it to the US government. Another of Vernon's coups was a type of infra red gun with camera attached. When used at night from an aeroplane, it could photograph mineral deposits in the ground. He sold this also to the US government for several million dollars, plus the Otter and a huge long range Catalina flying boat. Maybe not Gerald's foremost export customer, but in exports, you have to keep on trying.

India

Another overseas drama was quite sudden. In 1975, Gerald received a letter from the Commonwealth Secretariat, describing their quest for someone to go to India to revive the copper and brass tableware industries there. He told Janet: the government of India wanted someone to help to get 2,000,000 people back into employment in their traditional metalwork skills. Gerald was feeling stale and depressed by the devastating VAT increase in 1973 which had forced him to close the apple of his eye, his London workshops. Janet urged him to try the unique tonic offered by the vast colourful continent. Gerald got the job. His area, Uttar Pradesh, was enormous, stretching almost to Nepal, and to Benares, the whole Ganges area.

Gerald went to live in a local house in Moradabad, the old brass-polishing centre. The population was 250,000. Of these, 25,000 were metal-polishers, compared with about 16 people in the centre of British metal polishing, Sheffield. There were no Western hotels and very little sanitation. He spent weeks visiting workshops in the appalling slums. It was so hot that when the electricity, and with it the air-conditioning, cut off – it often did – in five

A group of Gerald's new designs was sold in London, but without local agents in India to supervise production, exports to Western markets could not be sustained

minutes all his clothes had become dark with sweat. He had to drink the local water – there was no other drink available since Coca Cola and Fanta, the best known soft drinks, had both been banished by the Indian government – and he got hepatitis twice.

The traditional local craft designs were mostly derived from luscious fruit and flowers and Hindu gods, embossed or cast in brass or copper dishes or jars. They would not sell in the West, specially not in the sort of smart shops which Gerald saw as the big market growth potential. So he tried to excite a local awareness of Western markets and fashions, by importing Western magazines. But he found the tradition of centuries was understandably difficult to shake, so he started to do the designing himself, adapting the local skills into a modern Western idiom. In the lower Himalayas, the traditional local product was huge hammered water carrying pots, beautiful shapes for which he contrived new spouts and handles. In Benares the only local aptitude was religious scenes of Krishna and the other Hindu gods and girls, embossed or chased onto big trays. He evolved a way of cutting out these scenes with a chisel and mounting them on hessian as a form of interior decoration which would decorate any living room in a cosmopolitan capital city. Next came his idea of casting geometric patterns into the surface of jugs and cups at the time they were cast, instead of

chasing and cutting them into the surface after the casting of the basic form. But these thin-walled innovative production pieces soon began to put too many craftsmen chasers and cutters out of work – once he had to receive a deputation of protesting chasers.

He kept at work designing copper, brass and enamels more stylish than anything ever seen before in India. Many thousands of pieces were made during his ten months in India. But nobody in Moradabad could imagine the export possibilities of his new designs. Nobody there could afford to go abroad, so there was no understanding of foreign fashions and needs. He may have been too European in his attitudes, and too impatient to achieve quick results.

Sadly, there was no infrastructure in India: he went to Delhi to try to rekindle government interest in his schemes, but a change of government personnel had led to inertia there. He failed to generate continuing faith in his visionary ideas. When he went home for a fortnight in Britain, the small momentum he had so painfully generated in Moradabad immediately died until his return there. The local craftsmen simply could not believe that he would return, still less that he might be able to help them to sell their products in far away places of which they had hardly heard. In India, action depends upon personal presence and persuasion, not on letters, memoranda and money.

Gerald evolved thin brasswork with elegant new enamelled designs, superseding the old hammered floral patterns, what we call chasing or embossing. The aim was to reach sophisticated Western markets with economical products

The new designs used old shapes. But because local producers were too poor to travel, they could not appreciate the potential of the world's distant export markets and therefore tended to stick with their centuries-old habits

Gerald's painter son Paul liked the new-style Indian products and tried to import them by the hundred. But, as there was no established production routine, and no easy transport, this proved too complicated, though the pieces, when they eventually did arrive, sold easily to an Indian dealer. Moradabad remains a sad memory for the Benneys.

But there was a happy Indian epilogue. One day Gerald's RCA silversmith friend Robert Welch phoned Gerald to tell him he was going to India tomorrow. Gerald said "Wait for me", immediately dropped everything and joined Robert on the flight which Robert had booked weeks before. Quick moving indeed, and evidence that Gerald had fallen under the spell of India, even if realisation of his Indian metalwork dreams still eluded him.

He spent a month with Robert and Robert's friends the architects of the Barbican in the City of London, Peter Chamberlin, his wife, and Gustav Bon. They visited all the buildings in India designed by Le Corbusier, or sketched out by him, noting sadly how impractical they were. This was partly because Corbusier himself had not bothered to visit all the sites, or supervise the construction works in detail. Also, the great architect did not seem to have understood the Indian way of life. Gerald now reminisces sadly that you have to be in India for at least a year before you can begin to appreciate that great country. He remembers seeing two incongruous examples of what looked like European arrogance and waste at Corbusier's new city, Chandigarh.

The expensive rubber flooring inside the spiral towers was covered by beggars. You could barely even enter the building, there were already so many people living on the floors inside. Outside, the huge empty squares, bigger than Aldershot's parade ground, were designed to give magnificent vistas from afar of "Corb's" sculptural buildings. But there was no maintenance, and tumbleweed, the local vegetation, loves to grow in cracks between stones and concrete blocks. So it grew till it was at least eight feet high, then broke off in the gales and made a frightening swishing noise against the sides of the buildings, or knocked you over as it blew about in the wind. But "Corb's" reputation was redeemed by the excellent training he gave to several Indian architects, now the enlightened leaders of their profession there.

Later, Indian affairs revived for Gerald in more manageable form. He was appointed Chairman of a new Indian Hallmarking Council. They eventually succeeded in establishing a voluntary hallmark to guarantee the metallurgical quality of Indian gold and silver. So his Indian experience was not all in vain.

Pewter designed by Gerald, part of his big series made by Selangor in Kuala Lumpur, Malaysia. The metal has its own qualities: it is very soft, never acquires the rich lustre of silver, and does not tarnish. For Gerald, Selangor pewter represented new opportunities

Selangor

Gerald's other main overseas industry client is a pewter factory: Royal Selangor, the three centuries' old firm in Kuala Lumpur, Malaysia. Poh Con Yong is a visionary leader. Every few years he features a different designer, at the same time continuing with his existing stable. He markets Gerald's pewter world wide with professional packaging featuring the (to him) magic words "Gerald Benney" much more prominently than the name of the firm. On his first visit, Gerald found about 200 very pretty girls in blue uniforms with white cuffs making pewter in immaculate surroundings. What a contrast with the dirt of Sheffield! He designed and made 38 working prototypes in three weeks, working with the firm's excellent Chinese model-maker who is deaf and dumb. Selangor now sell a large number of his pieces annually all over the word, even in the Malay peninsular where new designs were almost unknown. Gerald says modestly that his Selangor royalties paid the central heating bills at Beenham, which may sound a limited achievement. But if you have seen the size of Beenham, with its huge rooms and innumerable small rooms and corridors, you'll realise that the bill for heating alone here would be enough to keep most of us afloat for years.

Selangor have now bought the oldest British pewter company, Englefields, whose pewter tankards have improved the flavour of British beer in British pubs for three centuries past; Selangor have also bought William Comyns, one of London's best-known manufacturers of sterling silver. Gerald's future here is uncertain, but his past was bright.

Dubai

The Arab countries, newly rich from their oil, became important patrons for some British craftsmen, but Gerald has never flourished there. Maybe his style is too modern. New countries like these usually yearn for traditional, ornate designs with an Oriental flavour, and that is not where he wants his art to lead him. But he has made one important collection in Arab territory: for The Mahdi al Tajir, Foreign Minister and ambassador of Dubai, perhaps the most energetic patron of them all for British silversmiths and jewellers. He hopes for more!

Though he much prefers direct factual conversations, he does digress occasionally into generalisations. He recalls "I got some awful jobs from public bodies, like reproducing the clock tower in a county town; I usually managed to avoid the worst travesties of modern art, but I'm a designer, not a diplomat, and practise does not make perfect when you' re dealing with wealthy philistines. You want their commissions, but you dislike their taste, always a nasty pull for any artist!"

Viners of Sheffield

It is often said that the valid expression of our time is not handwork, not painting and sculpture, but product design for mass production. Gerald does not entirely share this shibboleth because he loves using his hands and he knows that handwork gives quality which no machine can ever approach. But he is not a dogmatic person, and he has been lucky with his industrial clients.

The first of his metalwork factories was Viners of Sheffield. They were a newish company in that city, where silver workshops started to grow up along the River Don three centuries ago. Founded in 1907 by Ruben Viner's father and two uncles, they became quite big under Ruben and Leslie Glatman, with some 1,100 employees, quite mechanised, with machine polishing and automatic welding. Viners were international, too, with exports, agents and factories in Japan, Hong Kong and other distant places whose importance was not yet generally appreciated in the West.

Gerald designed for Viners for thirteen years, between 1957 and 1969. He earned maybe £ 2,000 annually as his salary, but he also negotiated 1½ % royalties on all products designed by him, because, as he says, " I was confident I was on to something big." He earned his best royalties, sometimes as much as £60,000 annually, from four patterns of flatware, called Chelsea, Studio, Design 70 and Sable.

Their new extra-shallow bowls allowed automatic robot polishing. This was a revolutionary and huge economy over the traditional hand polishing. With this old process, each piece had been placed separately by hand against a revolving felt wheel, roughened with River Trent sand. The power to

It was Gerald's elegant designs which ensured the huge success of his industrial pioneering for Viners. His first big breakthrough was the "Chelsea" pattern with its two-tone finish, part bright polish, part soft or "butler" finish. The bowls, blades and prongs were bright, whilst the handles were matt finished. It was launched in 1960 in his Chester Street home, the price of a 7-piece place setting in its box being two pounds five shillings and sixpence. By 1967, Viners production had spread to the Far East, and "Chelsea" sales world-wide were enormous, as many as 4,000 dozen pieces weekly.

Left: Chelsea
Right: Studio, featuring deep texturing which Gerald's industrial ingenuity had by then made possible in hard stainless steel

rotate the wheel was originally provided by water-wheels driven by the fast-flowing River Don which frequently surged under or beside the factory concerned. Thus, the steep hills of Sheffield with its cheap power available from its local river, made possible the Sheffield cutlery industry, which in the 18th century became a world leader.

Gerald has never received proper credit for his mechanical genius. He has expressed it over the decades in everything he makes, never being content to use the accepted production routine, always wondering if there may be a quicker and better way, a spectacular departure from the norm. I remember that when I was studying silver factory methods in Sheffield for six months during 1952, there was already some talk on the shop floors of the few progressive firms, that automatic polishing and automatic knife sharpening were an important and horrible dream, but that they would never be made to work efficiently. It was Gerald who made that dream a reality, and gave to Viners one of their great successes in new technology.

Even more important was Gerald's other great invention, the no-scrap blank. Flatware starts life as a sheet of metal, from which the flat silhouettes or blanks of the flatware are cut by machine. These silhouettes are then tapered, shaped, and textured until they become knives, spoons and forks. The sheet of metal minus these silhouettes then becomes scrap and is

melted down for reuse, an expensive and wasteful process. This is what happens with valuable silver, but in the case of harder, less valuable stainless steel, the scrap is quite literally scrapped.

The no-scrap idea almost eliminated this perforated scrap sheet. The resulting flatware pieces were of more or less conventional shape in plan, but in section the bowls, prongs and handle ends were thinner than the stems. This thinness is the result of rolling or pressing these ends, and it does not lose its curved shape because stainless steel is such a hard metal. Thus the silhouette cut from the sheet could be almost rectangular, leaving almost no metal between one silhouette and the next. Almost no metal was wasted, which gave Viners a certain edge over all their competitors world-wide.

The Chelsea pattern was probably the first entirely machine-made stainless steel flatware in Britain, the achievement of semi-flow line production which took four years to evolve, 1958–62. By 1967, sales figures were enormous: Chelsea might sell 3,000 or 4,000 dozen pieces weekly, Studio maybe 1,500 dozen. Total flatware weekly production was around 25,000 dozen pieces, or nearly half a million pieces, and an order for three million pieces for contract use was normal.

Such were the wages of his being as practical as he was innovative. His royalties at one time earned him more than the Chairman of Viners himself, an astonishing reversal of roles. Usually in Britain, designers were poorly paid and the Chairman not only took the credit for any design achievement, but the cash too. Alas, marketing and computer troubles caused Viners to lose their position, and to abandon with it their valuable links with Gerald. The name Viners survives today, as it was bought from the Viner family at the time of the collapse, but the significance of the name is sadly diminished without the spark which Gerald gave it.

Cocktail set by Viners in pewter with rolled-on texture and fine polish, the contrast emphasising the softness of the metal. Gerald is always aware of the potential of his raw materials as well as of his machines. The jug retailed at £4.10s, the tankard at £2.5s.

8 Business Growth

Business grows from Beenham – enamels – Burch and Zürich – Jewish synagogue plate – Israel visit – outworkers lead to stability.

Gerald had been an enameller for years, and in 1968 this skill came to his rescue. He was feeling the sort of lassitude and staleness which can assail any artist or craftsman after a long period of intense activity, and he decided to look for the necessary tonic by developing, refining and mastering this ancient technique. He knew enamels were capable of much greater variety than he had so far been able to achieve, so he set out to conquer the expressive vocabulary of this difficult art form, so common from the time of the ancient Chinese until the French Art Nouveau jewellers, now generally neglected because almost nobody could still do it properly. Janet, not for the first nor the last time, gave him the crucial impulse. She put into his hand a return air ticket to Zürich, saying "what your silver needs is colour, and that means enamel … Go and find a craftsman who worked for Burch Korrodi in Zürich, and bring him back with you".

Burch had inherited some of his skills from the Fabergé team, and had evolved his own special mastery, with much more modern designs than Fabergé ever achieved, and with much bigger areas of continuous colour. He had exhibited often, and in 1954 produced a good book which won him some fame, and which brought a regular trickle of pilgrims to his studio in Zürich. I had assumed, and I think he had too, that there was some special magic about the air he breathed or the purity of the Swiss water he used, which would explain how he achieved his purity of colour without streaks or blemishes, and how he caused the enamels to adhere to flat surfaces instead of cracking off. I met him occasionally in Germany, where the regularity of his finish was much admired, and found him thorough and unassuming, not at all the flamboyant showman which the originality of his output might have suggested. This was the master whom Gerald now pursued through the winter snows, rather resenting having to desert the glorious English country spring in favour of the urban ice in Zürich.

He walked up Zürich's main shopping street, Bahnhofstrasse, then skidded and fell, spraining his ankle outside one of the best jewellers there, Turler. Mr. Turler kindly helped him inside, treated the ankle and in the course of their subsequent talk, told Gerald of one of Burch's craftsmen, Berger Bergersen from Norway, who had worked for Burch and for Bolin in Stockholm, a fine enameller who spoke good English. Gerald tracked him down and soon he was working for Gerald in England, where he stayed for several months, a typical Norwegian who was very popular and taught Gerald's team everything he knew.

Gerald had always been able to use simple enamels, but now he proved what he had always suspected: enamel is the most unpredictable and infuriating material known to man. Beenham must have helped, because of its clean atmosphere compared with some polluted urban workshop

From 1968 Gerald steadily improved his mastery of enamels to satisfy his yearning for more richness and colour. Enamels involve heat, dust and dirt as well as high precision and courage. This box lid is the biggest known piece of opal matrix, 4½ inches across, cut for a centrepiece in the great exhibition of 1851. Thirty years ago, Gerald was already master of most of the difficulties of enamelling, where one mistake can mean total ruin

settings. As Gerald says, London is too dirty for enamels: you get small bits of metal dropping out of the chimneys in London. Nevertheless, despite everyone's skill and devotion in the workshop, six man-years were spent at Beenham after Bergersen's departure, making enamels not one of which was fit for selling. Not until the early '70s did Gerald start to generate his present reputation as one of the world's foremost modern enamellers.

Another unexpected, refreshing new impulse for him was his Jewish religious synagogue plate. There had been some modern stirrings initiated by Richard Norton of S. J. Phillips, Bond Street jewellers, in the two West London synagogues of which he was Chairman. But it was Jonathan Stone, silver connoisseur and writer, who became the leading pioneer of new design in Jewish ritual plate. He convinced his mother Dorothy to commission from Gerald a large eternal light (like a sanctuary lamp) for the New London Synagogue in Abbey Road. This was followed by a set of Torah Bells, breast plate and pointer commissioned by Ethel Wix. The basis of Jewish worship is the Torah, which has an oval case containing the Torah Scroll. This is surmounted by either a crown or a pair of objects which contain bells called Torah Bells. Many other pieces for private ritual use were then commissioned, proving that this ancient faith could present a modern face to its young new worshippers. The complicated rules for ritual gradually became clearer. Arnold Horwell, a new friend of Gerald and a good art patron, helped to explain them and himself placed many commissions, including an Hannukah lamp, a Mezuzah and a Havdalah set.

Most spectacular was the initiative of Jacob Rothschild, now Lord Rothschild, the banker turned Chairman of the National Gallery, turned

Silver vase with red enamel commissioned by the Worshipful Company of Goldsmiths

Silver jug with carved ivory handle and black enamel, commissioned by the Victoria and Albert Museum

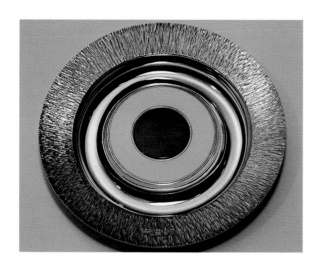

Varieties of enamel colour. The translucent effect of enamels changes with the quality of light. But enamels cannot often parallel the varied texture of stones, like Lapis Lazuli for instance, with its unique flecked blue colour

A gift from Wills Tobacco expressing the full potential of colour and texture offered by stones with enamels

By 1993, Gerald had gained the confidence to mix lapis stone with the enamelled coat of arms of his private client, achieving a ceremonial panoply. Enamels have a domestic function as well as their more normal use in ceremonials. Enamels can receive much handling, but do not need regular cleaning

Thermos flask 1991 for Geoffrey
Lawson featuring his racing
colours in enamels. His father in
law Lord Samuel commissioned
many pieces from Gerald

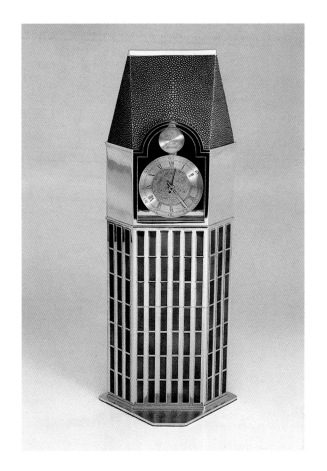

Enamelled clock 1993
commissioned by W. H. Smith for
their collection to celebrate the
connection with the firm of the
Hornby family, Michael and his
son Simon

Enamel can act as a focus for
attention, as with this domestic
clock. One of an edition of three.
This was a difficult job
technically because the
electrotype case, which was
produced by the BJS company,
had to be formed over a metal
pattern which was made by
hammering. Owing to the shape
this was very difficult to control

The enamels on this small mug act as a visual junction between the vertical bowl and the horizontal table beneath. The owner, Jonathan Stone, helped to launch Gerald into making Jewish plate

head of the National Lottery, finally combining all these fertile interests into a flow of charitable initiatives for Israel. After some big pieces of silver, the culmination of the Rothschild – Benney links to date, is the recent commission by the Rothschild Foundation in Jerusalem (Yad Hanadiv) for a painting by Gerald's eldest son Paul. Paul painted the twelve eminent Jews who were chiefly responsible for the new Supreme Court building in Jerusalem.

Rothschild had generously invited Paul, who was back in Britain after years as a painter in New York, to visit Israel and stay there for as long as the job needed. It took nine months, both in London and in Jerusalem, and Paul had to assemble his subjects one by one as they could never all be in the same place at once. The big picture, measuring 170 by 230 cm, was exhibited in the National Portrait Gallery in London in 1994–5, and was very successful there. Now, it is a major feature of one of the great new buildings of Jerusalem, the Supreme Court.

The impressive group is one of only a small handful of modern masterpieces showing men of affairs pursuing their discussions together; another is the Directors of Penguin Books by Rodrigo Moynihan. The difficulty is not only to make such people look as interesting as they in fact are, rather than making them look like dead totems; but also, the artist must fabricate a coherent composition out of rather static colourless male dress. Paul succeeded admirably, disposing his figures round a big model of the new Supreme Court building in Jerusalem. After this, it will be very difficult for Paul to resist the temptation of commissions, emulating in paint the successes of his father in silver.

One by-product of the Supreme Court commission was an exhibition for Gerald. Paul, while living in Jerusalem, had met a jeweller, Oded Gera, who had a shop in Tel Aviv. Oded visited Gerald at Beenham and staged a large show of Gerald's silver in the Tel Aviv shop. Gerald had made a quantity of Judaica – Jewish ritual art, which earned enthusiastic attention and publicity. But, surprisingly, it was the beakers and ice buckets which sold. This was Gerald's latest export venture and confirmed his experience over decades, that exports for him are an expensive effort. Perhaps he tries to move too quickly for the markets concerned, instead of returning regularly and cultivating local goodwill patiently until it turns into local business.

Gerald reminisced to me in a different context about the religious message conveyed by silver. He made the altar cross for one of Britain's famous public schools, Charterhouse, and he was under no illusions as to the meaning of the cross: "you've got to get the lighting right – you're probably competing with a great big window behind, or maybe a clerestory round the sides. Then your design must somehow have dignity. I'm not sure how many boys at Charterhouse actually reflect on the symbolism …

Hannukah Lamp 8 ins high, silver and silver gilt, for private ritual use by Arnold Horwell, who taught Gerald some of the meaning of Jewish ritual, and some of the niceties of Hebrew script. The Maccabees took eight days to defeat the Assyrians, so there are eight lights with the servant and oil holder

Business Growth

Spice box for Mr. Astaire

Torah Bells for New London Synagogue, one of Gerald's principal clients for Judaica

Torah Crown used in Synagogue ritual, symbolising the Tree of Life

I hate to say it, but I think that out of the 500 boys at morning service, the cross is the last thing most of them are thinking about … But, if it is elegant, complementary to the chapel, it can be rather like a nice pair of gates when you come into a house … it must do something for their education, even if it's subliminal. And occasionally the symbolism of Jesus on the cross can bring a great deal of comfort in your beautiful church with your own cross on the altar."

Jewish youths are not so different from Christian. If you compare the 250 years old Jewish plate at Bevis Marks synagogue in Spitalfields in London's poor East End, with Gerald's newest work, you can see how skilfully he has stripped away the old technical visual complications, to leave the clean lines of the essential modern faith.

It is sometimes claimed that the Jewish peoples cling together to the exclusion of Gentiles. It is good to be able to record that Jewish attitudes towards Gerald have been absolutely liberal, even in the intimate matter of religion. Gerald, a Gentile, was invited by Jews to bring their faith visually into the new millenium, and he succeeded.

9 Honours and Public Offices

Honours and public offices – RDI – Goldsmiths' Hall and resignation from Goldsmiths' Court – apprentices – Silver Trust.

Gerald tastes celebrity: receiving the Freedom of Reading in 1984 with the Mayor and a civic party. The plate he had made for Reading was on display

Overleaf
The British hall-mark is unique throughout the world. It has guaranteed the quality of gold and silver for over five centuries. Its name means the mark of Goldsmiths' Hall in London. It is a link between the Hall, where it is applied, and Gerald, who loves to feature it on his work. This flatware was given by Janet's mother, Mrs Bridget Edwards, a lifelong supporter of Gerald, to her second husband Elie Mayorcas. She married him after her first husband died in 1990 and together they lived to enjoy the new shop opening in Walton Street, where they sat as distinguished senior citizens on camp stools side by side welcoming guests in the upstairs room

have touched on Gerald's inspirational qualities. They are rare and splendid, his invention, his speed, his warmth and generosity. These have earned him important honours. One of his earliest big pieces of silver was the big bowl with abstract erratic pierced cover given by Lord Adrian to Leicester University. It was so successful that the University in 1963 made him an Hon. MA, on the same occasion that Benjamin Britten received his Hon. Doctorate. As early as 1971 he was elected a Royal Designer for Industry at the Royal Society of Arts, a select body of some 65 creative designers of international repute, who include several of Gerald's friends: the silversmiths David Mellor and Robert Welch, the architect Alan Irvine, the illustrator David Gentleman, the graphic designer Dennis Bailey.

In 1984 he became a Freeman of the Borough of Reading, his home town, whose companies, institutions and citizens had been such good patrons of his, commissioning from him hundreds of pieces of civic plate and partly causing him to move to their region, making Beenham his workshop as well as his home. In 1990 he became an Hon Fellow of the Royal College of Art where he had studied and taught for so many years, and in 1994 a CBE, perhaps an acknowledgement of his loyalty to the Royal Family, as well as of his overall artistic distinction.

All this adds up to a great cornucopia of public goodwill towards him. Yet I cannot resist suggesting that if he had been another sort of artist, not our premier silversmith and product designer, he would by now be a household name, like musicians Benjamin Britten and Andrew Lloyd Webber, both Lords; architects Richard Rogers and Norman Foster, Lord and Knight with Order of Merit respectively; painter Howard Hodgkin or sculptor Anthony Caro, both Knights.

At this level, the honour is for the profession as much as for the person, and one need not look far to realise that craftsmen in Britain are alas not considered major artists.

Perhaps the most emotional honour for Gerald, is his membership of the medieval guild of British goldsmiths in the City of London, the Worshipful Company of Goldsmiths. In 1958 he was elected a Freeman of the 800 year old Company, at the same time becoming a Freeman of the City of London. Then came the next step up in the institution from which derived so many of his best and biggest commissions – he was elected a Liveryman.

Soon after, he joined the Company's Hall-marking Council, the national representative body which tries to pull together the various divergent practices and laws of the different Assay Offices: London at Goldsmiths' Hall, Birmingham, Sheffield, Edinburgh, Glasgow and Dublin, each started at different times with different procedures. Add to these, the imminent arrival of the European Community, each of whose countries has its own hall-mark activity, and you sense some of the complications faced by this

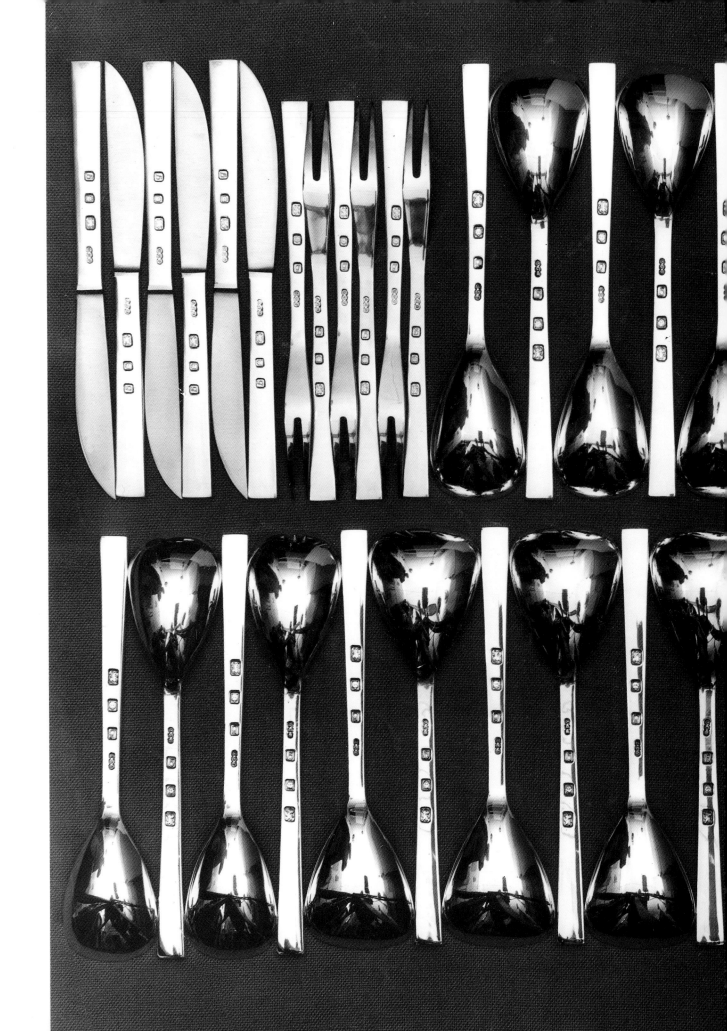

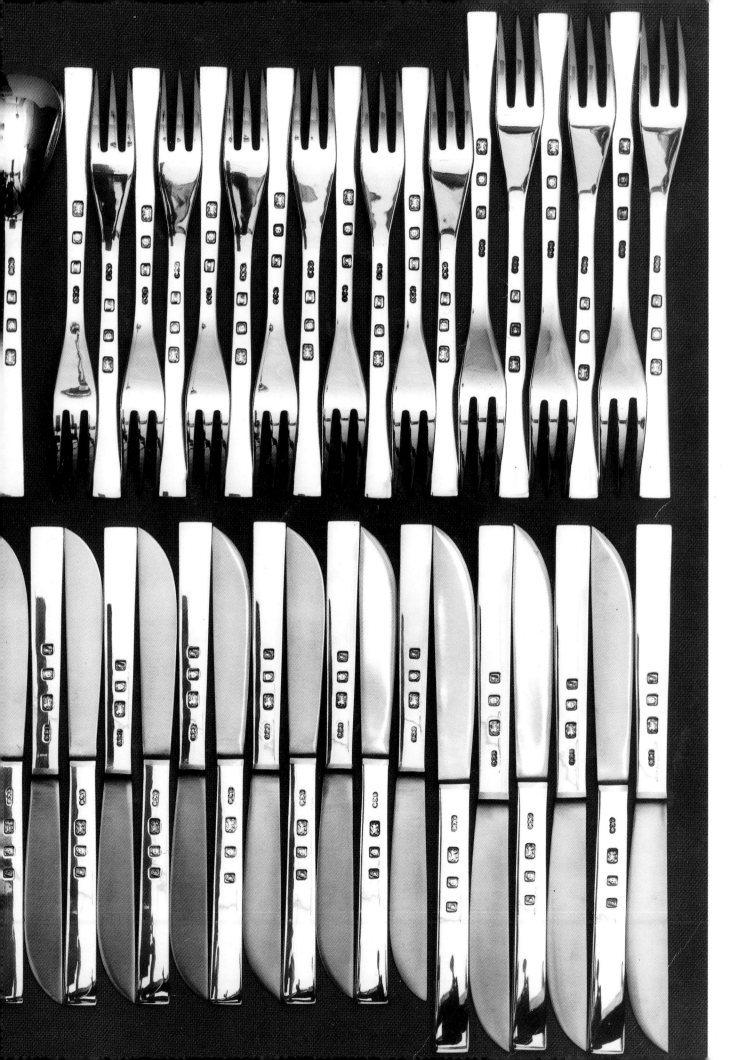

Council. Sometimes its good lunches at Goldsmiths' Hall lead to harmonious agreement, sometimes they lead to indecision and a postponement of action for another quarter or half year. Anyway, Gerald's six year membership of the Council enabled him to speak there with authority: he loves the Hall-mark and knows its guarantee and associations help him to sell his work. He always likes his hall-marks prominent, and he is sorry that the Goldsmiths Assay Office in London has not taken a strong pioneering line in its European negotiations. It might have persuaded our continental friends that the British system is not only far the oldest, but also by far the best in the world.

In 1980, Gerald was delighted to be elected to the governing body at Goldsmiths' Hall, the Court of Assistants, an honour which was specially dear to him. He wanted to be able to repay to the Company some of the kindnesses which he had received there so abundantly over the years. All began well, but the older members of the Court, who were used to supporting the craft, began to die, and the younger members did not share Gerald's enthusiasm for silversmithing. The decision was made to restore and rebuild large parts of Goldsmiths' Hall, mostly built in 1835, a huge cost which he believed was unnecessary and extravagant. Massive spending of many millions of pounds on the fabric and furnishing was reflected in a virtual shut-down of exhibitions and purchases of new plate, at a time when craftsmen badly needed support. Living art and craft no longer seemed important at the Hall.

Goldsmiths' Hall, mostly built in 1835, home of many of Gerald's dreams

The Court was then composed of captains of industry, scientists, stockbrokers, retailers and antique dealers including Arthur Grimwade of Christie's. Gerald was the only practising silversmith amongst them. He felt the Company was betraying the trust of centuries towards its own craft. After some emotional exchanges in meetings, at his last Court meeting he made his worries clear, but was told to sit down and only talk about things he knew about. He resigned, probably only the second resignation from the Court in the Company's eight centuries' history. He feels no bitterness, only disappointment that his view was proved correct within the decade. The rebuild seems to some outside observers to have been mismanaged. Anyway, its financial scars are alas all too obvious today in the much reduced scale of the Company's work for its crafts.

Gerald was not surprised when a friend of his on the Court said to him "Don't see you here so often nowadays, Benney". He replied "Well, actually, I resigned". "Oh, really" was the negligent end to the exchange.

Not every member of prestigious old British institutions like the Goldsmiths, engages in the Company's affairs with the intensity which comes naturally to Gerald. He thinks that his resignation was like a pebble dropping into a pool: when the ripple reaches the edge, it's gone, apparently forgotten. But ripples often touch something on the way, and he finds now that he is still active helping the Company to help its craft, and he enjoys his frequent visits to the Hall.

There is one tangible personal record of Gerald's five years on the Court, 1980–85. Each member is given enough money by the Company to commission a silver wine mug for his own use (there are alas no women on the Court). A few have been made by the member concerned, and Gerald's, finished in 1981, is one of his masterpieces. It is thick, hand-hammered, with a smoky, scrolly pattern picked out in enamel round the Company's arms. He did his own enamels because he could not find anyone else, not even the most famous enamellers in the country, ready to attempt what was an extremely difficult technical feat.

He cut deep grooves for the enamels – he likens his treatment to a ha-ha in a garden, with a wall on one side and a gradual slope on the other. The enamel goes easily into the deep side, but the meniscus, the natural surface layer with its centripetal tendency, makes the shallow enamel turn back on itself and become a longitudinal ball, losing the elegance of the tapered depth with its delicate colour shading.

There must be no bubbles or impurity, the enamel must be baked dry, which means the fine powder tends to fall off the curved silver and go down your sleeve, then you wiggle the silver on a fork into the tiny opening of your white-hot oven or kiln, where you balance it on a small brick and hope it will not tip over. It is fired at 850°, and in two minutes it has become glossy glass. After cooling, you file off the surplus surface glass and pray it will not crack or break off, because it is impossible to repair or adjust work of this extreme delicacy. One small fault will mean scrapping the whole and starting again, as the surface of the silver has been ground down during the process. It was a challenge at that large scale, the most tricky enamel that he had ever attempted. Malcolm Long of Yorkshire engraved with great subtlety both the scrolling pattern and the lettering, reading from Gerald's drawing almost more than the pencil could convey. This exquisite small mug is the best tribute to Gerald's decades of doing and wishing at Goldsmiths' Hall. Eventually, it will leave the Hall and join the Benney family as a reminder of their links with the ancient guild of Goldsmiths.

But the Company's permanent collection of modern silver, the biggest and best in the world, contains the true monument to Gerald's life at Goldsmiths' Hall. The earliest piece is 1950, made by him when he was a student at the Royal College of Art. The latest so far, is a coffee pot with striped enamel lid, a brother piece to the one commissioned by the Silver Trust and now in use for the Prime Minister at No. 10 Downing Street, made in 1997, the year he prepared to leave Beenham. Such a long unbroken record of half a century of brilliant creativity, is an unusual

testimony to his single-mindedness. In our age of violent change, not many artists or craftsmen manage to stick on their chosen course for as long as he has done.

When prosperity eventually returned to Beenham, Gerald no longer dreamed of recruiting again a comprehensive team of craftsmen who could do everything: what in business is called vertical organisation, so that you can make your product from beginning to end. He adopted a more flexible and economical system of using specialised outworkers, mostly in London. There he had engravers, polishers, spinners, and several smiths who could cope with specialised needs, and with fluctuations in demand, better than a static resident team. In the cutlery centre of Sheffield, he found some flatware craftsmen to help him. He had a normal complement at Beenham of perhaps three part-time craftsmen, compared with his maximum in London of twenty two, but in his last five years at Beenham plus Walton Street, he more than doubled his turnover, whilst at the same time he halved his staff and was able almost to forget those bugbears of any employer: health, redundancy and Pay As You Earn (PAYE) tax payments.

Altogether, he may have trained and employed about twenty five apprentices, quite a social and educational burden for him. During their five years they would do everything from filing up castings, sweeping the floor with its precious metal dust, making perhaps a dozen hinges at a time ready to fit to coffee pots, cutting out the blanks for spouts, bending them into shape and soldering them, making handles in some heat resistant material, which might have been ivory but may now be ebony or holly, perhaps doing some polishing, though that tended to be kept for specialists. After five years, the boy would be practical, but he would need another five years to become proficient.

Now, the system is changing fast. Under the old procedure thirty years ago, an apprentice would be indentured by a factory like C. J. Vander Ltd. of London through Goldsmiths' Hall, the Cutlers' Company of Sheffield, or his local trade association. Wage rates, conditions of employment, training standards, and regular visits to an art school, were to some extent determined by national or regional agreements. Some of the few dozen factories employed their own designer, but most of them did not; they purchased designs from free-lance designers who had learned to draw at an art school, or from the retailer for whom the factory was making its silver.

Gradually, as mechanisation reached our skilled craft industry, apprentices were displaced by trainees. Apprentices, with their long training period, were qualified in a big range of handwork skills. Trainees by contrast had a short, technical training which equipped them to use maybe one or two specialised machines. The distinction between apprentices with their versatile hands, and trainees with their machines, became blurred.

Each member of the Court at Goldsmiths' Hall is given enough funds to commission a wine mug for his use there. Gerald made his own, and it is a superb example of his design and enamel skills, together with Malcolm Long's carving

A generation ago, artist-craftsmen like Gerald were few and far between. Probably not more than a dozen of them throughout Britain made their living entirely out of producing silver. They designed and made their own pieces and usually sold them direct to their clients without the services of an intermediate retailer.

Now, there are very few firms able to train apprentices in the old way. Most craftsmen today are not indentured apprentices. Instead they are creative artists, taught in art schools, who then set up in very small workshops working on their own. It is an exciting change, partly because there are now many women craftsmen, whereas there used to be no women apprentices – Gerald had no woman among his twenty five boy apprentices. Equally important, the emphasis in art schools is naturally on art, whereas for apprentices it was on technique. Most of these small workshops earn less money than the apprentices used to do, and the quality of their work is much more varied. But they are creative, whereas the apprentices usually were not. There are now hundreds of tiny studios all over the country making enterprising new work designed by the owner/manager, with perhaps under a dozen traditional factories training their own apprentices in the traditional way. Art schools and artists are burgeoning in Britain, whereas the highly skilled craft factories are suffering from the competition both of the machine and of the small artist. Gerald's friend David Mellor is a good example of modern trends: he is finding it necessary at the time of writing, to enlarge his model workshop at Hathersage near Sheffield, to accommodate more sophisticated machines for his cutlery manufacture, and fewer people.

The Silver Trust is the most optimistic and unexpected silversmithing innovation of the '90s. It was the brainchild of Lady Mary Henderson, wife of Sir "Nicko" Henderson, lately British Ambassador in Washington. She contacted Gerald, David Mellor and Robert Goodden for discussions. Perhaps the seeds had been sown when Margaret Thatcher discovered that there was no official Prime Ministerial plate in her residence, No. 10 Downing Street. Prime Ministers like the Duke of Wellington, had always been expected to provide their own table plate. But Prime Ministers in the 1980s were no longer like the Duke, and Mrs. Thatcher tried to fill the gap by borrowing some big new pieces from Goldsmiths' Hall, to stimulate her friends to give new plate to No. 10. They did not do so. Until two dynamic women founded the Silver Trust about 1985, there was still no official silver for the Prime Minister.

Gerald, as a founder Trustee and as a friend of these ladies, tells how the initial fund collected from industry and individual well-wishers some £400,000, which was spent commissioning young craftsmen to make a

Beaker given to 10 Downing Street by the Silver Trust for the use of the Prime Minister

range of pieces which would reflect credit on the users and earn publicity for an art at which the British have always excelled.

It was upsetting for him when he asked that a Trust meeting might be held at Goldsmiths' Hall – he was still a member of the Court there. The Clerk at that time, refused and thereby lost the opportunity for the Company to lead a splendid, well-financed initiative. The Trustees had to walk from the steps of Goldsmiths' Hall to the offices of Hambros Bank for their meeting. Soon, David Mellor and Robert Goodden phased themselves out. Rupert Hambro the banker succeeded them and provided an office for Trust meetings.

Lady Marcia Falkender, colleague of Prime Minister Harold Wilson, joined them with Carla Powell and Jocelyn Stephens, then Rector (or head) of the Royal College of Art, who became Chairman of the group. Jocelyn, dynamic and cathartic, much admired by Gerald, organised a competition for 70 silver plates in record time, working with his partner Vivien Duffield. Doubts about the possibility of co-ordinating 70 mostly young, inexperienced and different designers, using various untried techniques, were soon dispelled as action succeeded discussion.

The results were impressive Later, Gerald felt that he should be available to make some plate for the scheme, which would have been impossible for a Trustee, so he resigned. Since then, he has been awarded two commissions. Now, the Trust is managed by Christopher English and continues to thrive, still organised from the office of J. and O. Hambro. It is successfully collecting its second round of financial support, and Lady Falkender remains the courageous fund raiser.

10 Painting

Painting – Solomon Gallery exhibition – pictures at Beenham, Newbury, Walton Street.

As Gerald de-centralised his production, using fewer permanent employees, more out-workers, and as the pressures of life mounted, so he needed positive relaxation. He found it in painting. He had always been an accomplished draughtsman, drawing anything from his own silver, to the Mediterranean landscapes visible from Nigel Broackes' ocean – going yacht, to architectural details of buildings he loved. That was therapeutic and sensible, the sort of relaxing fulfilment which may be enjoyed by any artistic person in need of a tonic.

But the painting bug became a roaring lion. There was by then spare space at Beenham, and the energetic visitor might be allowed to trespass through the ground floor leisure rooms, into a sequence of what might be defined as artist's free expression. Easels, stretchers, canvases, piles of paper were everywhere. Tables were laden with paint brushes in dirty beakers, paint tubes and pots. Round the walls were paintings of all sorts and sizes, many of them of a distinctive long thin shape, with a long dreamy landscape and a setting or rising sun, many with a gorgeous girl in varying stages of undress. Gone was the passion for order and logic which typified the rest of the huge house . Here was total freedom. This was Gerald out of harness, and having real fun.

Perhaps these large oils gave an outlet to his subliminal dreams of sun, women and landscapes. He started painting seriously about twelve years ago. He spent perhaps every other week painting, a recreation for him of his creative spark, which may have become a little jaded after so many years of hectic inspiration. He asks "why do people paint? I suppose it's fundamental to any artist because with tools, you are limited by technique, whereas with paint you can do whatever you want. Silver is discipline, paint is freedom".

His models were stable girls and girls connected with Janet's new racehorse and horse eventing business, his views were what he already knew in his own park at Beenham, in Scotland and in the nearby Berkshire Downs. His first public display was in Philip Solomon's new gallery in Dover Street, and he sold 28 pictures there. Good, he thought, but the figures did not thrill Philip.

Temporarily, Gerald's painting has taken a back seat because he finds so little uninterrupted time after dealing with his other affairs: a huge increase in silver sales since the end of the recession, and the opening of his son Simon's shop at 73 Walton Street. To paint well remains one of his goals. Rather pessimistically, he compares it with light at the end of a tunnel, and he says he is still trapped inside that tunnel. Perhaps his sale of Beenham in 1998, his painting exhibitions in Henley and at the Benney shop in Walton Street will reignite the incandescent flame.

As to the art, this is not the place for a detailed assessment. Suffice it to say that the colours are usually autumnal, the very opposite of this ebullient artist's normal mood. His palette is usually soft and quiet, between the autumnal and the icy, mostly dun browns and steely greys, quite a contrast to the taut, dramatic lines of his silver. These greys and silvers, browns and whites are the foil for occasional flashes of bright yellow or red in the sky, in the landscape, or on the furniture near the nude figures. The sureness of the linear construction may reflect his long experience of making designers' plans and sections for others to interpret: there, clarity must come first. But in these paintings, the sharp pencil of the designer has given way to the broad brush of the artist. The tools are different, but the language they express remains surprisingly similar. I expect the peaceful country monochrome will eventually yield to some of the rumbustious turmoil which is Gerald's inner character. I think the restraint of his paintings may soon be influenced by the riot of innovation presented nowadays by the youth of London.

Rumanian Friend

Portrait of Sukie

Imminent storm at sea.
Gerald knows stormclouds,
literal as well as metaphorical

Wreck, Dominica

An agreeable foretaste of the future was his large one-man retrospective in the Century Gallery, Henley-on-Thames in May 1998. The nudes were mellowed by the sunshine reflected off the rippling water of the River Thames outside the windows. The grey landscapes, in truth seeming almost icy at dusk, began to radiate a mysterious warmth. The pen and wash drawings enticed us mentally to share Nigel Broackes' yacht in the Mediterranean with its raked masts and funnel, and Denis O'Brien's in the Caribbean islands with their tiny buildings clustered up the coastal hills. Appetising was one word which came to mind. Another was variety. If we did not see overwhelming colours, thick impasto or metaphysical perspectives, the clarity and grace of line was a tonic in the context of the pretentiousness of too much modern art. Enjoyment was probably the theme of the pictures, just as it is the inspiration of the silver.

Martinique visited by Gerald on holiday in the yacht of Sir Nigel Broackes

11 Newest Commissions

Newest commissions – Lichfield Cathedral, Dublin Cathedral, Derby race trophies –
Janet becomes more independent, horse eventing, catering, managing the estate –
Simon becomes partner, organises successful new shop at 73 Walton St. near Harrods.

Delivering a trophy can be anxious in case the client does not like it, or tedious in case there are long speeches. Here was a recent moment of real pleasure: the Whitbread Round the World Trophy is on dry land before the boats set sail

Gerald decided to diminish his personal involvement in producing his stock pieces, leaving the making to others, those trusted free-lance craftsmen who had been working for him intermittently for years. He gave more responsibility to Simon who assumed responsibility for everyday business affairs, and who began to design not only the jewellery which had always been his province, but some of the silver too. This left Gerald free to specialise in the area which he had always enjoyed most, designing special pieces of silver for commissions from private clients. Nobody knew whether there would be enough of these commissions in the rather austere new political climate of Prime Minister Thatcher, to absorb his still impressive energy. But he hoped that a few complex jobs would be enough to compensate him for the loss of some of the smaller routine work. And events in the last few years seem to be proving him right.

In August 1989 John Harley Lang, Dean of the fine medieval cathedral at Lichfield and his wife, visited Gerald and Janet at Beenham. An immediate sympathy sprang up between the four. They had met to discuss the cathedral's need for a new chalice to use when the cathedral's benefactors were celebrated. But they were soon planning much more challenging schemes to commission a succession of pieces.

Then they dreamed not of a succession, but of an instant cascade, that "they should commission everybody all at once", so as to meet Lichfield's need and promote the silversmith's craft at the same time. It would be a deliberate act of patronage, "in the grand manner" as the Dean recorded. In February 1990 the eighteen participating silversmiths visited Lichfield, and Gerald recorded "We are all taking part in something special". The Dean raised the funds from local well-wishers and others including Goldsmiths' Hall, and only a year later the collection was finished, ready for the Lichfield Festival. The speed was intoxicating, the impact of the opening exhibition in the Chapter House was magnificent, the enthusiasm and generosity of the donors was infectious. The project coincided with the Dean's retirement; never was the spirit of youth more in evidence.

Another amazing surprise took Gerald to the big medieval Anglican cathedral in Dublin, St Patrick's, where Dean Swift used to officiate nearly three centuries ago. Cecil King of the Daily Mirror had been a friend and client of Gerald's for years, and used to visit Gerald's workshop to see what was going on. One of the dreams they had together, was a solid gold goblet, whose special appeal lay in its stem. This stem was three inches long and one and a half inches diameter, and it was hollow, and open at the top. So the contents of the goblet would go down the stem without being seen from the outside. King used this remarkable stem to conceal from his friends and from his wife, his generous appetite for brandy. Alas, the goblet was stolen, but the owner's gratitude to Gerald lived on in a very useful way.

Processional cross for Lichfield Cathedral, 1997. Local firms, encouraged by John Lang, the Dean, commissioned eighteen silversmiths to make new plate for the Cathedral, a magnificent cooperative effort

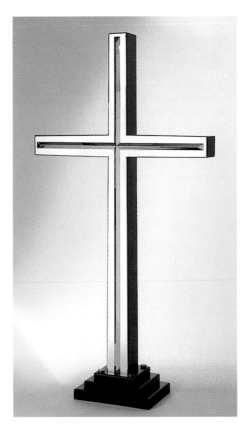

Altar cross for St. Patrick's
Cathedral, Dublin, 1997,
commissioned by Cecil King in
his will

King was an Irishman and an Anglican. In his will, he bequeathed cash to pay for a new cross on the High Altar of St. Patrick's Cathedral, Dublin, to be made by Gerald. There was a delay of years while the Executors tried not very urgently to trace Gerald. Eventually Cecil's widow, Dame Ruth King, found Gerald through the Goldsmiths' Company, and he gratefully received the big commission as it were from the grave. Gerald tells me in a rather Irish way that he will go *anywhere* to stay in the Shelbourne Hotel because it is so comfortable and has such delicious bacon and eggs; that's an Irish comment because there is only one Shelbourne, and it is in Dublin, so you can't go anywhere else to get there. Gerald made the splendid cross and in 1997 went to Dublin for the consecration.

Another Irish joke transpired. The lighting had to be installed over a Bank Holiday, and the electrician was on hand to meet Gerald by the altar. He cheerfully announced to Gerald that he had miles of the necessary wiring. Gerald asked about the light bulbs, and was told there were none, and, worse, none could be obtained during the holiday. Gerald had to return to Britain to get some bulbs and tubes, because lighting for an altar cross in a big cathedral is absolutely crucial; here, the lights had to be concealed behind columns in order to reflect from the prism surfaces of the cross, as it were bright lights from Heaven radiating onto the worshippers.

For the consecration, the cathedral was full and the design was deemed magnificent. It was, as usual there, a friendly ecumenical congregation of Catholics and others praying together in the Anglican cathedral, because there is not enough space elsewhere in Dublin to hold so many Christians together: an example which inspired Gerald in the context of other "Christian" behaviour elsewhere in Ireland.

The point of the Dublin cross, apart from showing how Gerald continues to design with startling originality and always fresh style, is to illustrate how an artist may develop his clientele during a whole lifetime. Gerald has never advertised, yet the number of his clients has increased steadily, sometimes rapidly. The King connection, culminating in the Dublin cross, lasted for four decades. It was nourished no doubt by Gerald's sociable instincts and King's excellent brandy, but the real cause of the bond between them was the continuing vitality of Gerald's art. King, like most of Gerald's other distinguished clients, was capable of dropping people as quickly as he might pick them up. Discerning clients like King have stuck with Gerald partly because they like him, mainly because his art is unique.

The Derby horse race at Epsom initiated what was perhaps Gerald's largest recent commission sponsored by industry: Vodafone launched themselves into this, the most famous flat race in the world, with an initial £ 3 M. Gerald's obelisk for the Oaks was only one of seventeen magnificent

fantasies with which he extended the fancy of the smart set beyond their horses, towards his silver.

Janet meanwhile had filled the gap left when her children grew up and left home, by starting a new business in catering. She is a good cook and realised that most meals in most public places were flabby and unappetising. The idea of good cooking as an art form and as an intellectual pursuit, was still not generally accepted in Britain. But she knew that Haute Cuisine could be supplied to anyone who wanted it, by using the new process of vacuum packing.

Her catering company, Sean's Kitchen, had a young professional chef called Sean Kellingray, who had trained at the Savoy Hotel. They built a kitchen in Lambourn, near Newbury, in the middle of training yards for race horses, where visits by wealthy race horse owners were therefore not unknown. Refrigerated vans distributed the meals, and eventually Janet was able to sell her share in the business to Sean, who is still going strong.

Horses became Janet's new interest. She bought several racehorses, which she ran in partnership with her mother, helped with family capital from her father's building business in Basingstoke. Their trainer was David Nicholson (the Duke), and they did well until one week the fates struck: a week old foal died, two horses broke their legs and had to be put down, another was badly injured and took months to recover. There were no horses left to race.

Then, in order to do a good turn to a friend, she bought an eventing horse. Through that, she met another friend's jockey son, Mark Corbett who joined her in a new company: the European Bloodstock Society. She

The Vodafone Trophies showed impressive variety

Overleaf
Gerald's earliest jewels, made in silver all in one day about 1957 (he could not then afford gold) and bought for the Goldsmiths' Hall collection

now goes to France several times a year to find young stock, which Mark and his wife Sian and their team train and "bring on", based at Janet's old home, Rawlins Farm in Hampshire. The horses all have the name prefix "Society" and are sold for dressage, showjumping and eventing at home and overseas, including America. Finally comes the Highclere Castle Horse Trials, which she has raised into being a big international event with French government backing.

Add to all this her still running Gerald's office, and still entertaining their many friends and clients, often the same thing, and you see how dynamic she is. Over four decades, the charming young wife of Gerald's imagination, has become the sinewy business partner. But the charm still remains dominant in her personality, ready to enslave the unwary males in the double world she now inhabits, the equine and the golden.

The hand of Gerald's imagination was fitting well into the glove of his production. But he was 67, Beenham had 52 rooms now being used by only two people, and Janet's two dozen horses were neighing for attention. The shoelace which tied this straggle together was the new shop at 73 Walton Street.

Gerald's son Simon financed and opened the shop in 1993, and sales there were, as Gerald described them, "miraculous". For the first time ever, stylish advertising was begun on the back page of the Covent Garden Opera Friends' magazine, using soft-focus photos taken under water. Walton Street displaced Beenham as the business headquarters. Gerald and Janet now prepare for the Millenium, brave and optimistic as ever.

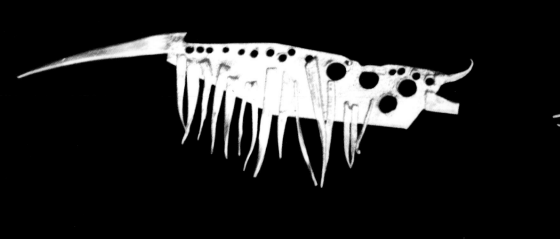
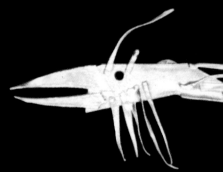

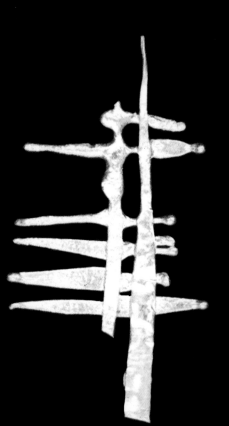

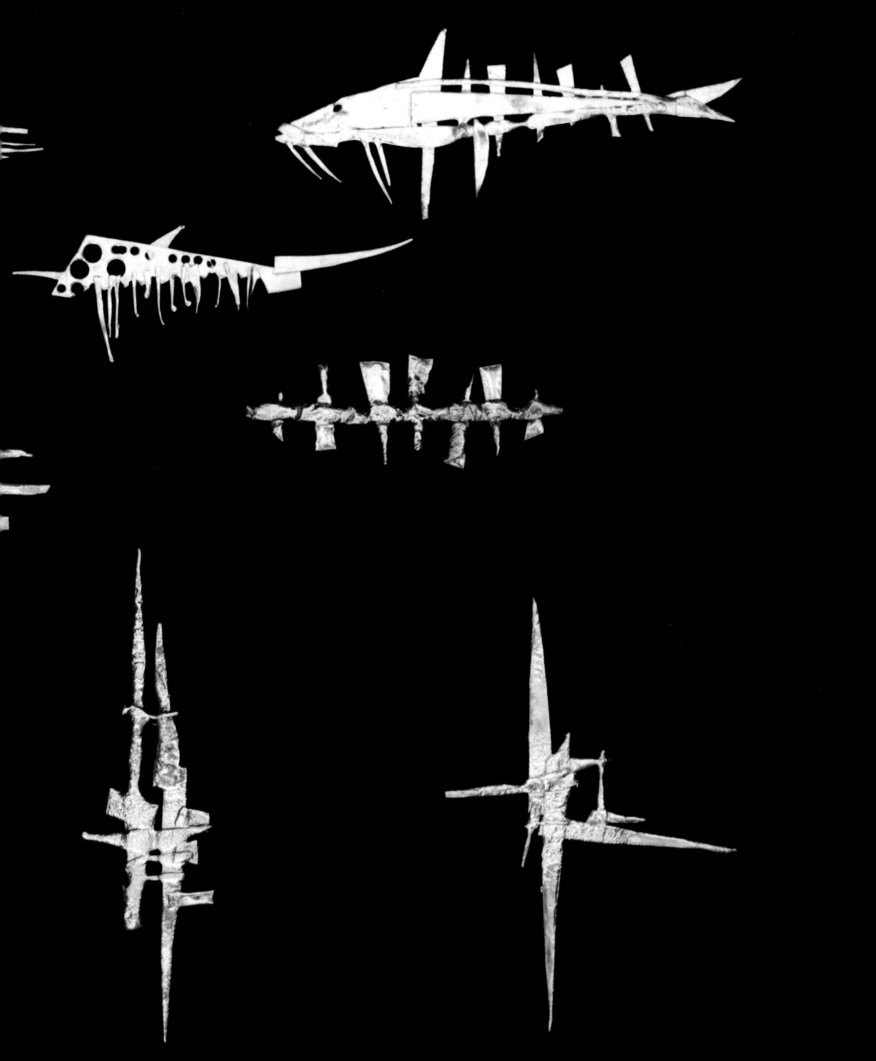

His first gold jewel. The gold, topaz and peridots in this pendant of 1961 show more abstract design skills than feminine grace. Gerald's interest in the fantasy of personal ornament came later. Goldsmiths' Hall collection

Pendant jewels designed by Gerald in 1997 for sale at "Benney", the family shop at 73 Walton Street, London SW 3. Containing opals, gold, lapis lazuli, diamonds and enamels . All represent an interesting contrast in materials

Necklace, earrings and ring in 18 carat with rubies and diamonds

12 Technique and Design

Technique – joy in handwork – texturing, raising, evolution of attitudes and style.

Texturing on the surface of silver was at first an accident because Gerald was using a hammer with a damaged, uneven head. Then texturing became a valued and unique expression of his own skill on his own work. Then his idea was widely imitated and became an asset for the silver industries everywhere. But texturing, now a well-known and easily recognised process, has seldom been fully understood, still less fully publicised. It is an interesting story, as important scientifically as it is commercially.

Silver is known and admired for the soft lustre of its surface, for its malleability which can be coaxed into such lovely shapes, for its scarcity which gives it a steady value, for its ancient history which associates it with great events and people, for its British hall-mark which guarantees its purity and which tells its pedigree. But silver presents one big problem to its owner, and that is tarnish. Gerald's invention of texturing partly solved that problem.

It began with a surprise, like some other semi-legendary inventions and discoveries of benefit to the human race: Newton and his apple falling from the tree disclosing the force of gravity, for instance, or Archimedes' water overflowing from the bath when he got into it, deducing from the displacement of water, that mass is constant. On the gastronomic front, it was the ancient Chinese who by chance dropped some pork into the fire, thus discovering that pork fat could easily be transformed into the delicacy of crackling. Coffee reached the West when the Turks retreated from their siege of Vienna, and burned the huge mounds of coffee they had to leave behind them, attracting the pursuing Viennese armies to this new taste.

In the mid-sixties, soon after moving into Beenham, Gerald started hammering a cup into shape with a hammer whose surface, unknown to him, had been damaged by banging onto hard nails and other hard household products. After half a dozen blows, he realised he had inadvertently imposed a pleasing pattern onto the silver. He filed the hard end of the hammer to make the pattern more emphatic, and produced a few complete beakers and goblets in order to test his new idea.

It worked in at least three ways: it looked good, and any artistic novelty tends to sell well. Secondly, the ripples on the surface meant that damp human fingers, a prime cause of tarnish when they press onto flat silver, could not press continuously onto the metal, so the corrosive effect of finger prints was dispersed and diminished.

The third effect of the new ribbed texture was more scientific, and therefore more difficult to describe in common language. The process of changing a sheet of silver into a shaped cup or bowl, either by hand hammering or by machine stamping or pressing, involves compressing the metal, which hardens it. This work-hardening has to be softened

The sculpture of files and hammers shaped by experience to fit the various jobs, the handles rubbed by hand till they have tactile appeal

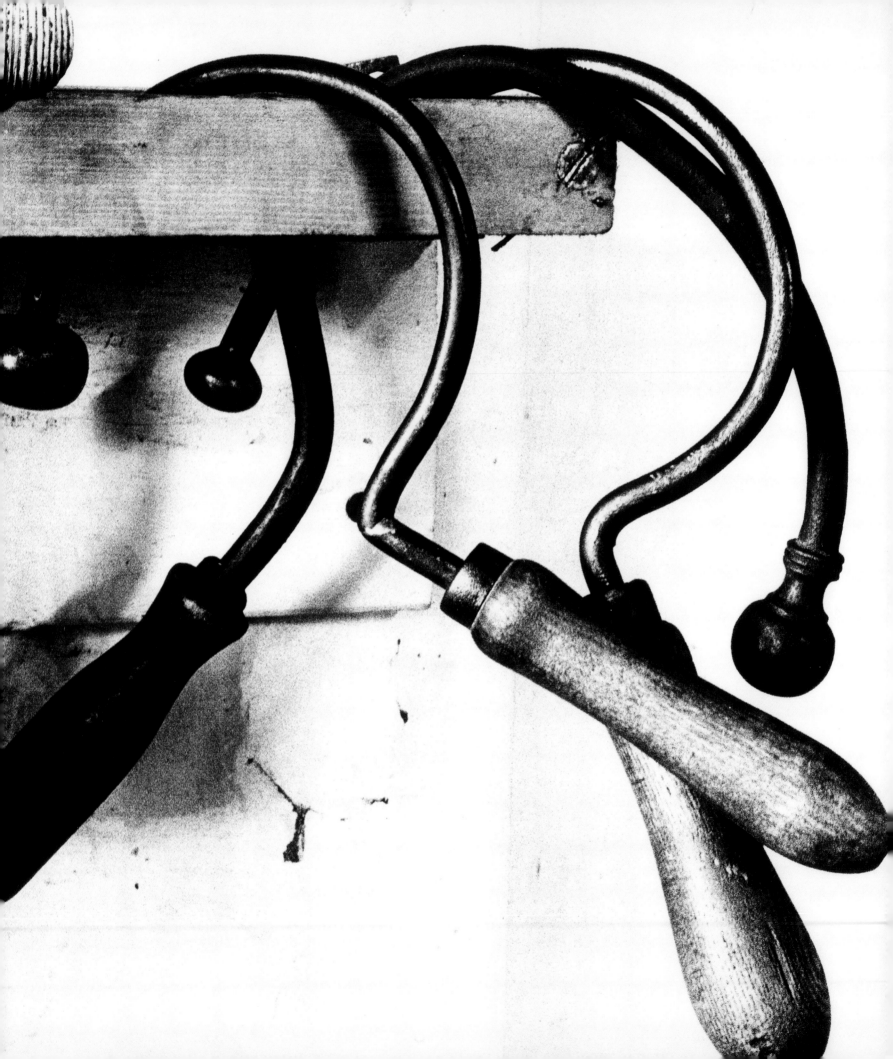

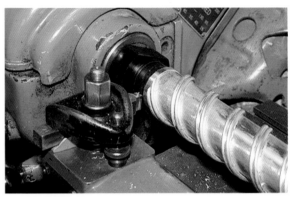

The process of making the parts of the Commonwealth Mace and assembling it, requiring a combination of creative imagination, craft skills and mechanical finesse

A basic skilled goldsmithing process is 'raising'. Here, the cup-shaped mace head (top) is hand raised or hammered into shape from a flat sheet of gold

occasionally, by a controlled heating process called annealing. The heating oxidises the copper in the alloy, which is then burned off in acid. The cleaning acid leaves a surface of vulnerable, very soft pure silver, a characteristic colour of white or grey-white. The robust mixture of silver alloys beneath is hidden by this layer of silver. The term "firestain" as used in the trade refers to the dark patches which occur when the outer thin skin of fine silver is worn or polished through.

The texturing hammer strengthens and leaves intact this top surface layer of fine silver, which cannot be polished off in the normal way. And fine silver is hardly subject to tarnishing by oxygen in the air, very little by sulphurisation. So, in one move, Gerald had achieved a surface which was easy to handle without making finger marks on it, he had cut down dramatically the need for and therefore the cost of polishing, and, years before the advent of modern improved silver polishes, he had invented an almost tarnish free silver.

His texturing soon came to be known in the trade as "Benney Bark Finish" but there was scant public acknowledgement to him for his important invention. Indeed, within a year or two, his invention was being used generally in the silver industry and often by craftsmen who had been trained by him. It was chagrining for him at first. But it is a token of his generosity of mind that he never showed any resentment at the ease with which his discovery was copied and sometimes debased by lesser hands than his own. The importance of texturing diminished during the eighties when new, wholesome chemical silver polishes became normal, but half his production is still distinguished with this charming, useful technique.

The formal name of the governors of the Worshipful Company of Goldsmiths includes the words Wardens and Commonalty of the mystery … of Goldsmiths, the word "mystery" being the same as the old French word métier. This is rather unfortunate, because it has indirectly led to a detachment of skilled craftsmanship from ordinary life. Too many admirers of the crafts may think today "very fine – it's a pity I cannot understand it and it does not seem relevant to my way of life". Consequently, these same people, instead of taking the trouble to locate what they really like, namely a good piece of hand craft, instead buy a ready-made machine piece off the shelf.

There are plenty of manuals of silversmithing, explaining the difference between the basic processes for making a shape from a flat sheet of silver. Raising is hammering your bowl shape from a flat sheet. It is the fine craftsman's preferred method, because it usually results in a more sensitive form, it flatters thicker, heavier metal, and the hammer marks can give a pleasing rhythm to the surface. Spinning forms the bowl by rotating it on a lathe, often against a wood shape. It is quicker and cheaper than raising, but seldom achieves such a sensitive shape. The metal sheet for spinning does not have to be thin, but for hand-raising, metal both looks better and responds better to the hammer if thick.

Casting in sand is still commonly used to make such parts as need to be rigid and solid, like the thumb-pieces of tankards. This type of cast unit normally emerges from its sand mould with a rough surface which has to be finished by carving or chasing by hand. The more sophisticated lost wax casting, with or without pressure, gives a more precise finish; Benvenuto Cellini in his autobiography, tells how he did it when he cast his bronze figure of Perseus in 1554. Casting procedures have not changed much over the centuries, although few goldsmiths today have to burn their furniture and melt their cutlery in order to provide their raw materials for casting. Centrifugal casting yields pressure in a neat, clean way, and is useful for the mass-production of light jewellery. Stamping, pressing, vacuum evaporation, electroforming, all have their uses in more or less high-tech mass-production, but are hardly adaptable to the small-scale activity of a skilled craft workshop. A good craftsman will know the potential of all these methods and, even if he cannot execute them all himself, he will know which to use to gain the desired effect, and he will know how to get specialists to make their necessary contribution to the whole effect.

Gerald's special aptitudes as a silversmith are many. Perhaps the most striking is his attitude: he does it fast, in direct contradiction to Chaucer, who wrote six centuries ago of the life so short, the craft so long to learn. I can hear Gerald snorting and saying "rubbish, all you've got to do is try hard and think quickly … "

One of Gerald's deceptively simple achievements: illusion cutting. It looks deep, is in fact shallow

Alan Evans and Robert Winter have made nearly all the really complicated silver and gold pieces over the last 30 years and are masters, not only of the traditional techniques, but also of new methods which in most cases, have been developed by the Benney team. The most important skill which they both have is the ability to interpret a pencil line into a three dimensional shape and know when to vary it marginally in order to improve the appearance or balance. This is an instinctive skill which they have accquired over the years.

When he was young, he used to work away, at a teapot for instance, constantly adjusting and fine-tuning such details as handle sockets or the pouring part of a spout, or indeed the body shape itself. Later, he decided that it was a more productive policy, both from the aesthetic and the economic point of view, to carry out the whole design as originally conceived without alteration. This he calls his "one-shot" technique. It relies on incorporating any considered improvements or adjustments into the next design, and so on …

In order to analyse Gerald's designs, it is useful first to put them in context, to look at the work of other artists and then consider how Gerald compares. Extreme cases are Beethoven and Picasso. There is a clear difference between early, middle period, and late Beethoven or Picasso. The first is carefully formed according to a pattern which is generally accepted at the time for that type of work. In mid-life, these great creators stretch the accepted idiom until the artist's personal vision becomes more evident than the conventions within which he expresses it. In later life, the artist says "To Hell with the inherited wisdom of ages. I am myself, and that is that." Late Beethoven quartets take us on marvellous journeys through an endless uncharted territory of the imagination. Late Picasso drawings, with their ecstatic pleasure in the basic human senses of touch and sex, give us another exciting shock, making us concentrate on what is normally hidden.

Some painters don't change much. Turner, for instance, loosened his early almost photographic images until, in his later visions, light and colour have become more important than line and silhouette. But you can usually identify a Turner because his strong personality shines through his varied subjects. Other artists – Picasso is the classic case – enjoy novelty. For a time he may thrive on blue, then it may be the red period, and so on. You cannot always be sure what is by Picasso because he was such a chameleon and so much enjoyed dramatic change.

For applied art designers, variety of expression may be more difficult, because the techniques are so slow to acquire. Without a new technique, it may be difficult to evolve a fresh vocabulary of ornament. The work of famous silversmiths cannot therefore easily be dated simply by its personal style. Paul de Lamerie nearly three centuries ago, for example, may have swung slowly from the Huguenot style of his youth towards the rococo, then to the neo classical, but these were the universal fashions of the time, not expressions of personal idiosyncracy. In our own century, early and late Fabergé or Leslie Durbin cannot easily be dated simply by changes of artistic style. It is their use of new materials or technology which enabled them to achieve new colours or shapes. For Fabergé, his growing mastery of enamels, and the availability of coloured stones from newly accessible Siberia, gave his work a new vitality. For Durbin, his increasing use of cast ornament with a rough finish, contrasting with precise details sometimes turned on a lathe, gives his later pieces a distinctive variety.

Silversmiths cannot express their occasional moods, as painters or musicians may do, because silversmiths are the slaves of something more constant than their moods, namely their hammers and tools, their sheets of metal and their reels of wire. Craftsmen can express themselves only within the limitations of their materials. They are not free as air. They are only as free as their materials allow.

There is much discussion nowadays about the correct description of craftsmen. According to one view, craftsmen must be ruled by their apparatus and their logic, so they cannot ever approach the true magic of art. Therefore they should not be called "artist craftsmen". "Designer craftsmen" is more accurate because craftsmen must design before they can start making.

The other view, which I share, holds that anyone can be an artist, regardless of what medium he or she works in. It is the quality of the end result which counts, not the materials, nor the methods used to achieve the results.

Unfortunately, the world at large seems to think that the only true artists are those who make something from nothing, like musicians or painters, and it is this sort of magic creation which earns high prices. Craftsmen often dream of breaking through the price barrier between craft and art, but alas they seldom succeed. Craft is in some sense earth-bound because it depends upon the products of the earth and takes time to make. Art is closer to Heaven because it is pure creation and, like magic, can be spontaneous.

Whatever we call Gerald, he is obviously a big creator, and his designs do give us a sniff of personal evolution: throughout his five decades of creative smithing, his designs have changed and matured in close harmony with his developing techniques. What all his pieces have in common, is an organic quality, in contrast for instance with a mass-produced aluminium kitchen kettle, or a machine finished spherical ball-bearing. You need not stretch your imagination too far, to feel a Benney silver teapot reminding you of the dynosaurs in London's Science Museum, very slowly moving towards each

Francis Bacon wrote nearly four centuries ago "There is no excellent beauty that hath not some strangeness in the proportion". This cup for Imperial College of Science and Technology illustrates Gerald's taste for a startling silhouette. The stem, in the hands of a conventional smith, might have tapered inwards as it moved upwards, forming a normal cone, big at the bottom, thin at the top, as was the practice for standing cups in the 17th, 18th and 19th centuries. Gerald's inversion of the norm gives the piece a characteristic brilliant quality of surprise

other and eating each other. Or observe how a Benney ceremonial cup bounces upwards from its flat base, much as a salmon will leap up from a Scottish torrent, suddenly defying the forces of gravity with its shiny muscular grace.

Compare a Queen Anne style cup of 1700 with a Benney cup of 1960. The first is noble, with classic, balanced proportion, good counterpoint between its convex and concave curves, pleasing, gentle mouldings to lead your eye from the straight sides and the rounded top and foot, a uniform soft polish overall. The Benney cup, on the other hand, has dapples and grooves like the skin of a lizard where its legs join its body. He gives us no mouldings to caress your eye upwards, the pointed top shooting straight out of its horizontal base, just as the hard shiny beak of a bird comes at you directly out of the soft feathered head, without any visual preliminaries. The boldness of form, the mixture of colours, the delight in asymmetry, the deliberate use of uneven measures, all these features of Benney work come not from the calculations of the measuring board but from the wild ecstasy of the jungle and the wilderness of primeval nature.

I choose the word organic to identify the Benney style. In another mood, though, I can see in Benney work, echoes of those modern rockets and space engines which enliven the scenery at Cape Canaveral in a uniquely modern manner. Aerodynamic shapes express energy, and energy is a Benney characteristic. But aeroplanes have to be symmetrical in order to survive, whereas Benney makes his pieces eccentric in order to charm. Either way, Benney silver will excite overtones of surprise, will cause raised eyebrows as the solemn, precious medium suddenly reveals a hidden joke, some sense of fun in the decorative fantasy. You may think that silver is soft and gentle. So it often is. But a Benney piece is more likely to convey vibrations of fierce defiance of the accepted artistic customs and rules.

Amusing imagery as with this 18 carat gold hedgehog cup originally made in 1969 for Lord McAlpine, may conceal enormous effort in the setting of hundreds of stones each in its own separate stem

This mace given by the Times of Australia to Flinders University was designed by Gerald with a hangover in a hurry to catch his flight from Sydney back to London after the Worshipful Company's exhibition in Sydney. Alcohol may have eliminated elaboration, speed led to nobility and simplicity. The University wanted to clinch an immediate deal, but he had neither cartridge paper nor a table big enough to support a full-size drawing of a mace. So he used a felt tip pen on a double spread of the "Times" newspaper stuck together with Sellotape and laid out on a table in a local bar. The mace head suggests the pages of a book opened by the teaching of the university. None of his designs was ever more warmly received, none had a more speedy birth

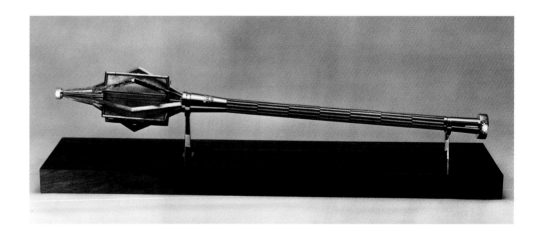

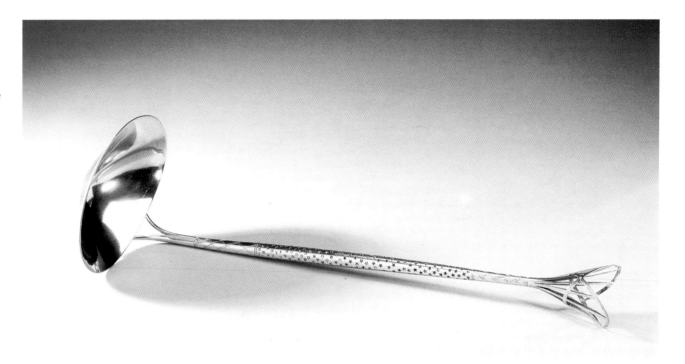

Ladle, gold and silver, made by Gerald when a student at the Royal College of Art 1952, the first of his pieces bought by the Worshipful Company of Goldsmiths. He stamped each of the stars into the handle with a tool he made for the purpose

Big cigar box in silver, gold and mahogany, 14 inches long, given in 1955 by Sir Foster Robinson, past Master in 1943 and 1944, to the Society of Merchant Venturers, Bristol, the ancient guild. Gerald's biggest early commission

He begins in his youth with details evolved instinctively under the hammer. A fair example is the ladle of 1951, demonstrating a sleeve wrapped round the stem, saw-pierced with stars to suggest a defiance of its solid nature; the same idea of piercing the solid handle occurs with the suggestion of latitude and longitude symbols constituting the terminal at the end. The bowl is sensitively hammered, and gilt until it suggests a sort of bluebell flower, delicate and discreet. The whole small piece demonstrates early Benney: the joy in complicated processes, the sudden transitions from one surface finish to another, the element of fantasy at the handle end where many smiths would have put a simple round knob. The ladle remains a delight, full of joy, but the sum of the parts in this student piece, do not add up to a convincing whole.

By 1955, with the box given by Sir Foster Robinson to the Merchant Venturers in Bristol, perhaps the earliest big piece, we see the next stage. As with the ladle, there is abundant imagination: the coloured enamel arms, the silver strips inlaid into the wood, the gilt balls nestling in their oval sockets round the sides, all these provide a ceremonial panache which suits the stately setting in Bristol. But, unlike the ladle, this casket has functional elements. The big flange on the lid front means you can open the heavy lid without its crashing shut onto your fingers, the tapered section of the flange means it is easy to get your fingers underneath, the balls round the side, being gilt, do not show your finger marks, and the raised sockets are easy to grasp, thus minimising the risk that your hand will slip and let the heavy box drop. Most important, the bulging sides and end, hold these elaborate decorative elements into a comfortable generous frame. The visual abandon of the ladle is still here, but now we have mature early Benney at its best.

Then comes the greater artistic confidence bred by batch production and industrial design: the style is more direct, often simpler, and there is less fiddling, less detail. The bowl given to Leicester University by Lord Adrian in 1957 may be the first good example. It has only two themes: the rough surfaced abstract cover, like the skeleton of some great primitive organism, and the deep cut lettering in the circular frame. Two ideas may be enough if they are as visually strong as these. Another instance of a few ideas well used, is the gold hedgehog cup for Alistair McAlpine. An amusing shape plays with sinuous curves as luscious as the feminine body. But look! You cannot stroke it as your instincts may urge you to do, because the sides are encrusted with precious stones, each sticking out and sharp like a porcupine quill. The stones have their function, to make the cup easy to hold and difficult to drop, but they also make a typical Benney joke, denying your fingers the obvious pleasure of caressing beauty. For me, this bowl and the cup, with their concentration on one idea powerfully presented, characterise the style of the middle Benney period.

For late Benney, I look to his technical virtuosity. First are his enamels which have not received the public acclaim they deserve. They are so difficult to achieve that nobody can imitate them and they have therefore not received wide distribution. The second flavour of late Benney, is his hammered and carved textures which, unlike the enamels, can be and have been imitated, so that they have changed the appearance of much British silver of the past two decades. His coffee pot of 1997 commissioned by the Silver Trust for use by the Prime Minister at No. 10 Downing Street, has a hinged lid with enamelled stripes of rare eloquence. These stripes suggest heat and movement. They invite you to open the top to pour in your water, then again to discover how much coffee remains inside. The subtlety of the enamel colour implies the subtlety of the taste and aroma of good coffee, and the contour of the stripes accentuates the satisfying fecundity of the dome. As to the pot beneath, I can see a sureness and maturity of line which needs no ornament to emphasise it.

My second illustration of the late Benney virtuosity, as shown in his texturing, is his processional cross of 1990 for Lichfield Cathedral. It might appear to be a simple matter to contrive meaningful reflections from a shiny metal. In fact, silver reflections can easily hide the silver rather than enhancing it, because the reflections pick up the light and colour of their surroundings, rather than glowing with inner strength. This is where angles and rounded tubes, as in the Lichfield cross, can be so eloquent. And texturing, as on the Dublin cross, can be important as well as beautiful. It can help to emphasise the whole architecture of the precinct, giving

"Hand-finished" means the human spirit is behind it. Cutting out from a whole piece of gold is the sort of difficult process which is only found in hand craft and which is called perfectionism

prominence to the object in the context of what is happening nearby. And it can ensure visibility from every angle, not just from front and back. This cross, because of its skilful texturing, and the angles of the metal planes and rods, remains a powerful symbol of the Cross wherever it moves up and down the Nave and Choir of the great building, and to some extent, the more it moves, the better it is seen. Late Benney is economical in design, powerful in effect.

To set his work in the context of other living silversmiths would be complicated and invidious. Comparisons often fail to do justice to anybody. Other smiths may concentrate on suave logic, or ease of function, what is called ergonomics. Others again may load their pieces with fantastic ornament, more labour than inspiration, hardly leaving a single inch of uninterrupted metal, much as was the custom in Victorian times. Or there are some who prefer rough to smooth, achieving a sort of barbaric power, the opposite of modern architecture with its straight lines and lack of individuality. Each of these has its own merit. But the unique character of Gerald's work can be summarised in one word: it is adventure. He always gives us concentration on the present moment. He is sure that the next design will be even better than the last. "One-shot" may not be the language of art criticism, but it identifies his powerful appeal, which is his spontaneous, compulsive urge.

Exhibitions

A select list of the more important exhibitions in which Gerald participated.

* indicates a one-man show

"The Worshipful Company" is "The Worshipful Company of Goldsmiths, Goldsmiths' Hall, London"

1955
British trade fair, Copenhagen, in the Worshipful Company's display in the Tivoli Gardens.

1958
British Week, Brussels, Belgium, in The Worshipful Company's display under the medieval vaults of City Hall in the Grand' Place, and small displays in retail shops throughout the city.

1959
Stoneleigh Abbey, Warwickshire, The Worshipful Company's display.

1960
British Exhibition, New York.

1962
British Week, Stockholm, in The Worshipful Company's display in the city's fairground, and in small displays in retail shops throughout the city.

1963
British Week, Zürich, in the Worshipful Company's display in the Hallenstadion and in retail shops throughout the city, including Meister.

1964
Reading, inauguration of Benney collection in the Town Hall.

1964
Sydney, Australia, in the Worshipful Company's display in David Jones store.

1964
Düsseldorf, British Week, The Worshipful Company's displays in retail shops throughout the city.

1965
Tokyo, British Exhibition, the Worshipful Company's display in Ginza.

1967
Detroit, USA, in the Worshipful Company's display in the world's biggest department store, J. L. Hudson.

1968
*Rutland Gallery, London.

1968
New York. The Worshipful Company's display in the Lincoln Centre foyer and in the Cartier shop in Fifth Avenue.

1970
Farnley Art Fair at Farnley Hall, Otley, Yorks, with the Crafts Centre of Great Britain.

1973
*Benney retrospective at Goldsmiths' Hall, London.

1992
*New York

1994
Modern enamels at Goldsmiths' Hall.

1995
*At Oded Gera's shop in Tel Aviv, Israel.

1998
*Painting retrospective at the Century Gallery, Henley-on-Thames

Bibliography

Many booklets and catalogues published over the past half century by the Worshipful Company of Goldsmiths at Goldsmiths' Hall, Foster Lane, London EC2V 6BN feature Gerald's work, often with accompanying essays by myself. Among the more substantial are:

Modern Silver, new booklets in 1954, 1959, 1963

New Gold, Silver and Jewels commissioned by industry at the Institute of Directors 1964

The Reading civic plate 1961 – 66

Public Treasure at Leeds City Art Gallery 1967

Pomp at the Royal Scottish Museum, Edinburgh 1969

Gerald Benney exhibition at Goldsmiths' Hall 1973 with foreword by the Prime Minister, Edward Heath

British Master Goldsmiths 1997 features two dozen leading craftsmen including Gerald, exhibited at Goldsmiths' Hall

Gerald Benney himself has published half a dozen of his own distinguished catalogues, some of them available from "Benney", 73 Walton Street, London SW3 3HT.

The German Goldsmiths' Society, Deutsche Gesellschaft für Goldschmiedekunst, Altstädte Markt 6, D 63450 Hanau near Frankfurt am Main, has useful international reference material to set Gerald's work in a world context. The Society of North American Goldsmiths (SNAG) c/o American Crafts Museum, 40 West 53 Street, New York, NY 10019–6112 also spreads its net very wide.

Modern Silver, by Graham Hughes, Studio Vista, London 1967 remains the most comprehensive international coverage, with many of Gerald's pieces.

A good introduction to enamels is *A Thousand Years of Enamel,* the catalogue of the diamond jubilee exhibition 1911–1971, organised by Wartski, Grafton Street, London W1.

Gold-Silberarbeiten aus der Werkstatt Meinrad Burch-Korrodi, Sakrale Kunst, Schweizerische St. Lukasgesellschaft, ed. NZN Zürich, 1954 (German language): introduces pre-war Swiss sacred work, interesting to compare with Gerald's teacher Dunstan Pruden; shows Burch's enamels, a run-up to those of Gerald.

The Worshipful Company of Goldsmiths as patrons of their craft 1919–53, Goldsmiths' Hall 1965, London, catalogue of the silver collection of those years with biographies of many craftsmen. British silverwork including ceremonial plate by contemporary craftsmen exhibited at Goldsmiths' Hall 1951: introduction to the big Festival of Britain exhibition, covers the immediate pre-war years, setting the scene for Gerald's arrival. There are very many more books on modern art jewellery than on silver. The huge literature on silver concentrates on the past, and alas seldom gives prominence to new work. Modern silver is badly publicised except in Scandinavia, where it remains a popular and much respected art form.

Pioneers of Modern Craft, ed. Margot Coatts, Manchester University Press 1997, has good essays covering a dozen masters of different crafts including Gerald. ISBN 7190 5059 6

The Crafts Council, 44a Pentonville Rd., London N1 9BY publishes useful catalogues and keeps good records e.g. Living Silver 1995

Contemporary Applied Arts (once the Crafts Centre of Great Britain) 2 Percy Street, London W1P 9FA, celebrated its fiftieth birthday 1998 with a book of essays on the main crafts ed. Tanya Harrod

David Mellor's retrospective exhibition at the Design Museum, Shad Thames, London 1998 included furniture he made aged 17, street lamps, the altar set for Liverpool Anglican Cathedral with Crucifix by Elisabeth Frink, and, new in 1998, his welded high-tech cutlery and the trolley he designed for the Italian manufacturers Magis

Commissions

Public patrons of Gerald whose pieces are illustrated, are credited in the captions, and are in the index. Other notable customers include Marks and Spencer who gave a coffee set to Bootle Corporation, and a gilt covered cup to Cardiff Corporation; Glasgow University mace; Wokingham District Council Chairman's badge of office; the Borough of Rushmoor's gift of a Freedom Casket to the Royal Military Police; the Sunday Times Business News Export Success Trophy; Lord Normanby's gift of an altar set to Lythe parish church; the Archbishop of Canterbury's light portable travelling processional cross. We are accustomed to base metal being silver plated or gilt, pretending to be silver or gold. Gerald, with customary wit, did it the opposite way round. He made an 8 inch silver paper weight look like a rolled steel joist, which Margaret Thatcher as Prime Minister gave to Rosehaugh Stanhope Developments when she opened their Broadgate office development near Liverpool Street Station, London.

One family made and is still making an exceptional contribution. Michael Hornby, Prime Warden of the Worshipful Company of Goldsmiths and Managing Director of WH Smith, guided many commissions to Gerald. Sir Simon Hornby, his son, became Chairman of WH Smith, helped to stimulate Gerald into using more stones and into marketing his ever-improving enamels, promoting them from the experimental to the classic level. Sir Simon is now one of Gerald's close friends, treasuring the personal links as much as he does the silver and jewels.

I hope I have shown in this book that Gerald's work never allows you a dull moment. He likes people and he welcomes visitors. If you want an agreeable, unexpected surprise, he will probably give you one if you can accept his open invitation to meet him. And like many others before you, if you went to him as a friend, you will probably come away from him as a devoted client.

Acknowledgements and Photography

I am specially grateful to Alan Irvine, architect and friend of Gerald and mine since student days at the Royal College of Art, and to Susannah Horton-Fawkes who used to run the Crafts Centre of Great Britain, who has known us for almost as long. They both read my text and made characteristically shrewd comments on it.

Isambard Thomas designed the book and made beauty out of chaos. Nobody who has not digested the visual confusion which precedes a book like this, can imagine the mental poise and discipline required. The pictures are of many sizes, some tiny 35mm slides, others works of art too big to fit on a table, some in colour, others black and white. They all have to correspond to the text, and, equally, to fit the budget. Isambard kept his head, and our readers are his beneficiaries.

It has not been possible to trace the copyright of many of the photographs taken so many years ago, and I apologise to any friend who has not received due recognition. Peter Parkinson took many of the silver photos for the Worshipful Company of Goldsmiths at Goldsmiths' Hall, to whom the book owes so much, and Gerald acquired them from him. Spike Clift inherited Peter Parkinson's photographic mantle, then Alf Barnes of Barnes and Webster. Robert Winter recorded the developing activity at Beenham, and John Goldblatt enabled us to enjoy some of his imaginative views and details of tools, architecture and silver in and around Falcon Wharf. More recent subjects are by David Cunningham, Philip Tull and myself. It will not surprise readers to know that the versatile Gerald is an excellent photographer; he knows exactly what he wants, and he gets it, as with his cutlery on the double spread on page 176, where the hall-marks chime so neatly with his taut design. I thank all these artists, whose pictures give to the book so much of its appeal.

G H

The Hornby family, Michael and his son Sir Simon Hornby, are long-term friends and patrons of Gerald. Here, Michael Hornby wears his gold badge as prime Warden of the Worshipful Company of Goldsmiths, at the opening of their display at the British Week, Brussels 1967. Gerald explains his big bowl to Lord Snowdon, who opened the exhibition

222

Gerald and Janet, painted here by their son Paul Benney, married in 1957 and have helped and loved each other ever since, a remarkable record. John Donne four centuries ago summarised the cumulative effect of sharing experience:

"If your mine of pleasure in equal thankfulness you both unlock: so we each other bless"

Index

SWIMMING FOR TRIATHLON AND OPEN WATER

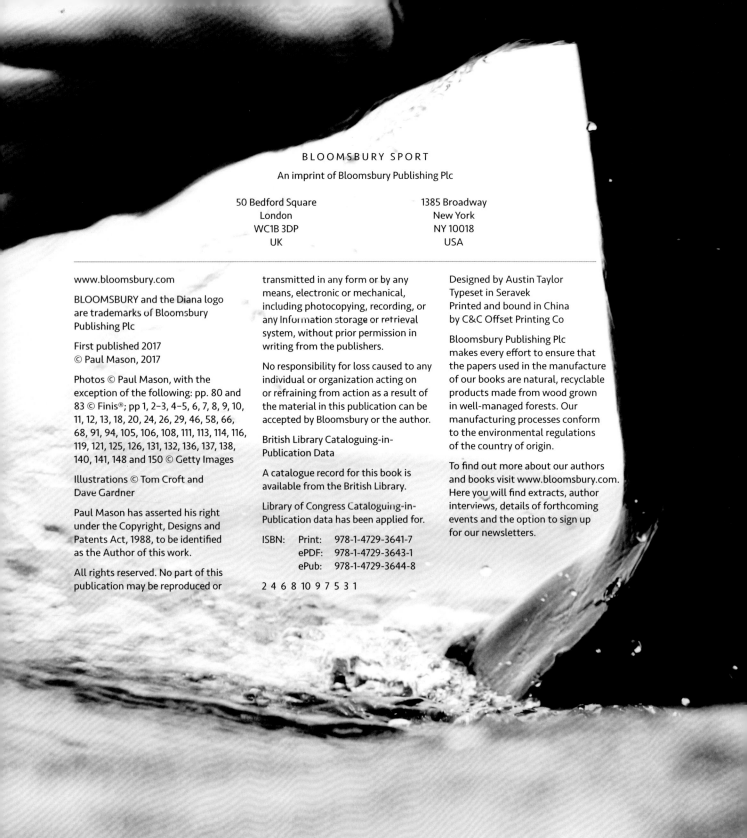

BLOOMSBURY SPORT

An imprint of Bloomsbury Publishing Plc

50 Bedford Square	1385 Broadway
London	New York
WC1B 3DP	NY 10018
UK	USA

www.bloomsbury.com

BLOOMSBURY and the Diana logo are trademarks of Bloomsbury Publishing Plc

First published 2017
© Paul Mason, 2017

Photos © Paul Mason, with the exception of the following: pp. 80 and 83 © Finis®; pp 1, 2–3, 4–5, 6, 7, 8, 9, 10, 11, 12, 13, 18, 20, 24, 26, 29, 46, 58, 66, 68, 91, 94, 105, 106, 108, 111, 113, 114, 116, 119, 121, 125, 126, 131, 132, 136, 137, 138, 140, 141, 148 and 150 © Getty Images

Illustrations © Tom Croft and Dave Gardner

British Library Cataloguing-in-Publication Data

A catalogue record for this book is available from the British Library.

Library of Congress Cataloguing-in-Publication data has been applied for.

ISBN: Print: 978-1-4729-3641-7
       ePDF: 978-1-4729-3643-1
       ePub: 978-1-4729-3644-8

2 4 6 8 10 9 7 5 3 1

Designed by Austin Taylor
Typeset in Seravek
Printed and bound in China by C&C Offset Printing Co

Bloomsbury Publishing Plc makes every effort to ensure that the papers used in the manufacture of our books are natural, recyclable products made from wood grown in well-managed forests. Our manufacturing processes conform to the environmental regulations of the country of origin.

To find out more about our authors and books visit www.bloomsbury.com. Here you will find extracts, author interviews, details of forthcoming events and the option to sign up for our newsletters.

SWIMMING FOR TRIATHLON AND OPEN WATER

Gain confidence and unlock your ideal front crawl

PAUL MASON

BLOOMSBURY

LONDON · OXFORD · NEW YORK · NEW DELHI · SYDNEY

Contents

Want to swim better front crawl?

If so, this book is for you.

In particular, it's for you if you swim front crawl in open water. Whatever your standard, from novice to expert, you'll find useful ideas about technique, training, racing, equipment, tactics, safety and the psychology of open-water and distance swimming.

▲▶ Johnny Weissmuller (above) and Sun Yang (right): world record holders almost a century apart, and at two very different distances (100m and 1500m). They had very different styles, too – but they share one crucial technique with almost every other great front crawl swimmer: a high elbow catch.

Most useful of all, *Swimming for Triathlon and Open Water* will give you the key to unlock the secret of great front crawl.

'What should I work on?'

At least one of these questions has been asked at every technique clinic and coaching session I've ever held:

'What's the ideal pull?'

'Should I always use a 2-beat kick in a 3.8k race?'

'What's the perfect head angle?'

'Does my recovery need to have a high elbow?'

The truth is, there isn't always a correct answer to questions like these – unless it's 'what works for you'. But at the same time, there are some skills and techniques – shared by all top-level swimmers – that you do need to learn if you're going to be a really effective swimmer. These skills may only form 20 per cent of your armoury, but they produce far more than that in terms of results. *Swimming for Triathlon and Open Water* identifies these crucial skills – the things that will make the biggest difference to your swimming and allow you to get the most benefit from your training time.

Triathlon and open water technique

For triathlon and open water swimming, what you need most is an efficient stroke, one that:

- Allows you to swim at a strong, even pace for an hour or more
- Utilises your underlying aerobic ability
- Delivers you to the finish without leaving you drained of energy (unless you choose to make a sprint at the end, of course)

This book will show you the technique you need, with a focus on the single key element that will improve your swimming more than any other. This key element has been shared by top swimmers from the time of Duke Kahanamoku

Last, do it fast

This is an old saying from the world of martial arts, but it applies equally well to swimming:

FIRST, DO IT.
NEXT, DO IT RIGHT.
LAST, DO IT FAST.

Applying this approach to the technique drills in this book will yield the best, quickest result possible.

(1912 and 1920 Olympic 100m freestyle champion) until today – and now it can be yours, too.

OPEN WATER BASICS

Many people get their first taste of open water swimming when they take part in a triathlon or charity swim. You may have bought this book with just that sort of swim in mind. But open water swimming encompasses a tremendous range of types of swimming. The simplest is wild swimming – taking pleasure in being somewhere other than a chemically sterile pool. Then there are swim-trek holidays, triathlon and open water races. Some of these are marathon swims in which the top swimmers may spend hours in the water.

Natural hazards and safety

Whether you're swimming in the ocean, a lake or reservoir, or a river, open water is potentially hazardous. The best way to experience it safely is by finding a local open water club or training group. They'll have established safety procedures which you can just slot right into. But although open water is getting more popular every year, there still aren't that many clubs. What hazards should you consider when swimming outside an organised environment?

Water temperature

Some open water events do not allow wetsuits, despite taking place in relatively cold water. If you've entered one of these, you'll need to acclimatise. Take care: really cold water can quickly impair your judgement and senses. It can take months to get used to; you may initially only be able to manage a few seconds. Your body *does* eventually adapt, but this is a test of will: it can be a long and uncomfortable process.

Warmer water than you're used to also poses problems, the main one being the risk of dehydration. You can mimic the effects of warm water by swimming in a heated pool wearing a wetsuit.

Water conditions

The obvious challenges are chop and waves. These are usually easy to forecast, so you should know they're coming. Even so, if you haven't trained in similar conditions they present a challenge.

There's advice on preparing for rough conditions on page 125.

Local sealife and conditions

The open-water racing at the 2007 World Aquatics Championships in Melbourne was an event for tough nuts. The competitors had to swim through large blooms of jellyfish; some of the favourites failed even to finish. It's an extreme example, but it does show that open water swimmers need to be ready to face unexpected challenges. (Others include boat exhaust fumes, seaweed and fog.)

Currents

My first open water race was a 2k pier-to-pier. The opening 1.95k went OK: I wasn't first, but I wasn't last. Then, in the last 50m, the wheels came off. The tide had properly turned, and I'd spectacularly misjudged my effort (I was only 11). Try as I might, I couldn't get around the moored-up finish boat. That's no disaster in an organised event: I just swam ashore, prickly tears of shame and frustration slowly filling my goggles. In open

water, though, currents that match themselves against your dying strength can kill. Always be aware of currents, tides, flows from river mouths, etc. Always plan to swim well within the limits of your endurance.

Training partners or groups

As with any sport, your training should mirror the thing you're training for. If you're taking part in an open water event, this obviously means at least some of your training should be done in open water. If you're not in an organised group environment, it's a good idea to do this with a training partner (or partners). The two key benefits are:

Safety: Open water, particularly the ocean, is potentially a lot more dangerous than pool swimming. Having someone with you makes things a little safer.

Motivation: The open-water environment can be a bit off-putting on cold, wet days. Knowing someone else is relying on you to come out helps. Having someone swimming alongside might also help you to push your level, rather than sitting back and taking it easy. Of course, you'll also get to share the joy of lake sunrises on misty mornings, swimming in to a warm beach at sunset and so on.

Ideally you want at least one other swimmer of about the same standard as you; if you're venturing far from shore, add a kayaker, SUPer, paddleboarder, or someone on another vessel you could hang on to in an emergency.

Open water swimming equipment

The basics of open water swimming equipment are the same as for pool swimming (see page 16–17): goggles, swimsuit, hat and (if you wear them) earplugs. All open water swimmers need a brightly coloured hat, to warn other water traffic that they're there. Silicon hats are noticeably warmer than standard latex ones.

Some contests – Olympic open water races, for example – have strict rules about the type of costume you can wear. In these, the only additional equipment you're likely to need is petroleum jelly (or a similar product such as Body Glide), to stop chafing and prevent other swimmers from grabbing hold of your shoulders or feet.

Swimming wetsuits

One crucial piece of kit for most open water swimmers is a wetsuit. In triathlon swims in water below 14°C you're usually required to wear one of these. You can buy them relatively inexpensively; the alternative is to rent a wetsuit for the event, but this is expensive, you can't get used to it beforehand and there's no guarantee the fit will be spot-on. You also miss out on the chance to practise swimming in a wetsuit, which isn't the same as swimming in skin.

WETSUIT THICKNESSES
Swimming wetsuits are available in different thicknesses. The thinnest, swim skins, are actually somewhere between a costume and a wetsuit. They provide the least insulation and flotation,

so they feel closest to swimming without a wetsuit. Swim skins are often available in armless cuts, which allow complete freedom of movement.

Thicker swimming wetsuits tend to cover everything except your head, hands and feet (and usually a cheeky glimpse of ankle). They're available in different thicknesses, but these suits don't run to the kind of neoprene some surfing suits use, 6–7mm. This is far too buoyant, and changes your stroke dynamics so much that swimming feels unnatural.

For cold water, most open-water swimmers add a neoprene hat, gloves and socks. Bear in mind that anything thicker than 2mm will make it hard to feel what's going on with your leg kick and pull.

CHOOSING A WETSUIT

Never be tempted to swim in a wetsuit that's not specifically designed for swimming. It won't have articulated shoulders, and fighting the cut of the suit with every arm recovery will drain your arms and shoulders of energy very quickly.

Swimming wetsuits are available at a wide range of price points. In general the fit is more important than the brand or whether it has expensive shave-seconds-from-your-1500m-time features. Around your body the fit needs to be as tight as possible without being constrictive. From neck to ankle it should be neither uncomfortably short, so that it pulls downward on your shoulders, nor so long that there are wrinkles in the neoprene. The best way to find the right suit is to decide on the style/thickness and price point you want, then try on as many as you can.

Trying on a wetsuit

If you're trying on a variety of wetsuits and you might have to return them, watch out: thin neoprene is much easier to tear than you might expect. Here are a few tips:

- *Take off any jewellery that could snag, especially rings and watches.*
- *Shield the suit from your nails by putting on socks and soft gloves. (Plastic bags and the see-through gloves they have in petrol stations will do the same job.)*
- *Step into one leg of the suit and gently ease it up until the end of the leg is above your ankle. Repeat with the other leg, then ease both sides up to your hips.*
- *Wriggle your body into the suit, pulling the legs up towards your torso if you need more room.*
- *Finally, when the suit seems to be properly in position on your body, slide your arms into the sleeves and do up the zip.*

You'll probably need to ease the body of the suit up or down to get a feel for whether it really fits. Key things to check for are whether you feel it's pulling down on your shoulders at all, and whether there's a big air gap either in the small of your back or between the suit and your crotch. If you can't adjust these out, the suit isn't a great fit.

To remove a wetsuit, unzip, then carefully peel off both arms, the body and the legs. Never stand on one leg to get out of the other – unless it's a suit you own and you're in T1 (the transition from swim leg to bike leg in a triathlon).

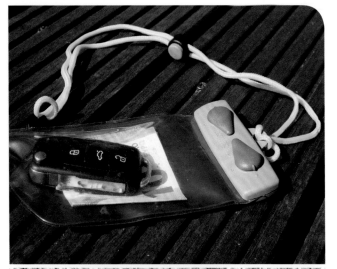

◀ A waterproof pouch for money, keys, etc.

▶ Some of the equipment you'll need: hand paddles, swim fins, googles and a swimming hat.

Buoys and bags

Sharing the water with other users can be dangerous, especially if they're in powered craft such as jetskis or sailing boats. To make themselves more visible, some open water swimmers tow an inflatable buoy behind them. These are easier to see than a simple hat, which can easily be obscured by chop. The buoys also sometimes have a waterproof section for carrying things like car keys, snacks, a phone or wallet. Some even have a hydration bladder for use during long swims.

If you don't need or want to tow a buoy, a variety of waterproof pouches is available. The best hang on a cord around your neck, and tuck inside your wetsuit.

General training kit

Swim training doesn't require a huge cupboard full of equipment, but you may end up needing a large-ish box. There are a few pieces of kit that everyone needs, plus several things that will help with the drills in this book.

You don't need an expensive specialist racing costume: they're actually a real pain to get on and off, and quickly wear out. But a fitted costume *is* important, because anything that flaps or drags (such as baggy shorts for men) will affect how

◀ A specialist tri suit like this is worn under a wetsuit, then kept on for the bike and run legs.

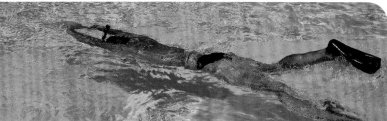

▲ Three basic tools of the pool – swimmer's trade: a snorkel, fins and hand paddles.

streamlined you are in the water.

Goggles are also crucial. Without them, it's impossible to see clearly what's going on underwater: what your hands are doing, whether there are other swimmers close by, etc. Many open water swimmers choose large goggles, but smaller ones may actually be better as they cause less drag around your head. If you have hair that's anything but very short, a hat is always a good idea for the same reason.

Equipment for the technique drills

Most of the technique drills in this book can be done without special equipment. There are one or two things you will need, though:

- **Swim fins** – not diving fins (swim fins are shorter and usually less stiff). They need to fit closely without being super-tight
- **A kickboard** and **a pull buoy.** Most pools have these available for customers to borrow if you ask
- **A swimming snorkel,** which rises in front of your face while it's in the water. These are good for practising kick and some drills. Some people find snorkels more comfortable to use with a **noseclip**
- **Hand paddles.** Basic hand paddles can be used to build strength, but Finis makes two styles that can actually help you improve your stroke. The Freestyler (for front crawl only) and Agility paddles (for all strokes, shown above) actively help you to pull in a direct, powerful style

01

TECHNIQUE BASICS

basics *noun, pl.* the essential facts
or principles of a skill or subject;
fundamentals, essentials, foundations

(NOT THAT)
FRONT CRAWL IS ∧COMPLICATED

At root, front crawl is straightforward – which is not the same as saying it's easy – but many swimmers find it harder than it has to be, because they're unsure what's important and what isn't. This chapter is a basic outline of the stroke; chapters 2–7 will break down the constituent parts, show you how to improve each one, and tie them all together.

These are the basic elements of an efficient, effective front crawl:

With each stroke, your feet kick in a steady rhythm and your body rotates along its long axis. Forward power comes from the arm pull:

1 Your hand enters the water ahead of your shoulder, rather than your face (see the diagram on page 21)
2 At the start of the pull, keep your elbow high and use it as a hinge to begin a down-and-back movement with your hand and forearm
3 Pull back, towards your hip

4 Repeat with your other arm; the first recovers to its starting position over the surface

You're unlikely to see this technique in an Olympic 50m sprint final, but it dominates almost every other front crawl event. It's especially good for medium and long distances.

Arm stroke

The ultimate aim is for every arm stroke to be one smooth, accelerating movement – but when thinking about technique, it's useful to divide the arm stroke into four stages:

1 Entry
2 Catch
3 Pull
4 Recovery

In the underwater part of the stroke (stages 1–3), the aim is to use your forearm and hand to pull yourself FORWARD for as much of the stroke as possible. This means pulling downward or up for as *little* time as possible.

Stage 1: Entry

Your arm should go into the water ahead of your shoulder, rather than reaching across to the centreline of your body. (Most untrained swimmers put their hand in at or even across this centreline. There's more on the problems this can cause in chapter 3.) Your hand should go in fingertips first, and ideally parallel to the surface when seen from the front. (So, someone watching you swim towards them would see your hand go in flat, rather than sliding in sideways at an angle, thumb first.)

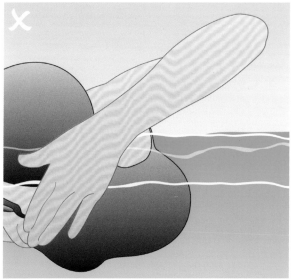

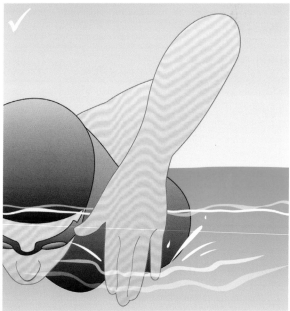

▲ The top image shows the swimmer's hand entering the water at her centreline, which is not ideal. In the lower image, her hand goes in at the right place, ahead of her shoulder.

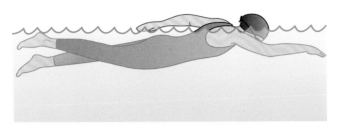

▲ Stage 1: Entry

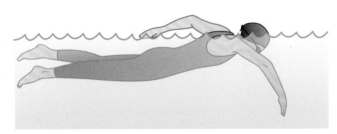

▲ Stage 2: Catch

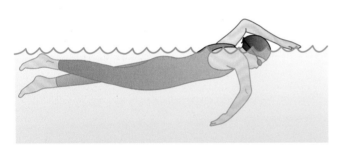

▲ Stage 3: Pull

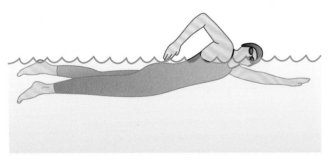

▲ Stage 4: Recovery

Stage 2: Catch

As your hand enters the water, your body should have rotated so that the pulling side is lower than the side where your other arm is recovering. (see the photo on page 23.) Next comes the 'catch', the start of the pull. AN EFFECTIVE CATCH IS THE SECRET TO SWIMMING FRONT CRAWL WELL.

Keeping your elbow high, bend your arm and use the joint as a hinge to sweep your forearm and hand down and back. The idea is to get your forearm vertical as early as possible, which is why this high-elbow technique is sometimes called Early Vertical Forearm (EVF).

Stage 3: Pull

This is a progression from the catch: carry on pulling straight back towards your hip. (On video, you'd see that your hand actually sweeps in towards your hip after the catch. For most people, though, the feeling is of pulling straight back.) At the end of the pull, your hand comes smoothly out of the water, without any splash.

Stage 4: Recovery

The recovery stage is led by your elbow, rather than your hand; your arm should be relaxed, especially at the wrist. Apart from this, the only things to really worry about are whether your hand leaves and re-enters the water in the correct position.

Breathing

If you're worried or tense about swimming, you'll almost certainly have trouble with your breathing. The flip side is that feeling relaxed in the water will make learning good breathing technique simpler. If you feel tense when swimming, there's an exercise in chapter 4 (page 62) that will help you learn to relax in the water.

Technically, taking a breath should be part of your stroke, rather than being a separate element. When your face is underwater, breathe out steadily. Then, when you need a breath, turn your head at the same time as your body rotates during an arm stroke. Having blown out all your waste gases underwater, a smooth in-breath to grab some oxygen is all you need.

▲ A snapshot of front crawl technique: the pulling arm is extended and flat in the water, the swimmer's body is rotated, and the recovering arm has left the water cleanly at the lower hip.

This breathe-out-underwater, in-above rhythm is crucial to good swimming technique. If you hold your breath with your face underwater, you have to breathe out *and* in with your face out of the water – which leaves you with two options:

1 Keep your face out of the water for longer
2 Take in less air with each breath

Chapter 4 explains how each of these is likely to hurt your technique and affect your stamina over distance.

The myth of glide

Lots of swimmers think glide is the Holy Grail of technique, an arcane way of making apparently effortless progress through the water. Simple (well, Newtonian) physics says this is not possible. If you stop swimming and instead 'glide', you'll slow down. You then have to expend more energy getting back up to speed than it would have cost to maintain your speed.

Watch underwater footage from any top swimming event and you'll see that even swimmers with a slow stroke rate don't glide at all: as soon as their arm is fully extended in the water, they start the catch. Any glide you consciously add to your stroke is guaranteed to result in decreased speed.

Body position

Aim to swim with your body in a straight line, pointing in the direction you're swimming. It can rotate, but it shouldn't kink or bend off that line. Many coaches invite you to imagine yourself as a human kebab, with an unbending metal stick running from head to toes. You may find it more comfortable to think of yourself swimming your body through a narrow tube: you can rotate inside it, but your body mustn't touch the sides.

Your body should also be almost parallel with the surface of the water. If your hips and/or legs drop down too much, they become like a sea anchor being dragged along behind you. This problem will be familiar to many heavy-legged triathletes: the solution often begins with improving your catch technique.

Leg kick

Do not bend the knees! At least, not deliberately. A big, splashy bent-knees kick creates so much turbulence and drag that it will actually slow you down drastically. It also wreaks havoc with your body position.

Your knees shouldn't be bent, but they also shouldn't be stiff and rigid. The aim is for your legs to be held straight but without tension, with loose ankles. The kick comes from your hips, and with each downward kick your foot flicks as if you're trying to free yourself of a smelly sock.

Most swimmers use a 2-beat, 4-beat or 6-beat kick, which is 1, 2 or 3 kicks per arm stroke. There's no hard-and-fast rule about which is best: there's advice on finding your rhythm on page 70.

Key skills

- *Learn a high-elbow catch: this is the secret of effective front crawl.*
- *Remember to breathe out underwater.*
- *Avoid artificial pauses in your arm stroke, or you will lose speed.*

▼ Kick practice using a swimming snorkel

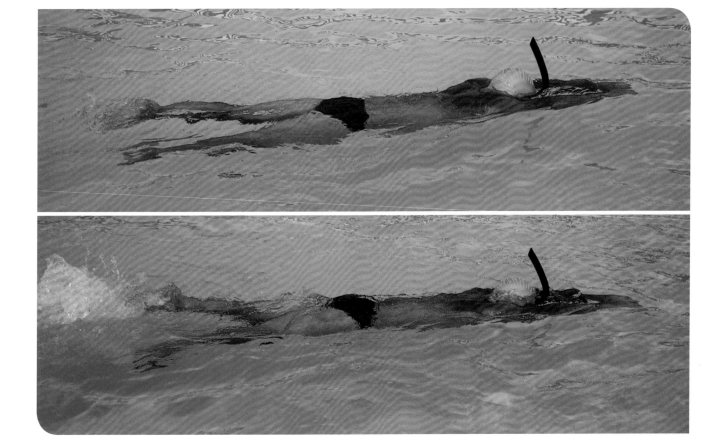

02

ARM STROKE

stroke *noun* in swimming, a single complete movement of the arms and/or legs

ARM STROKE

There's a lot of confusing (and confused) advice out there about arm technique. Should your hand go into the water thumb first, or fingertips? Do you pull in an S-path or not? What kind of recovery is best? The answers to some of these questions are important; others, not so much. Knowing what to aim for – and even more, which element to focus on – isn't easy.

It's important to get this right. About 90 per cent of your forward drive comes from your arm stroke: it's an area where small improvements have a disproportionate benefit.

Time for a bit of science.

Sir Isaac Newton and swimming theory

He probably wasn't thinking about it at the time, but Sir Isaac's third law of motion has a direct bearing on swimming technique. It says, in part:

'Whatever [body] draws or presses another is as much drawn or pressed by that other... The changes made by these actions are equal, not in the velocities but in the motions of the bodies.'

In other words, applied force always moves you in the opposite direction to the one in which the force has been applied. In front crawl, if you want to move forward, apply backward force. Greater backward force will equal greater forward movement.

So, the primary aim is to exert backward – *directly* backward – force for as much of the pull as you can. To do this you need a high elbow catch.

Forward drive v streamlining

Your ability to move through water is affected by the force of the water pushing back at you. You can minimise this force by presenting as small a surface area as possible to the water you're moving through – in other words, swimming with a streamlined body shape.

There's advice throughout this book on streamlining, which is an important skill. But never think that streamlining alone can make you a good front crawl swimmer. (If it could, all the really good swimmers would have narrow, streamlined body shapes, rather than wide shoulders and powerful arms.) The key to good front crawl is developing your arm stroke.

The entry phase

Each arm stroke starts when your hand enters the water. There's advice about this on page 35. In general, a flat hand entry is the simplest way to set yourself up for the rest of the pull. This isn't crucial, though – the most important thing is that you don't throw your hand inwards, to (or even across) your centreline.

▶ Top front crawl swimmers have wide shoulders and powerful arms for a reason: the stroke gets most of its forward power from the arm pull. Developing a strong-but-efficient pull is the key to swimming well in triathlon and open water races.

Arm stroke

The catch phase

The catch sets up the rest of your arm pull. It's the transition between your hand going into the water and the part of your stroke when you generate most power. Keep your elbow high, and use it as a pivot to get your forearm and hand pushing backward as soon as possible. Practise the movement on dry land, and compare it with a straight-arm pull. You'll see that a high elbow catch allows your forearm and hand to pull backward much sooner.

To most people, the high elbow catch feels unnatural at first; it uses unfamiliar muscles that you have to work to develop. The drills on pages 39–43 will help you get used to the position, then integrate it into your stroke. The first time they get this technique right in the water, swimmers often compare it to swimming downhill.

▼ The top sequence shows a high-elbow catch. Direct backward force is being exerted from a point level with the top of the swimmer's head. The lower sequence shows a straight-arm pull, and here force is only directly backward much later in the stroke.

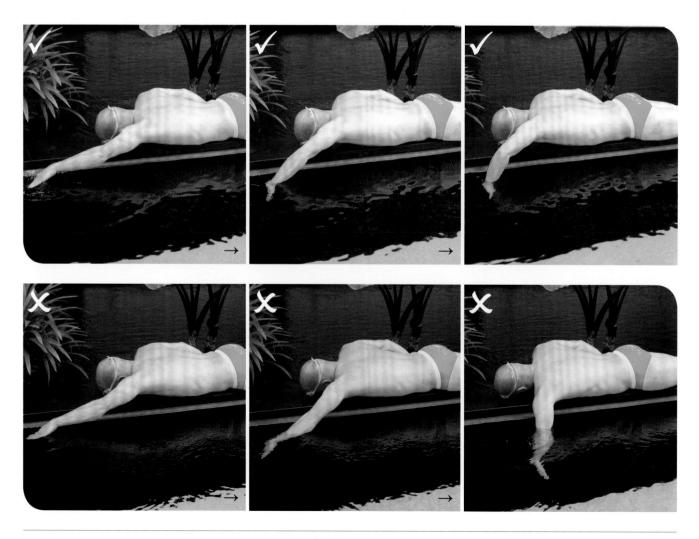

The power phase

Once the catch is complete, you're into the powerful part of your stroke. Your forearm and hand are now exerting force directly backward. Carry on pulling straight back towards your hip, more or less along the line of the outside edge of your body. The pull is unlikely to actually *be* quite straight, because it's affected by the rotation of your body: slight deviation is fine.

Throughout the pull, the aim is for your forearm and hand to point down (and your palm and inner forearm backward) for as long as possible. A good rule is:

- Fingertips always lower than your wrist
- Wrist always lower than your elbow

▲ The high elbow catch in action: the swimmer's upper arm and elbow are still close to the surface, his arm is bent at the elbow and he is pulling backward.

▼ Right at the start of the arm stroke, this swimmer's left hand is perfectly in line with his shoulder and the edge of his body.

▲ High elbow recovery

▲ Swinging arm recovery

The pull phase

The recovery phase doesn't move you forward, so of itself is not really important. The key issues are:

1   Does your hand enter the water at the correct angle and place?
2   Does it leave the water smoothly and without affecting your body position?

If the answer to both these questions is yes, your recovery is fine. That said, most people's arm recovery fits into one of two main styles:

High elbow recovery

Classic 'good style' in front crawl swimming is a recovery with your elbow coming up and your hand swinging through beneath it, close to both your body and the water's surface.

This isn't ideal for triathletes and open-water swimmers, because having your hand close to the water's surface in choppy water can cause it to get caught, interrupting your stroke. Additionally, there's some evidence that this high elbow style is linked to 'swimmers' shoulder', a shoulder impingement. The high training volumes and long race distances of tri and open water swimmers are likely to exacerbate this.

Swinging arm recovery

In open water and triathlon, a wider, more 'swinging' style of recovery is ideal. This is still led by the elbow, but the elbow doesn't come as high and your forearm swings out, rather than swinging through beneath your elbow.

Hand shape

One common query from untrained swimmers is what shape they should make with their hand as they pull. Many people think they need to cup their hand into a tight scoop to help them get a better 'grip' on the water. This is unhelpful in a couple of ways:

1 It diminishes the surface area that's pushing back against the water
2 A tight, tense hand tends to communicate itself up your arm and into your shoulder. Tension anywhere in your arms, shoulders or neck will inhibit your technique

A looser, more relaxed hand shape is best. It offers a larger surface area, and helps the rest of your upper body relax. Aim for a loose, *very* slightly scooped hand shape, with the fingers and thumbs slightly apart. Pressing back on the water as you pull will flatten this shape, increasing the surface area.

To thumb or not to thumb?

What should you do with your thumb? The answer seems obvious: hold it close to your fingers, increasing the size of your 'paddle'. But if you look at slow-motion video of top swimmers, it's clear that while some do this, many don't. So in fact, the answer is, 'whatever works for you'. It's definitely better to be relaxed with a sticky-out thumb than to tense up by trying to keep it tucked in.

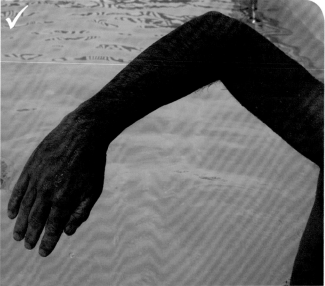

FISTS DRILL

Key aim: *To improve engagement with water*

This drill is a good way for getting a feel for how effective your hand shape is. Try swapping between your usual shape, a different hand shape (more relaxed? Thumb out?) and swimming with clenched fists.

1 Swim front crawl exactly as normal, but with your hands closed into fists for the whole stroke (including the recovery).

2 Mix things up: one hand in a fist, then the other; both as fists; six strokes with fists followed by six normal.

3 Pay attention to the feel from your forearm as you swim with a closed fist (try this for a whole length, both hands). You'll notice that as soon as your forearm is vertical in the water, you will feel the pressure of water against it. It's not only your hand that provides propulsion – it's also your forearm.

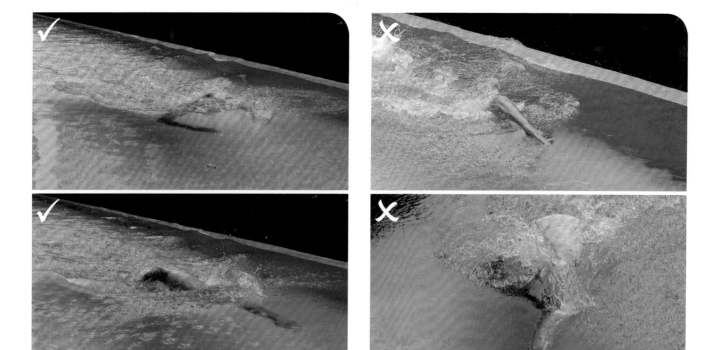

▲ Flat hand   ▲ Angled hand

Hand entry notes

Many swimmers have been taught to put their hand into the water thumb-first, with the palm of their hand facing slightly outward. The idea is to set up a catch that sweeps out, away from your body, and back in. Unfortunately, this type of catch is based on an incorrect coaching theory from the early 1970s.

We now know that the most efficient catch is one that goes straight back, instead of sweeping out and in. To set your stroke up for this, the best starting point is:

- Your hand enters the water fingertips-first
- The point of entry is ahead of your shoulder/in line with the outer edge of your body, not ahead of your face – this is one of the most common mistakes swimmers make
- The side-to-side angle of your hand (seen from in front) is parallel with the surface

Fingertips first

From the moment your hand enters the water, it's easy to remember what you're aiming for:

FINGERS, WRIST, ELBOW.

Throughout your pull, aim to have your fingertips lower than your wrist, and your wrist lower than your elbow.

BROKEN-ARROW DRILL

Key aim: *To practise effective hand entry*

What you need: *Swim fins*

If you're used to putting your hand in thumb first, this is a good way to get a feel for placing your hand in the water fingertips first.

1 With your fins on, push off and swim on your side, as in the rotation drills on pages 50 and 51.

2 Lift your trailing arm up out of the water and hold it vertically, at right angles to your body.

3 Bend your arm at the elbow and let it drop forward. As your arm drops down to the correct angle, spear your hand forward into the water. (Judging the angle takes a bit of practice.)

4 Make sure your hand goes ahead of your shoulder: it's easy to over-rotate and spear it in ahead of your face. It should also go into the water fingertips-first, pointing straight ahead.

5 Rotate on to your opposite side, and repeat with the other arm.

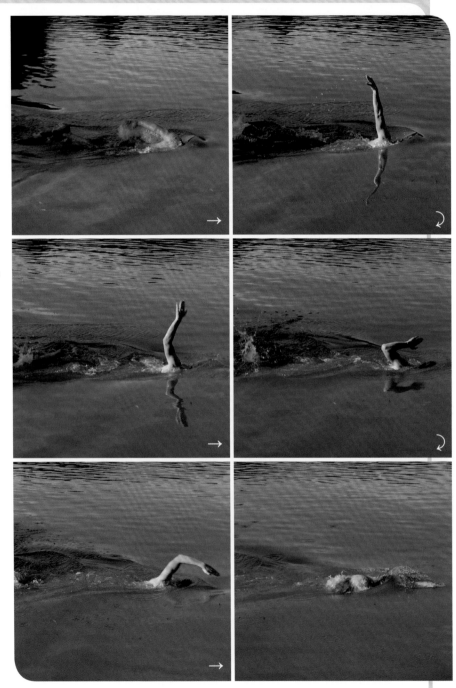

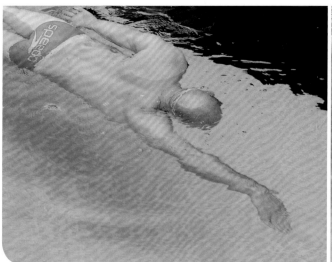

High elbow catch notes

The high elbow catch is the single most important element of good technique. It adds propulsion to your stroke, and as a side benefit helps you to maintain a good, streamlined body position. The high elbow catch begins with your arm pivoting down and back from the elbow. Your upper arm and elbow stay high in the water.

Few people naturally swim with a high elbow catch. Most start their stroke by pulling down and back from the shoulder, with basically a straight arm. This means that at first the high elbow catch feels unnatural, verging on uncomfortable. It takes time and focus to get this right, but it pays dividends. This technique has been shared by almost every top front crawl swimmer of the last century, male or female.

▲ In the sequence above the two images show a high-elbow catch: early in the stroke, the swimmer starts pressing water backwards.

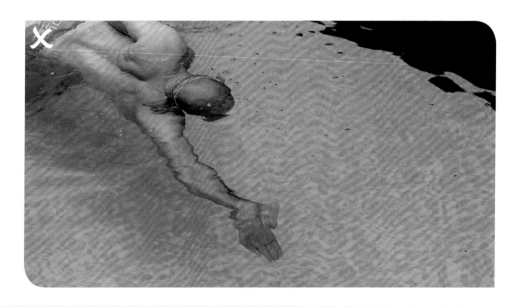

▶ In this image, the swimmer is using a less effective straight-arm catch; his elbow has dropped, but his hand and forearm are still not pressing the water backwards.

LANE-LINE INITIATION

Key aim: *To get a feel for the high elbow catch*

What you need: *A tight lane rope*

▼ As an alternative to using a lane line, this exercise gives you a feel for a high-elbow position. It's best done one arm at a time, instead of both together.

In this drill, your elbow *has* to stay high, because it's hooked over a lane rope. There's no need to do this for more than a few seconds: that will give you a feel for what a high elbow catch is like.

1 Float on the surface at right angles to the lane rope. Hold on to it with both hands, with bent arms and your face quite close to the rope.

2 Keeping hold of the rope with one hand, extend the other over the top of it. You're aiming for a position with your upper arm resting on the rope; if the rope is in your armpit, move back a bit. Have your arm extended and the palm of your hand facing the bottom of the pool.

3 Sweep your forearm and hand down and back as you would when swimming. (make sure your elbow is well clear of the lane rope, or this movement will be impossible.)

4 Once you've practised this a few times, try it with your face in the water (as it would be when you're swimming).

High elbow acclimatisation

The drills included here will help you get used to the position and sensations of a high elbow catch. Because you'll be using unfamiliar muscles it's a good idea not to do too much distance. Most swimmers find 50–100m of each is plenty. If you start to feel discomfort in the deltoid muscles on the outside of your shoulder, set these drills aside and come back to them another day.

CATCH DRILL 1

  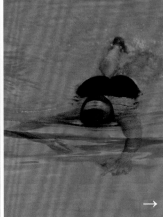 

Key aim: *To introduce/ improve high elbow catch*

What you need:
- *A fairly empty pool, as you'll be moving slowly*
- *Swimming snorkel*
- *Swim fins*
- *Finis Agility or Freestyler paddles (optional)*

▲ A single right-arm sequence of the catch drill; in the training pool this is practised with alternating arms.

Each pull mimics the catch phase of your stroke only, so the pulls should be short. Your hand recovers underwater, sliding up your centreline.

1 Push off the wall in a streamlined position (see pages 48–9). Use small kicks: they just need to keep your body flat in the water, rather than drive you forward. Have your arms relaxed and stretched out in front of you, and keep your neck and head relaxed. Breathe normally.

2 Pull with alternate arms. Focus on:
- Starting the pull from in front of your shoulder
- Keeping your elbow high
- Pulling straight back

3 As in full stroke, let your body rotate with each pull, but keep your head still. Unlike in full stroke, keep your elbow and upper arm still: the idea is to work only your hand and forearm.

CATCH DRILL 2

Key aims: *To improve catch; encourage a straight pull*

What you need:
- *A fairly empty pool, as you'll be moving slowly*
- *Swimming snorkel*
- *Swim fins*
- *Finis Agility or Freestyler paddles (optional)*

This single-arm drill makes a good follow-on from catch drill 1. Concentrate on the same elements of your stroke: start your pull in front of your shoulder, fingers pointing down, keep your elbow high and pull straight back.

1 Push off in a streamlined position. Allow your hands to drift shoulder-width apart, so that each is in the starting position for a stroke. Pull with one arm, starting the pull the same way as in catch drill 1.

2 This time, continue your pull straight back to your hips.

3 Recover over the surface as usual, then immediately pull again with the same arm. Continue for the rest of the length, then swim back down the pool using the other arm.

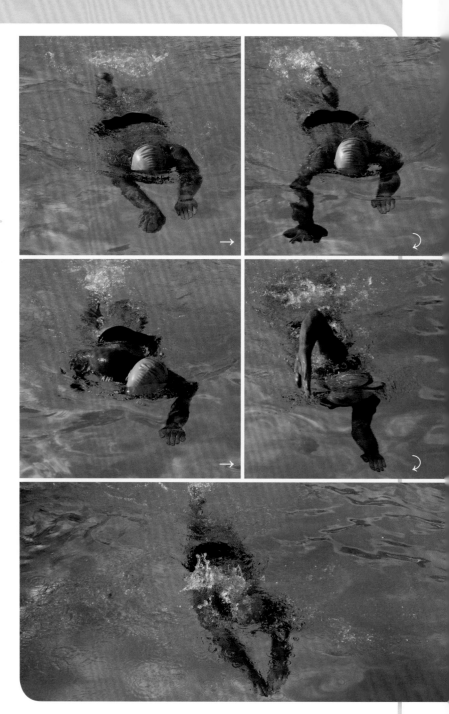

STRETCH CORD WORK

Key aim: *To improve muscle memory and strength for high elbow catch*

What you need: *Stretch cord*

Many swimmers initially find the high elbow catch challenging, partly because it's an unfamiliar movement and partly because it's physically taxing. In particular, the deltoid muscles of the upper arm/shoulder and the triceps may feel unaccustomed strain.

One of the best ways to address both issues is to practise the movement on dry land, using a stretch cord. If you can set this up in front of a reflective surface, it gives you a chance to watch yourself from an entirely different angle: is your elbow really staying still? Are you actually pulling straight back, from ahead of your shoulder?

Initially, use a light cord that offers minimal resistance. Once you have the movement set in both arms, you can progress to a heavier cord. This exercise needs to be done often, but for fairly short repetitions.

1 Anchor the cord above head height: you want to be able to bend forward comfortably with the cord and your torso in alignment.

2 To work on your right arm, take a step back with your left foot; bend forward and rotate your body as you would when starting an arm stroke.

3 You want the cord to be offering some resistance, but only a minimal amount. Adjust your distance from the anchor point accordingly.

4 Slowly practise the high elbow catch as described on page 30, taking care that your upper arm stays still and only your forearm and hand swing down.

5 When you have the movement right, increase the speed to roughly match your usual swimming stroke. At first do no more than 15 repetitions, three times on each arm.

The drill for (nearly) everything

This doggy-paddle drill is a great way to work on your hand entry position and high elbow catch. It lets you see what your hands are doing at the very start of your stroke.

When you swim full stroke, you can't really see where your hands enter the water or what they do next. It's easy to fool yourself into thinking that they're going in ahead of your shoulder, or that you're pulling back with a high elbow, just because what you're doing feels different. Usually, it needs to be a lot *more* different than you imagine – and doggy paddle shows you this.

▶ Once you have the knack of the doggy paddle drill (right), try swimming it underwater (on page 43). Half a length of this and half a length of full stroke is a great exercise.

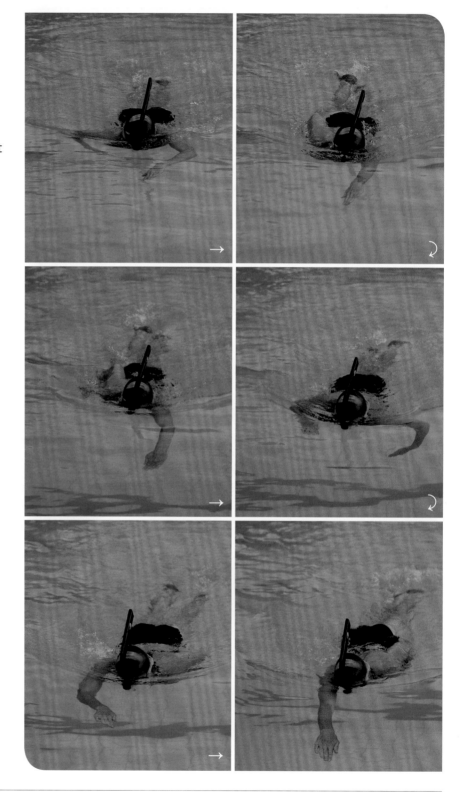

DOGGY PADDLE DRILL

Key aim: *To improve hand positioning and catch*
What you need: *Swim fins, possibly a snorkel*

Don't overdo this drill, as it can be hard on your lower back. In a pool it's generally best to mix it up by doing half a length of doggy paddle and half a length of full stroke.

1 Push off and start doing a front-crawl kick. Your arms will be out straight, and should be shoulder-width apart.

2 Lift your head and do a pull with one arm. Concentrate on making sure your pull starts in a line ahead of your shoulder, not your face. Begin the pull keeping your elbow high.

3 Pull straight back towards your hips (don't stop below your armpits, as a dog would). Pull right through, allowing your other arm to reach forward. Take care that your leading arm doesn't drift in towards the centreline of your body as you pull back.

4 Repeat with your leading arm, at the same time recovering your trailing arm by sliding it back up your stomach and chest, and out in front of you.

5 When you start to swim front crawl for the second half of the length, try to keep the same technique for your catch and pull.

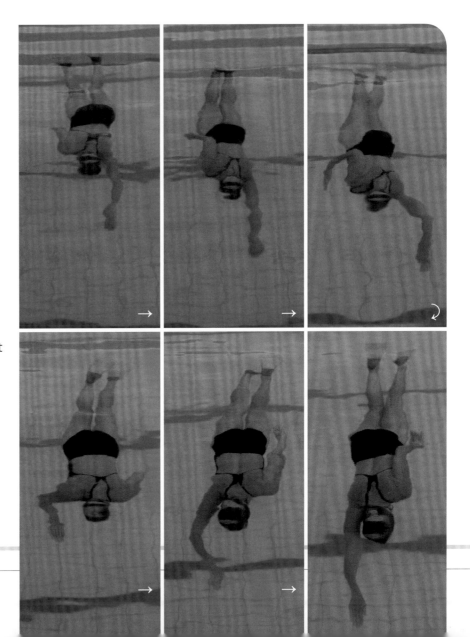

Arm stroke

Hand exit notes

The last phase of your arm stroke is the exit from the water and the recovery over the surface.

The exit seems a tiny detail, but it's worth paying attention to because getting it wrong can compromise your streamlined body position. The aim is to let your wrist relax at the end of the pull, then lift your forearm and hand clear of the water in a movement led from the elbow. Keeping your wrist rigid will lead to you pushing up as you finish your stroke. Doing this pushes your hips down, creating drag.

▼ This swimmer has finished his pull with a rigid wrist and the palm of his hand facing up. As a result he's thrown a scoop of water up into the air. The effect of this upward push has been to force his hips down, which in turn has led to an inefficient bent-knee kick.

Stroke counting: probably pointless

Many swimmers count their strokes per length, with the ultimate aim of decreasing the number. But what makes fewer strokes better? Watch an international race – especially an open water one – and you'll see that many top swimmers actually have a high stroke count. There's no rule that says to be a good swimmer you have to hit a certain number.

It's easy to get fixated on stroke count per length, but it often ends up being counterproductive. You start trying to glide, rather than swim – which will decrease your stroke count, but also slow you down (see box on the myth of glide, page 24).

Even decreasing your stroke count without adding glide may slow you down, if your stroke rate drops:

24 strokes per length @ 0.75 seconds per stroke = 18 seconds per length

22 strokes per length @ 0.85 seconds per stroke = 18.7 seconds per length

To work on this, go back to catch drill 2 on page 40. Instead of concentrating on your catch, think about making sure your wrist and forearm are relaxed as you start to lift them from the water. Pay attention to whether you are pulling back (good) or up (bad) during the last part of your stroke. You could also ask a fellow swimmer to check for the telltale signs of water being thrown up, as in the photo on the left.

◄ A few expert swimmers are able to adapt their recovery style to the circumstances. These photos show the same swimmer: practising a high elbow recovery style for the pool, and a swinging recovery for open water.

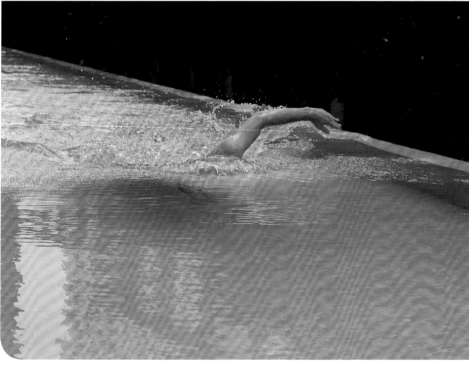

Key skills

- *Start your pull from in front of your shoulder.*
- *Keep your elbow high during the catch phase.*
- *Elbow, wrist, fingers – pull with your fingers lower than your wrist and your wrist lower than your elbow.*
- *Pull straight, not in a curved path.*

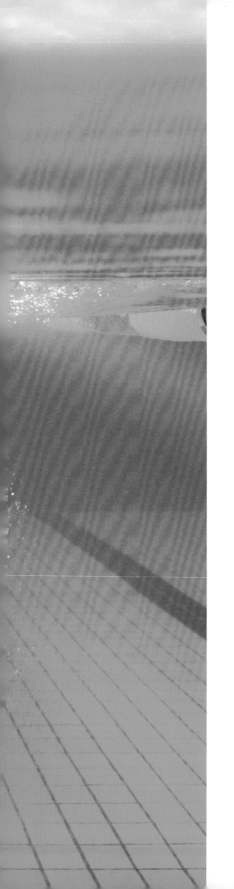

03

BODY POSITION

position *noun* the way or direction in which an object is placed or arranged; the posture that someone's body is in; place, arrangement, posture, location, situation, setting

47

BODY POSITION

The ideal body position balances a powerful forward drive against providing the smallest possible surface area for the water to push back against. This not only satisfies the scientific principles of bewigged sixteenth-century swim-spiration Sir Isaac Newton (see page 28), it also lets you use less energy, or go faster, than a large-area, high-drag position.

A low-drag, streamlined body position is almost straight and practically flat in the water, nearly parallel with the surface. (While actually swimming, your legs need to be just a little below the surface. That way, your feet don't end up kicking air half the time.) The practice below is a great way to get a feel for a streamlined body position, and there is also a good exercise for practising a streamlined shape on the opposite page.

STREAMLINE FLOAT

Key aim: *To establish muscle memory of a streamlined body position*

What you need: *Swimming snorkel (optional)*

This drill looks ridiculously simple – until you try it. Some people take weeks to achieve it; others get it right away. Even if you struggle, though, don't give up. It's a great test of getting your body into a streamlined position.

1 Take a deep breath, then let yourself float face-down in the water. Your whole body should be relaxed, with your arms and legs dangling down. (It soon becomes clear why this is sometimes called the 'dead swimmer float' – it's a good idea to warn the lifeguards what you're up to!)

2 Lift your arms and legs simultaneously, without kicking your legs or using your hands at all.

3 Point your toes back and your fingers forward, and keep lifting your arms and legs towards the surface.

4 You're aiming to get five points of your body all touching the surface of the water:

- Backs of your hands
- Back of your head
- Bottom
- Calves
- Heels

Try to stay relaxed, and keep looking straight down at the bottom of the pool. Just let your body slowly extend into a straight line.

SWIMMING STREAMLINED

Key aim: *To improve feel for streamlined position*

What you need:
- *Swim fins*
- *Swimming snorkel*

This is a very simple exercise that can have a big benefit. As always when swimming, try to relax and listen to your body. Feel how the water presses against your skin, where there's most resistance and where there's least.

1 Put on your fins and push off into the streamlined position from page 48. Lay one hand on top of the other, and look at the bottom of the pool rather than ahead. (Many swimmers find that the most streamlined head position looks down more than they expected.)

2 Kick with a steady rhythm, fast enough to feel water resistance as you move ahead. Take care not to bend your knees a lot, and make sure you're always kicking water, not air. Only your heel should ever come out of the water.

3 Experiment with different head, shoulder, hip and foot positions to see how they affect water resistance. Try pressing down with your chest, extending through the stomach, tightening up your back and bottom – but always come back to the streamlined position from page 40. (It's sometimes helpful to go back to that drill in the middle of this exercise, as a reminder.)

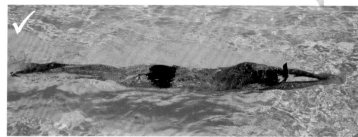

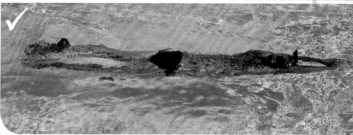

▲ A nice, flat streamlined position, with only the swimmer's heels breaking the surface as he kicks.

▼ The swimmer's head is too high and his hips and legs have sunk down.

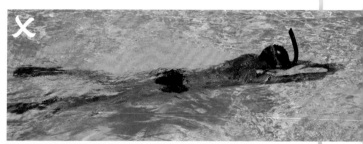

▲ The swimmer's head is low, his bottom is sticking up and his feet are coming right out of the water.

Rotation

Front crawl isn't really a great name for it, because you swim most of it partly on your side. As each arm lifts out of the water, that side of your body lifts up; at the same time, the opposite side drops down. This continuous movement is called *rotation*.

There are three advantages to rotating your body with each stroke. First, you're slightly more streamlined and slip through the water using less energy. Second, the roll helps your leading hand extend further forward at the front of your stroke, adding length to your pull. Third, rotation makes smooth breathing much easier to achieve.

Twist

Be careful not to confuse rotation (a good thing) with twist (so bad it should be made to go and stand in the corner). Twist is side-to-side kinking of your body as you swim, and is terminal to your efforts to be streamlined. Your body should stay in a straight, streamlined shape: never touching the sides of an imaginary tube around it, but constantly rotating inside it.

▶ This swimmer is throwing her arms across the centreline of her body, which is causing it to twist with every stroke.

ROTATION DRILL 1

Key aim: *To improve streamline position while on your side*

What you need: *Swim fins*

1 Push off, and do one arm pull with your right arm. After doing the pull, lay your right arm along your side.

2 Stretch your left arm out in front, dropping your shoulder. Your head will turn to the side – just let it turn with your body. Keep your neck in line with your spine, don't lift your head. Your right shoulder, arm and hip will lift out of the water, so you're swimming along on your side.

3 Swim like this until you need a breath. To get air, smoothly turn your head (or even roll on to your back), then settle back into position.

4 Swim a whole length like this with your right side up; repeat with your left side up on the next length.

Key skills

Use your vision to control your head angle. While you're swimming on your side, the edge of the pool should bisect your vision, leaving the world looking distinctly sideways. If it starts to look right-way-up, it's a sure sign you have lifted your head and broken the streamlined position.

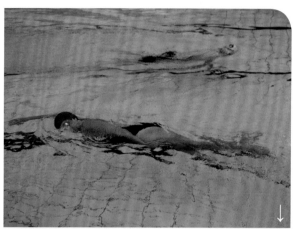

ROTATION DRILL 2

Key aim: *To work on combining rotation with a streamlined body position.*

What you need:
- *Swim fins*
- *Swimming snorkel (optional)*

Start by doing this drill on your back, then put on a swimming snorkel and try the same drill on your front.

1 Push off into a streamlined position on your back, with your arms by your sides. Use a small, steady kick to move yourself along. (Check whether your knees break the surface: if they do, it's a sign that you are kicking from the knee rather than the hip.)

2 Relax your shoulders and neck, and look straight up at the ceiling. It helps if there's a line of some sort to follow – most pool ceilings do point the same way as the lanes.

3 Once you are swimming smoothly, start to rotate your hips (i.e. tilt them so that one rises and the other drops). Try to make a smooth, continuous movement, first one way, then the other. As each hip rises in turn, the shoulder on the same side will also lift up. Constantly check to make sure you are not kinking your body shape: keep straight.

4 Watch for the backstroke flags, which warn that you're 5m from the end. When you reach them, turn on to your front.

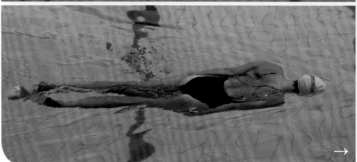

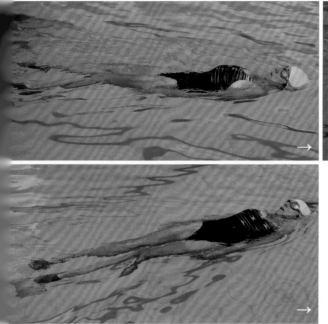

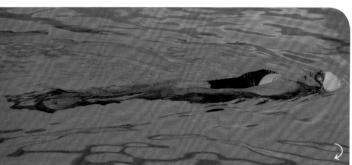

5 Once you have a feel for this drill on your back, try it on your front with a swimming snorkel. It's easiest if you follow a line along the bottom of the pool. Breathe steadily and keep your neck and head relaxed and still. Lift your head when you reach the end of the lane markings on the bottom of the pool.

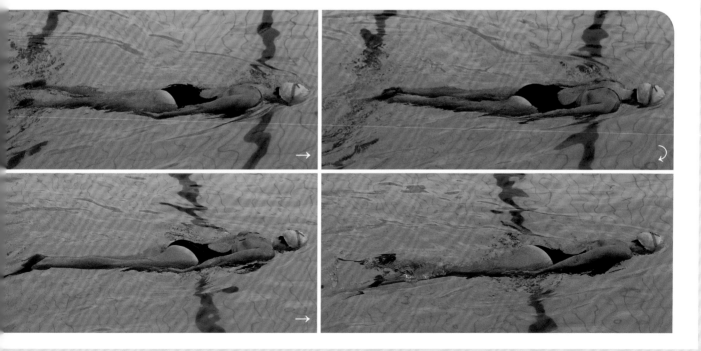

ROTATION DRILL 3

Key aim: *To improve streamline position during rotation*

What you need:

- *A pool with a straight line along the bottom*
- *Swim fins*

This is a development of drill 1, but it adds a change of sides. Don't worry too much if your breathing needs work (turn to chapter 4 for advice on that) – in this drill, the focus is on getting used to swimming in a streamlined position on both sides.

1 Push off along the line and take one stroke with your right arm, as in the drill on page 51.

2 Keep kicking on your side until you need a breath, then take a stroke with your left arm while recovering your right arm. As you do this, your body rolls to the other side. Continue the rotation to take a breath.

3 As you make the switch of sides, check whether you are still swimming along the line.

4 Repeat all the way down the length of the pool.

Once you have mastered this, try the drill with a swimming snorkel. You swim looking down at the line along the bottom of the pool the whole time; everything else is as above.

Common body position problems

These four things have a big effect on whether you achieve a streamlined body position while swimming front crawl:

1 Your head angle
2 Your flexibility
3 The catch phase of your stroke
4 Your hand exit from the water, at the end of the pull

▲ In the two images above, the swimmer's head is too high, causing his hips to sink.

Problem 1: Head angle

The angle at which you hold your head has a big effect because it's so closely linked to your upper body. For a demo, stand up straight then lift your chin forward and up. Your chest pushes forward; if you were in the water, your hips would also drop. This, though, is the position most people swim in.

Some people – often female swimmers – can swim looking forward without it affecting their body position. Most, though, would be more streamlined looking down rather than forward. Getting your head position right takes a bit of experimentation; ideally, get a friend to video you swimming, trying and reviewing various head positions until you find the most streamlined one.

▲ Here, his head is so low that his chest has sunk. As a result his shoulder is catching water and, in the side-on image, creating drag.

▲ Now the swimmer has found a good position. He's looking down and slightly forward, and his shoulder is clear of the water. His hips are higher, and overall this is a good, streamlined body position.

SHOULDER FLEXIBILITY

Key aim: *Check whether your flexibility is affecting your catch and body position.*

What you need: *A bench or stool, pushed up against a wall*

1 Start by sitting with your back flat against a wall and your arms relaxed, looking straight ahead. Next, raise your arms up and back until they are also flat against the wall.

　Did you end up bending at the waist, pushing your stomach out?

　Imagine that the wall is the surface of the water. Starting your catch at the surface, as most people aim to do, will have the same effect on your body as putting your arms flat against the wall. It will push your stomach down – in other words, mess up your streamline.

2 To get around this problem, go back to the wall and do the exercise again. Notice the point at which your back stops being flat against the wall.

3 The distance of your hands from the wall shows where your catch should start. For this swimmer it's shown in the fourth photo – his pull will be shorter, but his body position will stay flatter. He gains more from staying streamlined than from having a slightly longer pull.

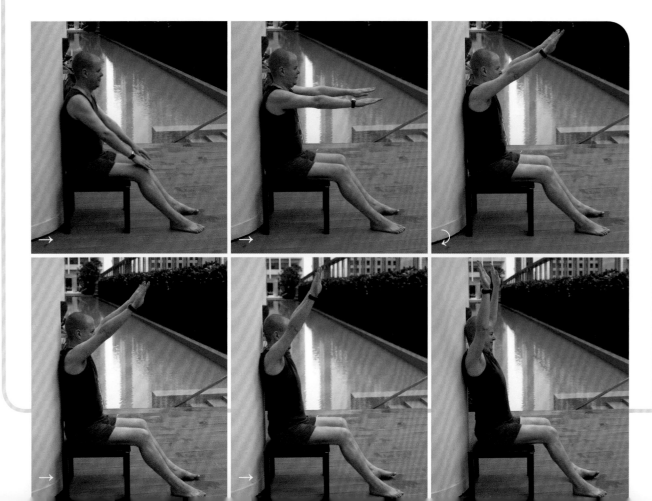

Problem 2: Flexibility and catch

The flexibility of your shoulders affects the position in which you start the catch stage of your stroke. Get this wrong, and it has a knock-on effect on your body position. This is a common problem for many swimmers, particularly those with powerful shoulders. Fortunately, it is simple to check and make adjustments accordingly. The panel opposite shows you how to do this.

Problem 3: Catch and hand exit

Your catch and hand exit can both have a negative effect on your body position.

Using a straight arm catch means that during the catch phase, you are pressing downward as much as, or more than, back. This lifts your head and chest, and drops your hips and legs.

In an effort to get more drive from their stroke, some swimmers continue to drive their hand as it exits the water. Their hand finishes the pull pressing upward, which pushes their hips and legs down.

In both cases, only part of their stroke is driving them forward; the rest is forcing them into a low-hip, draggy body position.

The cure is to adopt a high-elbow catch, which will emphasise the forward drive of your arm pull.

Key skills

- *Swim in the tube! Swim straight, without letting your body touch the sides of an imaginary tube.*
- *Use your vision to control your head angle.*
- *Pull backward – don't press down or scoop up.*

04

BREATHING

breathe *verb* repeatedly and alternately take in and blow out air in order to function; develop flavour through exposure to air; respire, take in air, gasp, pant, wheeze

BREATHING

If you're swimming more than about 50m, breathing is crucial to your performance. To keep your muscles supplied with energy, you need to expel waste products in the form of poisonous CO_2 gas and draw oxygen-rich air deep into your lungs. There are two key elements to front-crawl breathing: one psychological, the other technical.

The aim: psychological

In a word: relax. When humans are anxious, they tend to take shallow, fast breaths. As a swimmer, shallow breaths are not what you need. So part of a good breathing technique is to relax. If you're not relaxed, you won't breathe effectively while swimming – and if you don't breathe in enough oxygen, your performance will suffer.

The aim: technical

The overall aim is to match taking a breath seamlessly to the rest of your stroke. To do this you need a good catch, a streamlined position, and good body rotation. If you have good body rotation, you'll only need to make a slight movement of your head when breathing in.

- Keep your neck at the same angle as usual, so that your face turns to the side, rather than lifting up
- Make the breath a smooth movement, timed to fit exactly with the rotation of your body

▼ In these two photos you can see that the swimmer's body rotation is the same whether he is taking a breath or not.

▼ Here, the swimmer has lifted his head, instead of just turning it to the side. His hips have dropped and he's pushing a bow wave of water in front of his head.

BREATHING UNDERWATER

You can breathe underwater! This is a limited offer, because you can only breathe out, not in. Even so, breathing out underwater is a crucial skill.

If you hold your breath while your face is in the water it causes two big problems:

1 It means you are effectively swimming with a couple of air balloons in your chest. The balloons buoy your torso up, your hips drop, and you start to do an inefficient, bent-knees kick. It becomes difficult to maintain a good, streamlined body position

2 If you hold your breath while your face is in the water, you have to expel it when your face is *out* of the water. You could be using that time for breathing in! The result is that you either end up turning your head too far, keeping your face out of the water for longer than is really necessary, or you don't get enough oxygen. When fit athletes say they can't swim more than a couple of lengths of front crawl without getting out of breath, the cause is usually that they're holding their breath underwater

It's easy to hold on to all or most of your breath without realising it. The telltale sign is that as your face comes out of the water to breathe, you let go a puff of air like a surfacing whale. It will be visible, and maybe even audible, to a fellow swimmer on poolside.

THE SINKING DRILL

Key aims: *To build confidence; establish or improve aquatic breathing*

What you need:

- *A deep end*
- *A companion to watch you – this exercise is safest done in pairs*

Usually when swimmers hold their breath while their face is in the water it's because either a) a misguided swimming teacher taught them that way, or b) they're nervous and tense about swimming. Fortunately, this exercise is great for both groups. It's also useful if you find yourself tensing up while attempting another drill.

Warn the lifeguard that you're doing this drill, or you risk being rescued when they spot you sitting on the bottom.

1 Take a breath, and let yourself float vertically at or just below the surface.

2 Once you're still, start blowing air out through your nose and mouth.

3 Keep blowing, and you will eventually start to sink. It's important that you sink because of lost air/buoyancy: using your hands to swoosh yourself down is banned!

4 Carry on breathing out until you've sunk right down and can sit on the bottom of the pool.

5 Push back to the surface and take a welcome breath of air.

Breathing patterns

Your 'breathing pattern' is the number of strokes you do before taking a breath. Many people find it easier to breathe on one side than the other, and end up breathing every two strokes. Others can breathe on both sides and take a breath every three strokes. There are advantages to each pattern:

BREATHING EVERY 2 STROKES:
Advantage: You get more breaths per 100m, making it easier to swim longer distances without building up lactic acid in your muscles.
Disadvantage: It's easy for your stroke to become lopsided and unbalanced.

BREATHING EVERY 3 STROKES:
Advantage: Your stroke should be more balanced, because you have to learn to roll your body both left and right. This arguably makes it easier to train yourself to swim in a straight line. Being able to breathe both sides also allows you to adjust your breathing in open water, to avoid wind chop coming from the side.
Disadvantage: You breathe fewer times per length: sustaining this breathing pattern requires better technique and/or a greater degree of aerobic fitness.

Breathe better in doggerel

If you struggle to remember to breathe out, establish a bilateral breathing pattern, or both, try this trick. While you're swimming along, speak these words underwater in rhythm with your arm strokes:

HUBBLE, BUBBLE, BREATHE.

(Actually, you can riff any words you like on the same beat. I've heard: **Potatoes, bananas, cheeeese; Pepper, makes me, sneeeze;** *and* **Monkeys, live in, Belize.***)*

When swimmers feel they need to breathe every two strokes, it's often because they're not breathing out underwater. Making that simple adjustment is sometimes all it takes to give you enough air to breathe every three strokes.

Head position and breathing

As well as affecting your body position (see pages 54–5 for more on this), your head position has an important role to play in your breathing. Holding your head too high or too low will not only cause drag, it will also make breathing awkward.

The ideal head position for many swimmers is with their neck more or less in line with their spine, when viewed from the side. They look very slightly ahead, but more down than forward.

BREATH DRILL 1

Key aims: *To improve head position and movement for breathing*

What you need: *Swim fins*

This drill helps you get used to the angle you hold your head and the small movement you make when taking a breath.

1 Push off and begin to kick in a streamlined position, with both arms in front of you. Take one arm stroke, but without the recovery. Instead, leave your hand straight back, next to your hip.

2 Reach forward with your leading arm, dropping the shoulder and rotating your body. As you do this, the shoulder of your trailing arm will lift up, leaving you swimming on your side. Your head will be mostly underwater, and your neck should be relaxed and in line with your spine (not tilted up towards the surface).

3 To breathe, simply turn your head sideways, then lower it again. Make sure you rotate your head, turning your chin as well as your forehead.

4 Give a few more kicks, and repeat the breath. Do a whole length breathing on this same side, then change sides for the following length.

You might want to try this drill with 'Popeye' breathing, where you push your mouth upward, towards the air, as a way of minimising your head movement even more.

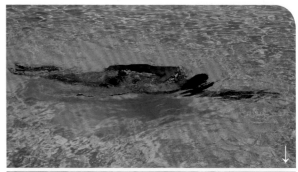
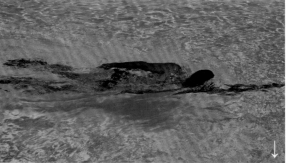
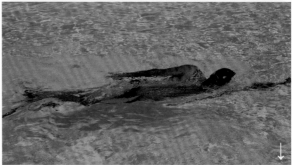

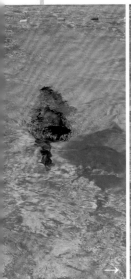   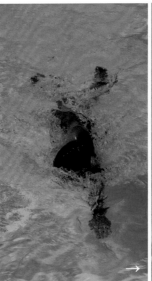 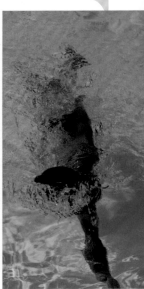

Key aims: *To establish timing of when to take a breath; work on breathing to both sides*

What you need: *Swim fins*

This is a progression from breath drill 1, but it adds a change of side. It can be helpful to go back and forth between them. If, for example, you find it easier to breathe on one side than the other, go back to swimming on just your weaker side for a while.

As well as fixing the timing of your breath on both sides, this drill helps you to swim with a balanced stroke, keeping a streamlined body position.

1 Put on fins. Push off into a streamlined position, and take an arm stroke without the recovery (see page 63).

2 Take a breath, then swim on your side for a slow count of three.

3 After the count of three, pull with your extended arm and recover with your trailing arm. Coordinate the two movements. As you roll to the other side during the arm stroke, leave the pulling arm trailing and the recovery arm extended, so that you're in the breathing position again, but facing the other side.

4 As you rotate on to the other side, take a breath. The key aim for this drill is for the movement of taking a breath to be a smooth continuation of the rotation of your body.

5 Swim on your side for a slow count of three, then change sides again. Continue like this down the length of the pool.

Try to keep your movements smooth – it's tempting to snatch at the arm pull. You'll find that a strong leg kick helps, as it allows you to concentrate on the motion of your upper body.

Physiological improvements

Most people only expel about 75 per cent of what's in their lungs when they breathe out. Fit people usually breathe more efficiently than that, but it is still possible to improve the amount of waste gas expelled. This is a double win: you process the waste products of exercise more efficiently, and you also have more capacity available for oxygen-rich air.

Key skills

- *Breathe underwater! Whenever your face is in the water, breathe out.*
- *Make taking a breath part of your body rotation.*
- *Turn your head to breathe – don't lift it.*
- *Always keep one goggle in the water.*

BREATH DRILL 3

Key aim: *To improve lung function*

What you need:
- *Chest-deep water*
- *A companion to watch you
  – this exercise is safest done
  in pairs, one at a time*

To do this drill well it's important
that you are comfortable and
relaxed breathing out underwater.
It doesn't work if you rush the
exhalation because you're in a
rush to get back to the surface.

1 Stand in chest-deep water
and relax. Bend your knees
until your chin is at the surface.

2 Breathe in deeply, then bend
your knees more until your
goggles are below the surface.

3 Breathe out slowly and
steadily, counting how long it
takes for you to completely empty
your lungs. Once you think your
lungs are empty, make an effort
to blow out a few more bubbles:
most people can.

4 Come back to the surface and
take one long, deep breath.
After one breath in, sink back
down and empty your lungs again.

5 Repeat the exercise until you
have done six exhalations.

05

KICK

kick *verb* propel, impel, strike out with the foot or feet | *noun* foot movement; leg movement; a thrashing movement with the leg or a swimming kick

KICK

You rarely have to go far in a crowd of triathletes before someone tells you no, you definitely shouldn't kick during the swim. Save your legs for the bike and the run. This is pure hokum. In front crawl, your leg kick is like the egg in a cake mix: leave it out, and you'll end up eating a slice of disappointment.

What *is* true is that as a triathlete or open-water swimmer, you're not really after forward drive from your kick. (Even good pool sprinters, with a kick like an outboard motor, rarely get more than 10 per cent of their drive from their kick.) The kick's job is to keep your legs and hips up, keeping you in a streamlined body position.

For a triathlete or open-water swimmer, front-crawl kick should be a balance of three things:

1 Most importantly, it should help you keep a streamlined body position. It needs to keep your legs and hips close to the surface, and the kick itself should be low drag. This means making small kicks with straight or almost-straight legs and toes pointing backward

2 Your kick should also be physically undemanding, so that you are not wasting energy on something that gives you next to no forward drive

3 The timing of your kick should be part of the rotation of your stroke

Kicking rhythms

In front crawl, kicking rhythm is counted over a cycle of two arm strokes (one stroke by each arm). This means kicking once every arm stroke gives you a 2-beat kick, twice equals a 4-beat kick and three times gives a 6-beat kick.

The 2-beat kick

A 2-beat kick provides little or no propulsion, but uses very little energy. The 2-beat kick is used mainly by distance swimmers, who place a premium on endurance.

The 4-beat kick

This is an unusual rhythm, but some swimmers just do it naturally. A 4-beat kick is obviously a compromise between the other two rhythms.

The 6-beat kick

This rhythm provides the highest potential level of propulsion, though a skilled swimmer can alter the power of the kick (and the level of energy it demands) dramatically. If used for speed, this rhythm uses a lot of energy.

Which rhythm you use is really a matter of what feels right. Over distance, a 2-beat kick demands least energy, but some swimmers find it's too slow and doesn't offer them enough support to keep a streamlined body position. It's worth experimenting, but it's a bad idea to force yourself into a kicking rhythm that feels wrong.

Timing

Whatever kicking rhythm you use, the basic timing of your kicks with your arm stroke should be the same. When your hand enters the water, your opposite leg kicks. If you're swimming with a 2-beat kick, this is the only kick you make per arm stroke.

In these images, notice the streamlined shape of the swimmer's foot: his toes are always pointing backward, in the most streamlined position possible. His legs are also either straight or almost straight throughout each kick. This is good technique – though in the last image he's kicking air, not water (see page 72), and was made to sit on the naughty step as a result.

▲ A 2-beat kick creates little turbulence, but also next to no forward drive.

▲ A 4-beat kick just feels right for some swimmers.

▼ In a 6-beat kick, a lot of energy may be expended in return for a relatively small amount of drive.

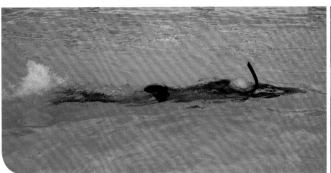 

Kick training

There are a couple of things to bear in mind when you're doing kick training:

1   Swimming snorkels are useful.
    When you're swimming legs-only, lifting your head to breathe will affect your streamlined body shape. It lifts your head and shoulders, and forces your hips down. Using a swimming snorkel is a good way round this (though in some places they are not allowed in public pools)

2   Don't get over-reliant on fins.
    Swim fins are a good training aid: they're useful in supporting your body during arm drills, they load your legs and build strength, and they encourage you to point your toes. Unfortunately, fins are also the crack cocaine of the swimming world: highly addictive. Nothing beats the feeling of bombing down the pool like a turbo-charged human/seal hybrid. Be careful you don't get hooked. Overusing fins gives your body a false idea of what can be expected from your legs. Then, once you take them off, your technique falls apart

Waving, not driving

When working on your kick technique, keep this simple rule at the front of your mind:

KICK WATER, NOT AIR!

Any time your feet come out of the water, they're waving at the spectators rather than doing useful work.

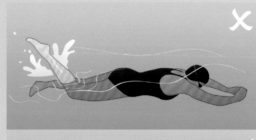

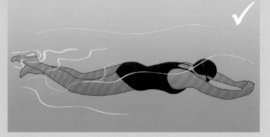

KICKING: SETTING THE KICK

Key aim: *To set muscle memory for front-crawl kick*

What you need: *A clear poolside with a raised edge (this drill is tricky in pools where the deck is the same height as the water surface)*

This exercise is also useful if you feel your kick has gone off-track in some way: just haul out on the side and run through it a couple of times.

1 Sit on the edge of the pool, with your bottom on the deck and your thighs clear of it. Lean back and rest your weight on your hands, then extend your legs out straight over the water.

2 Point your toes, and keep your legs close together. Lower your feet until they're about 30cm underwater. Make sure your toes are still pointed.

3 Keeping your legs straight, lift one foot steadily up, but don't let it break the surface. Lower it again, raising the other foot in an opposite movement. Your feet should be close together as they pass. Tilt your feet slightly inward so that your big toes actually brush as they pass.

4 Once you have the basic movement set, slowly increase your speed. Keep your feet, ankles and calves relaxed, and aim to make the surface of the water boil as your feet flick up beneath it.

SLOW KICK PRACTICE

Key aim: *To encourage a small kick from the hips*

What you need:
- *Kickboard*
- *Swimming snorkel (optional)*

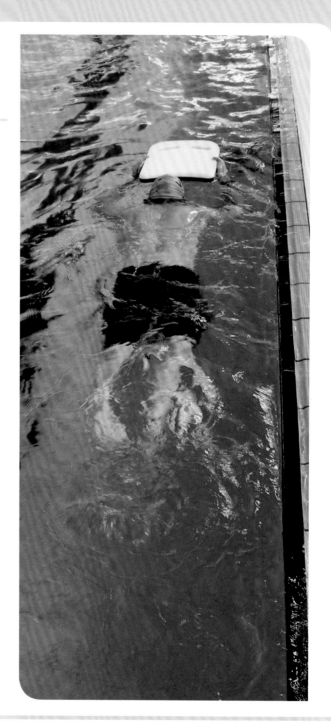

This drill is a way of practising a small, stream-lined front-crawl kick. It's especially useful if you're currently a big, splashy kicker. The drill is best done with a swimming snorkel, so that you don't have to lift your head to breathe.

1 Hold the kickboard by its sides as shown in the photo, with just your thumbs over the top and your fingers underneath. You're aiming to swim with relaxed wrists and bent elbows dangling down, rather than holding the kickboard out in front of you with straight arms.

2 Push off and start kicking. Keep your neck and shoulders relaxed. Use the limited range of movement from the drill on page 73: keep your legs straight, your toes pointed, and kick from the hips. Keep your calves, ankles and feet relaxed.

3 You'll feel a rocking movement in your hips; try to keep your head and your upper body still and relaxed. Breathe in and out steadily to help you relax.

4 If you're not using a swimming snorkel, lift your head to breathe when necessary, but keep kicking. Notice how lifting your head affects the angle of your hips and legs and forces you to start bending your knees as you kick.

Keeping your legs straight (ish)

Your kick needs to be streamlined, or it will slow you down. To achieve this, your legs have to be straight. Or at least, straight-ish. Obviously, your legs do bend slightly when you kick, because you're not holding them rigid. (Nothing should be held rigid when you're swimming.) The important thing is to avoid bending them too much. Below is a simple exercise that will tell you whether you're kicking with too-bent legs:

KICK ON YOUR BACK

Key aim: *To check for and correct kick from the knee*

What you need: *This kick can be done with swim fins if you struggle to keep a streamlined body position*

This kick is best done with a fellow swimmer: take turns watching each other for the telltale sign of a bent-knee kick.

1 Push off on your back into a streamlined body position. Look straight up at the roof, and keep your core tight to help maintain the streamline. (If this is difficult, putting on swim fins will help.)

2 Kick with your normal front-crawl technique and rhythm (front-crawl and back-crawl kick are basically the same). Swim a whole length with your fellow swimmer watching from the pool deck. They are looking to see whether you keep the streamlined body position and whether your knees ever break the surface.

3 At the end of the length, await the bad/good news from your partner. If you stayed streamlined and your knees never broke the surface, you are probably kicking with straight legs. Otherwise you are probably kicking from the knee, not the hip.

Increasing effectiveness

Once your kick is technically correct – with a streamlined shape, relaxed feet, ankles and calves, and movement from the hips – you can start working on increasing its effectiveness.

It's probably not a good idea to do this before you have the technical side right, as you'll end up bedding in bad habits.

PUSH-KICK DRILL

Key aim: *To improve kick effectiveness*

This drill is really simple, and really works. No equipment is needed.

1 From the side of the pool, push off underwater in a streamlined shape. Your arms should be out straight ahead, with one hand over the other. Your head is between your upper arms/shoulders, looking straight down.

2 Keeping your streamline, kick as fast as you can underwater. Stick to a streamlined technique – don't suddenly start doing big kicks in an effort to go faster.

3 When you come up, notice how far you have got. Swim back to the side, and repeat 4–6 times.

4 Immediately swim two or three lengths of full stroke. Don't worry too much about your kicking technique, except to remember that your big toes should brush together with each kick. You should feel as though you're swimming with less drag.

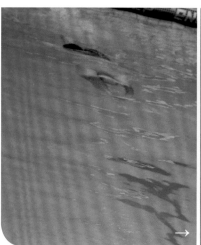
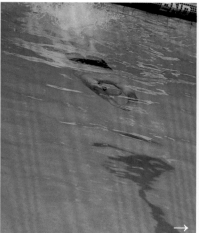

VERTICAL KICKING

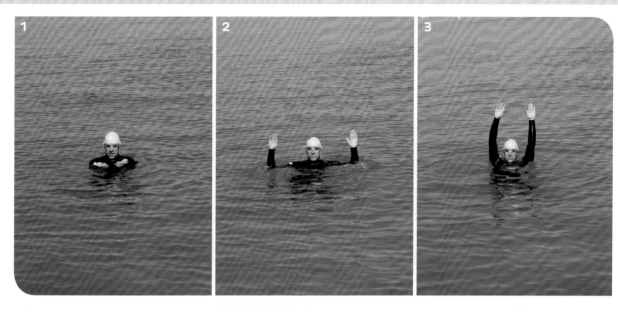

Key aim: *To improve kick effectiveness*

What you need: *A small area of water where you're out of your depth*

Many swimmers only really kick down, with the top of their foot and their shin. This drill encourages you to develop control of the other part of your leg kick: the upstroke, using the bottom of your foot and your calf.

There are three versions of this drill, each one increasingly difficult:

VERSION 1

Float vertically in water that's well out of your depth. Cross your arms over your chest, palms flat. Kick hard to keep your head above water, using the streamlined kick described in this chapter.

Ideally, try to maintain the exercise for at least 20 seconds before stopping for a 10-second rest, then repeating it. Repeat a total of five or six times.

VERSION 2 – HARDER

Instead of crossing your arms over your chest, lift your hands free of the water. Just keep your hands in the air, with your wrists above the surface. Keep the same timing as in version 1.

VERSION 3 – VERY TESTING

This time, instead of putting only your hands in the air, lift both arms clear of the surface. Only try this version when you're comfortably able to complete five or six repetitions of the second iteration of this drill. Otherwise you risk swallowing a magnum of pool water and putting yourself off swimming forever.

ANKLE WORK

Key aim: *To improve ankle flexibility*

What you need: *Towel or yoga mat*

For triathletes, it's not a great idea to try and make a sudden large improvement to your ankle flexibility. It's better to work on this over time, bringing a gradual improvement while letting your running and cycling styles adapt.

If you're an open-water swimmer, aim to improve as fast as possible!

1 Sit on the floor with your knees bent and your legs tucked under you. The tops of your feet should be flat against the ground.

2 Gently rock backward, stretching the tops of your ankles. If you find this too uncomfortable, support your weight by putting your hands on the ground.

3 Return to the sitting position, then repeat five to six times.

Ankle flexibility

Triathletes often lack ankle flexibility, especially if they come from a running background. This causes problems for their swimming, because ankle flexibility is a crucial part of your kick technique. If you can't point your toes to at least straight, each foot will act like a mini sea anchor as you swim along.

One way to improve your ankle flexibility is to include some kicking with swim fins in your training. The surface area of the fin tends to force your foot into a more streamlined position as you swim along, which over time will encourage greater flexibility.

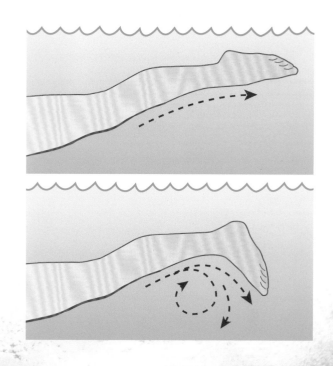

Key skills

- *Kick **water**, not **air**.*
- *Move from the **hips**, not the **knees**.*
- *Kick small, and brush your big toes.*
- *Have floppy ankles.*

06

TIMING AND RHYTHM

rhythm *noun* pace, tempo, cadence, pulse, a regularly recurring pattern of activity, or repeated functions of the body

TIMING AND RHYTHM

It's no accident that lots of people sing to themselves while swimming medium and long distances. The regular beat of a song helps maintain your timing and rhythm, the number of strokes you take per minute. This is also called your stroke rate.

The aim

This is Stephen Roche, the great Irish cyclist (bear with me...), on climbing behind Robert Millar in the 1983 Tour de France:

'When he was pedalling he had rhythm.
I had tempo.'

Roche was saying that Millar – arguably the best climber of his day – had a smooth, flowing pedal stroke, while Roche himself was stamping up the mountain, each turn of the pedals a downward thud of power. When swimming, always try to be a Millar rather than a Roche. The aim is to swim with a smooth, continuous forward movement.

   Earlier chapters covered the key foundations of a good front crawl: an effective catch and pull, a streamlined body position and an efficient kick. Good timing and rhythm flows from these, and is impossible without them. The drills in this chapter reinforce the advice from earlier in the book, and help you polish your entire stroke.

▶ A flowing, rhythmical stroke with constant forward drive is the most energy-efficient way to swim.

FINDING THE RIGHT STROKE RATE

What is the 'right' stroke rate to aim for? There's no single correct answer to this question.

Different swimmers swim at different stroke rates but are equally effective: just watch the final of an Olympic open-water race or triathlon to see the evidence. So, this is a very, *very* rough guide to stroke rates:

- At 2.00min for 100m: a stroke rate of 52–65
- At 1.40 for 100m: 54–68
- At 1.20: 57–83
- At 1.10: 61–96

If your stroke rate is outside these bands, using a Tempo Trainer (a little timing device that tucks into a swimming hat or goggle band) will probably improve your swimming. For example, say you swim 100m in 1.20, at 50 strokes per minute. Increasing your stroke rate will almost certainly make your swimming a) faster and b) less tiring (see the myth of glide on page 24). Set the Tempo Trainer to a stroke rate of 53: once you are used to the new rate, time yourself over 50m.

Keep increasing the stroke rate setting by 3–4 until your 50m times no longer improve. At this point, you have found a good stroke rate.

The process is the same if your stroke rate is too high: use the Tempo Trainer to train yourself to a lower rate.

REVERSE CATCH-UP

Key aim: *To improve catch and rotation, including breathing*

What you need: *Swim fins (optional)*

Reverse catch-up is good for many elements of your stroke. It emphasises good hand entry and catch phases. The drill also challenges your breathing technique and, in the fins-off version, your leg kick. It can be hard work aerobically, especially without fins, so is probably best tackled one or two lengths at a time.

1 If you want to focus on arm technique and timing, put on swim fins. For all-round stroke development, leave the fins on the poolside.

2 Push off and start kicking, concentrating on keeping your head still and your body in a streamlined shape. Catch and pull with your arm, but do not recover: leave your arm trailing at your side.

3 Catch and pull with the other arm. When this arm has reached the same position as the first (i.e. also trailing at your side), recover the first arm. Do a continuous recovery, catch and pull, so that you finish once more with both arms trailing at your side.

4 Repeat all the way down the pool. Stay relaxed and concentrate on keeping a straight, streamlined body position: it's easy to start throwing your arms around and waggling! Imagine your body passing along a thin, imaginary tube without touching the sides.

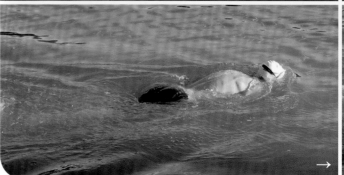

NOTE ON OTHER CATCH-UP DRILLS

There are several versions of catch-up drill. Probably the most common are three-quarter and full catch-up. However, few swimmers really seem to benefit from these versions.

In both, the 'stop' – where you wait for the other hand to catch up – is at the front of the stroke before you start your catch and pull. This is just at the place where many swimmers already have a stop that slows down their stroke, because they're searching for the illusory free speed of glide (see page 24). Drills that exacerbate this stop are often counterproductive.

Swimmers whose stroke rate is too high do sometimes benefit from a bit of three-quarter catch-up, because it forces you to slow down. Even so, the Tempo Trainer exercise on page 83 is likely to slow your stroke down more effectively.

▼ The questionable forward-stop catch-up drill in action.

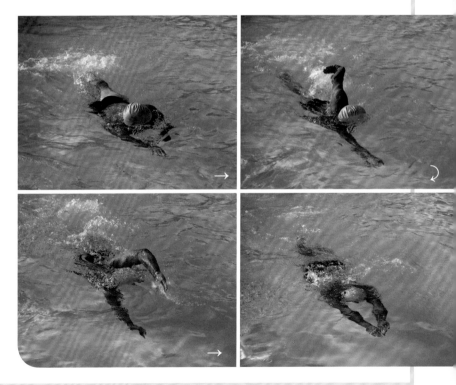

UNCO DRILL

Key aims: *checking effectiveness of pull; eliminating pauses; improving timing; improving breathing*

What you need: *Swim fins*

This one-arm drill was popularised, probably named*, and possibly even invented by the Swim Smooth organisation; whatever the level of their contribution, they deserve a big thank you. It's now used around the world as an all-round stroke development drill for intermediate and advanced swimmers.

Unco is Aussie for 'uncoordinated'.

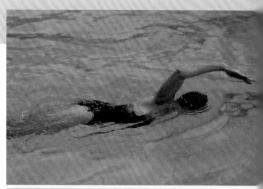

1 Push off into a streamlined position, both arms ahead of you. Catch and pull with one arm, and swim the rest of the length using only that arm.

2 With each stroke, breathe to the opposite, non-pulling side.

3 Pay special attention to the rotation of your body with each stroke. To get a breath you need to rotate not only to the pulling side, but also to the breathing side.

4 Once you feel the rotation is dialled in, pay attention to how your stroke feels. It's bound to surge and stop, surge and stop, because you're only pulling some of the time. But does it surge ahead, or leapfrog forward with an up-and-down movement?

5 Leapfrogging shows you that you are pressing down, rather than back, during the catch phase. Try going back to the catch and doggy-paddle drills in chapter 3 (pages 39–43).

6 Mix unco with some full-stroke front crawl, e.g. 2 x 25m unco, 50m front crawl, and repeat three times.

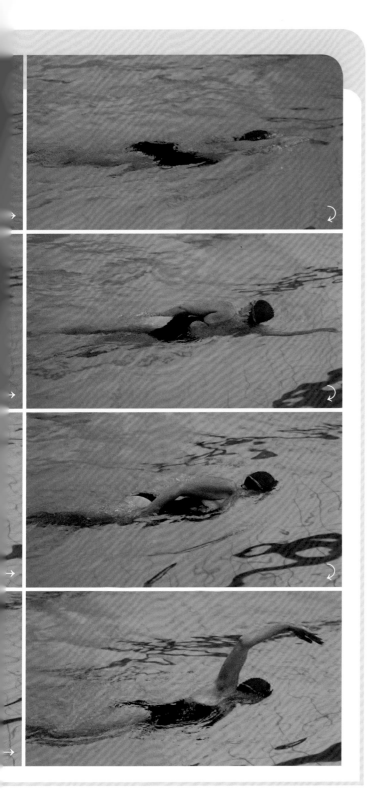

Swimming straight

Open-water swimmers, more than any other swimmers, get big benefits from being able to swim straight without looking where they're going all the time. Anyone who's ever zigzagged across a weedy lake, bounced off the banks of a river, or found themselves 10m further out from a turn buoy than everyone else will know how much energy you can waste by not swimming in a straight line. The exercises and advice on the next few pages will help you develop this skill.

▼ Swimming straight to the buoy (without having to look for it every other stroke) can save you a lot of time and energy.

TARZAN AND JANE

Key aim: *To improve your ability to swim in a straight line*

What you need: *Swimming pool with line along the bottom*

I started doing this drill when I was a kid, after seeing Johnny Weissmuller and Maureen O'Sullivan (Tarzan and Jane) swimming this way in a jungle pool.

1 Push off along the line, and take one stroke of front crawl. Reach ahead with your arm and let your body start to roll to the side as usual.

2 Instead of stopping the roll, let your body turn right over on to your back, with your leading arm still extended. Then take a stroke of backstroke.

3 Continue the rolling motion in the same direction back on to your front, taking another stroke of front crawl.

4 Restart the sequence of the same three strokes – front–back–front – by taking another stroke on your front with the opposite arm.

All the way down the length, aim to keep swimming above the line on the bottom of the pool. It does get easier!

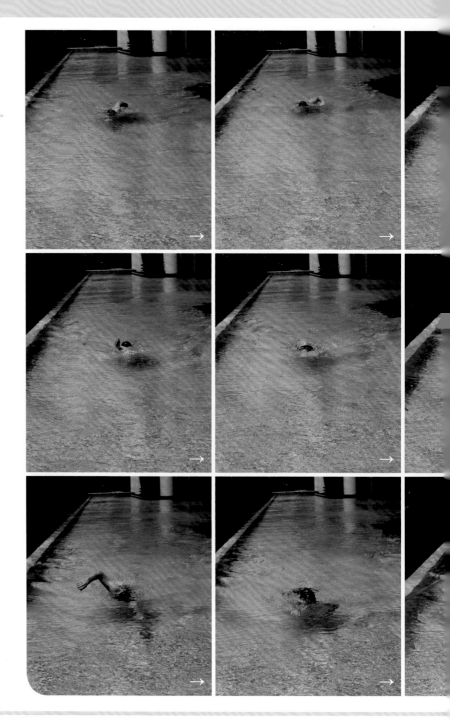

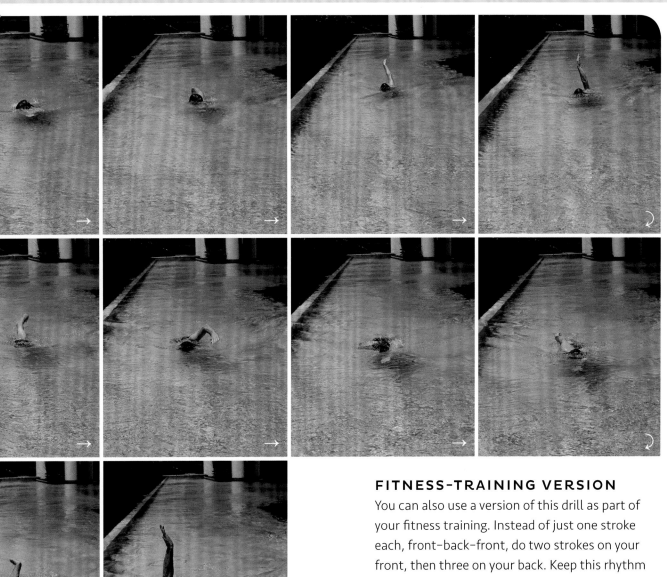

FITNESS-TRAINING VERSION

You can also use a version of this drill as part of your fitness training. Instead of just one stroke each, front–back–front, do two strokes on your front, then three on your back. Keep this rhythm all the way down the length. Do a length of straight freestyle to recover, then repeat. Sets of 100m or 200m at a time, with a 15- or 20-second rest between each, make a good aerobic challenge.

Swim blind

You do need an empty lane to try this, but it's a really good way to judge how straight and balanced your stroke is. Most of us are constantly making teeny little body adjustments to keep swimming in a straight line. These are based on visual inputs that you don't consciously register. Take them away, and a truer idea of how balanced your technique is will emerge.

I also find swimming blind is a useful way of concentrating on how your stroke feels. It's amazing how much easier it is to sense the effectiveness of your arm pull, or the degree of water resistance you're experiencing, with your eyes shut.

Start by swimming along above a line on the bottom of the pool. Initially, just close your eyes for three or four strokes before opening them to check where you are. As your feel for how to swim straight with your eyes shut improves, you'll probably be able to keep them closed for longer periods.

As an illustration of how useful this skill is, World Open-Water Swimmer of the Year 2009 and 2011, Keri-Anne Payne, attributes her success partly

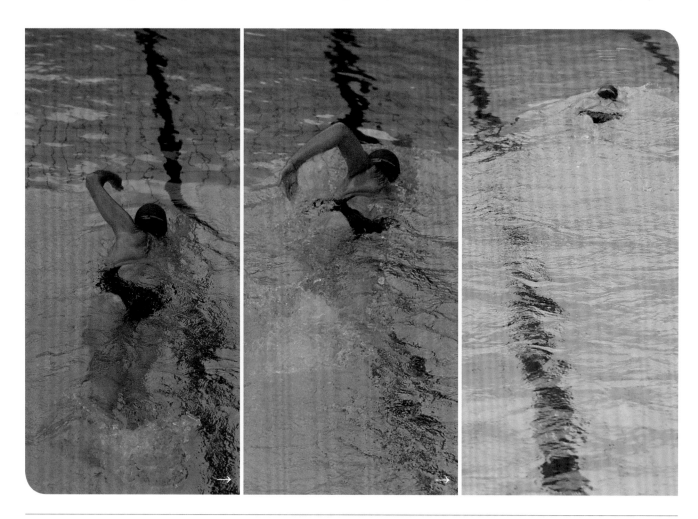

to learning to swim without goggles. She couldn't really see where she was going and had to develop a feel for swimming in a straight line.

If you find that you just can't get this right and keep bouncing into the lane lines, it may mean one of your arm pulls is stronger than the other. Try the correction exercise on page 92.

Watch yourself swim

We rarely look quite as we imagine. Years ago a friend of mine told me that she'd been very annoyed by some photos of herself at a wedding. 'I didn't actually look like that. At all. That woman's shorter and rounder than me. *I* looked like Lana Turner.' She did, too: just a shorter, rounder version of Lana Turner.

So, even looking in a mirror is no guarantee that you'll see things as they really are – but there's something about seeing yourself on video that forces reality on you. When someone films you, there's no escape. As a result, most people's swimming improves when they get a chance to watch themselves swim on screen. They immediately see whether their stroke differs from a really expert swimmer's. Armed with the knowledge from this book, you will probably also see how *your* stroke differs.

TEMPO TRAINER STROKE BALANCE

Key aim: *To encourage a balanced stroke*

What you need: *Finis Tempo Trainer*

This is a simple exercise that doesn't need to be practised for long. If your stroke is not balanced – i.e. if one arm is more effective than the other – try doing this little and often, just a few lengths at a time.

1 Set the Trainer to your normal stroke rate (see pages 82–3 for more information about stroke rate).

2 Swim a length at a steady pace. Notice whether your strokes on both sides hit the beep, or whether one is on time and the other ahead.

3 This missing the beep may mean one arm is pulling less effectively than the other.

4 If you breathe only to one side, swim as many strokes as comfortably as you can without breathing and check again for the imbalance. If it disappears or lessens, it may be down to your breathing technique. You could balance this by learning to breathe on both sides (see chapter 4).

5 If your breathing technique isn't to blame, concentrate on equalising your catch on both sides, as a way of matching the beep with both strokes. You could also spend some time doing the arm drills in chapter 3 in a 3:2 proportion, working more on your weaker arm.

Seeing yourself swim on video can have an electrifying effect. An age group squad I coached had spent months chucking their hands across their body line, instead of starting their pull in front of their shoulders. Finally, we got permission to film them, one by one swimming toward the camera. As soon as they could see what they were doing, they started to correct it. Within weeks, most were starting their pull from the ideal starting place.

Filming swimming

The ideal scenario is for a friend to film you swimming. This is likely to be impossible in a public pool, where concerns about the safety of children are rightly uppermost. So you may have to find another solution. If you can get access to a private pool, that's ideal. Alternatively, the sea (beside a pier will give a great overhead view, as well as side-on and in front), a river or lake will all work as long as the water is clear and calm. Wherever you are filming, warm up first, and do a bit of swimming before the camera rolls so that your stroke is working as it would in normal circumstances.

Key skills

- *Swim with continuous forward drive, and* **no stops or pauses in your stroke.**
- **Relax,** *and swim with* **rhythm.**
- **Practise swimming in a straight line,** *with a balanced stroke.*
- **Watch yourself** *swim.*

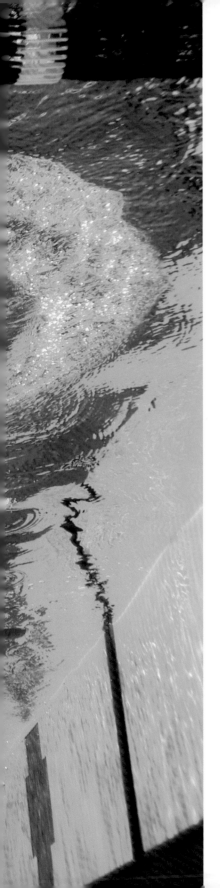

07

TURNS

turn *verb* twist, rotate, go round, roll, twirl, move to face a different direction, move around an axis

TURNS

Turns – in the sense of tumble or touch turns – have limited relevance for triathlon racing, and none in an open-water race. A few triathlons are swum in pools: in these, improving your turn technique can help you to a faster time. But where turns are relevant to your armoury is in the training pool.

Most of us train mainly in pools, rather than open water. Here, a fast turn achieves two things. First, it allows you to fit more distance into a given time. Second, focusing on your turns will help build endurance, especially if you currently touch the end and grab a sneaky extra breath or two before pushing off again.

The three key elements of a tumble turn are a fast tumble or flip, timing and a strong, streamlined push off the wall.

- For a fast tumble turn, you need to initiate the turn in a snappy way, and tuck your body into as compact a shape as possible
- Timing your turn relies on a combination of your distance from the wall and the speed at which you're approaching it
- A strong, streamlined push off the wall allows you to travel further underwater in a streamlined position

Open-water turns

Most triathlons have an open-water swim, rather than using a pool. The course is usually laid out around one or two buoys, which all swimmers have to pass at least once to complete the distance. Novice triathletes often get badly snagged up at these turns: turn to page 124, in the open-water chapter, for advice on how to avoid this happening to you.

◂ Turning around a buoy in a race is a very different skill from turning in the pool; turn to page 124 for advice on how to make buoy turns.

THE PUSH-OFF: STRONG AND STREAMLINED

1 Hold on to the side of the pool with one hand, and bring your legs up so that your feet are against the wall about 60cm below the surface. Have one foot above the other, with your shoulders similarly canted. Your other arm should be stretched out away from the wall.

2 Let go with your hand and let your body slide down under the surface. Keep your body bent into a compact shape, like a coiled spring. You should be facing sideways, with your feet firmly planted against the wall. Your arms should now both be stretched out into a streamlined position.

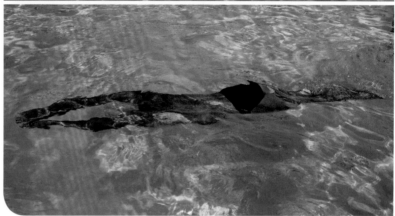

3 Push off as hard as possible. If one or both feet skid off the wall, or one foot pushes more strongly than the other, your foot position is wrong: have another try.

4 Once you've found a good, planted foot position, take a few goes to fix it in your head. This is what you'll be aiming for after learning to tumble.

5 Now add a streamlined glide, with your hands either one on top of the other or thumbs touching and your head tucked in. At the start of the glide you'll be on your side, and by the end of it you need to have drifted round on to your front.

6 Competitive pool swimmers add kicks, usually butterfly kicks, to their underwater phase. For triathlon and open water training this isn't necessary, but you could add a front crawl kick, as in the drill on page 76, as a way of improving your technique.

Bubbles avoid trouble

To avoid getting a snoutful of water while learning tumble turns:

KEEP BLOWING BUBBLES

Close your mouth, and keep letting a trickle of air out of your nose all the way through the tumble turn. This will stop water going up your nose and making you sneeze in an undignified manner.

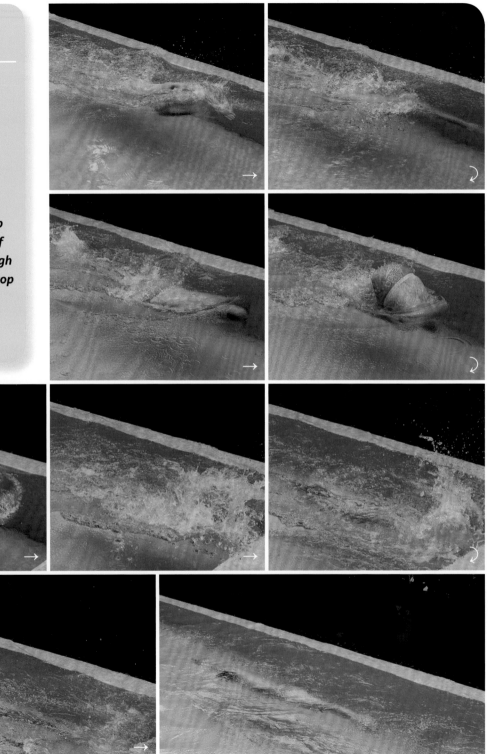

GET USED TO TUMBLING

If you get disoriented every time you try to do tumble turns, and come up facing a different way from the one you expected, this drill is a good starting point. The trick to learning a tumble turn is to break it down into stages. This drill is the first step: getting used to tumbling underwater.

1 Push off the wall, but instead of adopting a streamlined position, push off with both hands by your sides.

2 Before you lose too much momentum, tuck your chin into your chest and start a forward roll motion. Lead with your head, and aim for this to be a snappy and definite movement. Remember to keep your mouth closed and a trickle of air coming out of your nose.

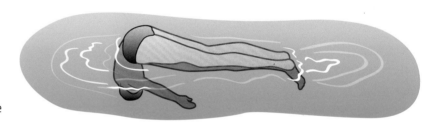

3 Let your body, then your legs, follow your head around. Make your body as compact as possible, so that you tumble over quickly, and bend your legs too. Only take a breath when you've come back to the surface, facing the same way as you started.

ARM STRETCH TUMBLE

This drill first adds an element of stretching your arm out in front of you to tumble over, then of swimming into the tumble.

1 Push off the wall as in the drill on page 97, except with one arm extended in the streamlined position. Have the other arm against your side.

2 Before you lose momentum, perform the tumble. The movement is similar to the one shown on page 97, but this time it's your arm and head that drives, rather than only your head: begin an arm pull, but continue the motion underneath your body, as if reaching back towards the space between your knees.

3 Let your head follow, and then the rest of your body as in a forward roll. As before, keep blowing a constant stream of bubbles from your nose: only stop and take a breath when your head comes to the surface.

4 Practise this drill with both right and left arm stretching forward: later on this will mean you can turn whether it's your right or left arm that makes the last stroke of the length.

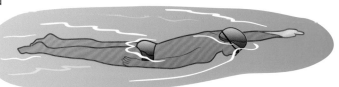

USING YOUR HEAD

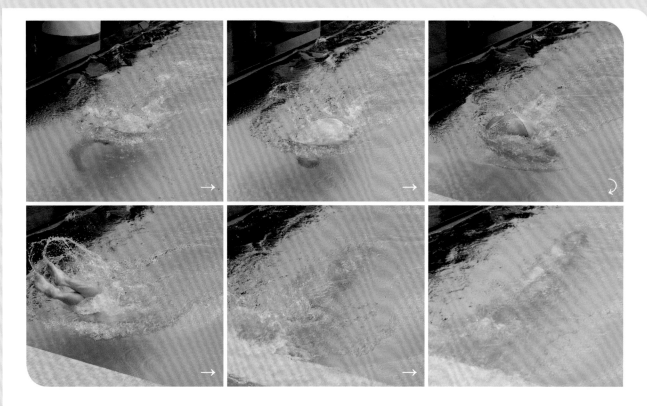

This drill simply puts together two skills you've already got: swimming front crawl and tumbling. It also gives you a chance to develop the final technique, leading the turn with your head, rather than your arm.

1 Push off the wall into the streamlined position, then start swimming. Take a breath as you come to the surface, then take three or four strokes.

2 As you finish an arm stroke, perform the tumble from page 100. This time, though, try to make finishing the pull and starting the tumble a continuous, one-after-the-other sequence. You will be leading the 'snap' of the tumble with your head, not your arm.

3 Practise this on each arm stroke, left and right.

Leading with your head rather than your arm means both arms will be at or nearly at your sides as your body goes over. This makes it faster and easier to get into a streamlined position, ready to push off, as soon as your feet hit the wall.

TIMING

Really the only way to learn the timing of your tumble turn – when to start the tumble in order to plant your feet solidly on the wall – is through trial and error. The variables that will affect how close to the wall you should be include your flexibility, the speed at which you tumble and the pace at which you approach the wall.

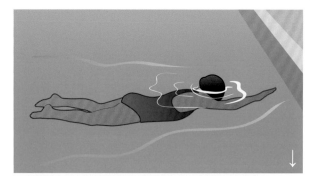

1 Swim towards the wall at the end of your lane. For the last few strokes, look ahead more than you usually would if your normal head position is quite 'down'. When you feel you're one pull from the end of the lane, allow yourself to glide forward with one arm extended.*

2 Once your hand is close to the wall, take a final pull. For most swimmers this is when their hand is 50–100cm from the wall, but it depends on your speed and the power of your pull.

3 Start the tumble just as in the practice on page 101. The aim is to 'land' on the wall in a tight shape, with your feet firmly planted.

4 At first you will hit the wall upside-down, looking up at the air. This is fine, as you can push off on your back and rotate on to your front after the push. Ultimately, though, most expert swimmers hit the wall sideways, with one foot higher than the other, rather than fully upside-down.

Glide is allowed FOR THIS EXERCISE ONLY!

Drive from the wall

The final element of a good tumble turn is your drive away from the wall. In a race, doing this well can gain you a lot of ground. It also sets you up to start swimming from a moving, rather than a standing, start. Follow this four-step sequence:

1 Push off strongly

This depends on having your feet planted firmly on the wall in a position that means they won't slip. If you find this is a problem, go back to the drill on page 97 and practise more.

Push off down, slightly towards the bottom of the pool, rather than parallel with the surface.

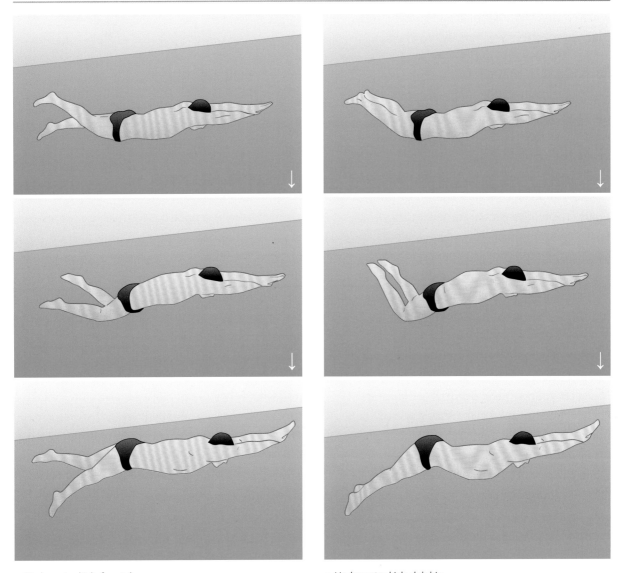

▲ Underwater kick, freestyle

▲ Underwater kick, dolphin

This way the force of your push drives you out and down, and as you kick back towards the surface your buoyancy adds speed and distance.

2 Rotate back to a face-down position

After pushing off, you need to rotate your body so that, instead of being on your side, you're facing the bottom of the pool. As this is achieved, step 3 will already have begun.

3 Kick underwater?

Top pool swimmers kick underwater to maintain speed and to delay the moment when they come back to the surface. Most use butterfly kicks.

As your training for triathlon or open water is aimed at distance ability, this phase is not really crucial, though it may help in a pool triathlon. Even then, always lean towards surfacing without holding your breath for too long, rather than staying underwater so long that you compromise your aerobic ability.

4 Surface strongly

Getting maximum drive from the wall requires striking a balance between distance and speed. Never let yourself slow down underwater to such an extent that you're moving more slowly underwater than you would be swimming. It's important to get back to the surface while you're still travelling at a good speed. Otherwise, your first few strokes will be spent wasting energy getting you back up to swimming speed.

Touch turns

Once in a while, a pool-based triathlon comes along that has decided tumble turns are not allowed. If you think you may one day swim in one of these, or if you're struggling to master tumble turns, it's worth practising some fast touch turns. They're noticeably slower than tumbles, but not by a massive amount if done well.

(If you can do tumbles but are about to do a tri where they're not allowed, give up tumble turns entirely for a couple of weeks beforehand. Otherwise, you're almost certain to forget yourself in the excitement of the event, throw in an accidental tumble turn and get disqualified.)

Practise this technique using both left and right hand to touch the wall; that way, you won't compromise your swimming by trying always to finish on the same hand.

1 One-handed touch

You only need to touch the wall with one hand. The best way to finish is very like a tumble turn, but instead of taking a stroke, you leave your arm extended to touch the wall. You need your hand either gripping a rail or the edge, if either is available at surface level, or flat on the wall of the pool.

2 Tuck in and push back

Bring your legs tightly in under your body, and at the same time push away from the wall with your hand, dropping your opposite shoulder back, away from the wall. Your non-pushing hand stays under the surface.

3 Plant your feet

Bring your feet through under your body in a tight, tucked shape. You should be sideways, with one hand pushing away from the wall and the other below your body. As your feet plant on the wall,

bring the pushing hand over the surface and into the water. At the same time, bring your other hand up to meet it.

4 Push off

You should now be in a tight, tucked shape with your feet solidly planted on the wall and your hands somewhere in front of your face. Push hard away from the wall, as on page 97.

Key skills

- *Make your turns **snappy and aggressive**.*
- ***Don't use turns as a rest** – lazy training technique leads to poor race technique.*
- *Turn in a **tucked-in shape** for maximum speed.*
- *Plant your feet so that you get a **strong drive** from the wall.*

 08
OPEN-WATER EVENTS

open water *noun* stretch of water not enclosed by land, ice or other barriers; natural or artificial body of water such as oceans, lakes, reservoirs, basins and rivers; area of water large enough for a boat or person to move around in

OPEN-WATER EVENTS

Open-water swimming has rarely, if ever, been so popular. Triathlon attracts more people every year, and most tri swims are in open water. Increasing numbers of leisure and competition swimmers are also opting for a non-chlorinated environment. Open-water events that used to attract tens of swimmers now close their entries with hundreds, sometimes thousands, of people signed up.

Choosing an event

There can't ever have been a better choice of events. You can swim in the ocean, rivers, reservoirs, lakes – in fact, the 70 per cent of the world that's covered in water is your playground.

You can choose a swim with an historical context, like the annual Bosphorus swim in Turkey, or a long lineage, like the Damme-Brugge swim in Belgium. You can pick from a variety of distances. In triathlon these range from 400m up to 3.8km and beyond. In open-water swimming, from 1–5km is generally seen as relatively short, 5–25km is medium to long distance, and 25km+ is a marathon swim.

If you're new to organised open-water swims, whether in a tri or not, pick a first event that's:

- Over a distance you're comfortable with
- Far enough in the future to allow proper preparation (see chapter 9 for advice)
- Likely to be in conditions (temperature, turbulence, currents, etc) for which you can practise

If you're at all nervous, a smaller local event is probably the best way to ease yourself in.

Preparation – the course

If it's possible, scouting the course by swimming it before the event will give you insight and confidence. If you're doing a sea or estuary/tidal river swim, work out the tide times of the event and do your recce at the same stage of the tide. I like to do this several times, starting a couple of months ahead; that way, if the distance or conditions come as a complete shock I have the chance to adapt my training.

If you can't actually swim the course, try to see it, even if it's only from the shore. Give yourself time to process the information, rather than rocking up on the morning of the swim and potentially worrying yourself.

On race day, try to get in and check the start and finish areas (are they slippery? Shallow, deep, rocky?). It's not always possible – but if you can, knowing what to expect will help your time and confidence.

Preparation – equipment

When the day of the swim comes, knowing you can rely on your equipment is key. It's a really bad idea to be trying out new kit in competition. Make sure your

costume, wetsuit, hat, goggles, earplugs, etc. are all much-loved companions, rather than blind dates. Spares are also a good idea: costumes, goggles and hats, in particular, have a habit of failing or disappearing just as you're being mustered.

For triathletes there are specialist bags with compartments for all your gear. These are really useful: having the structure with spaces for everything makes it harder to forget anything.

Preparation – fueling

This is very personal: with nutrition there's an element of needing to work out what suits you best. But if you're swimming for more than an hour, taking on some nutrition will be crucial. This could be in the form of drinks, gels or solid food. For swims of less than an hour, eating a little food between one and two hours ahead of the start seems to work for most people. Pre-race hydration is also important.

Registration and mustering

At all triathlons and open-water swims you'll have to register so that the organisers know you're there. You get a swim hat and race number. At open-water events you often get a bag to put your gear in, especially if it's being transported to the finish for you. You also get instructions for what happens next: where and how the swimmers will muster, and then start the swim.

Warming up

Warming up can be a bit tricky, as it's often hard to get in the water before the swim. Even if you can manage to get in, you rarely know exactly how long you have until the start, and dare not go far enough for a proper warm-up. It's often best to get yourself ready on land, for example using skipping, arm swings and other simple exercises.

Starts

Open water and triathlon events generally start in one of three ways: on the shore, in the water, or from a dock or pontoon. (There's a famous tri in

Pace yourself

Most swimmers use a different strategy in a triathlon from an open-water swimming race. One piece of advice holds good for both, though:

IT'S RARELY A GOOD IDEA TO GO FLAT-OUT AT THE START.

In general, pacing yourself to an even speed throughout the swim is the best strategy. In a triathlon, this should deliver you to T1 as fresh and as fast as possible. In an open-water race, it leaves you free to increase your speed towards the end, while others are tiring – especially if you've also conserved strength by drafting (see page 121).

Norway that starts by jumping off a ferry, but that is unusual.) From a dock you'll have to dive; in triathlons with more than one circuit of the swimming course, racers sometimes have to exit the water, cross the dock and dive in again.

Swims often begin with a massed start. If they have a choice, the racers will try to position themselves wherever they have the shortest route to the first turn buoy. When the starter's hooter goes, this area will be a churning maelstrom of arms and legs, as people sprint to get clear water and a good position.

The position you take at the start usually depends on your entry time and aims. If you've entered a fast time and want to compete at the front, you'll be mixing it with a bunch of ambitious, sharp-elbowed swimmers. If you just want to enjoy the swim and finish feeling you've done well, entering a slower time and taking a more relaxed approach at the start might work better.

◄ Massed start to an elite triathlon. In a race like this, the starting positions on the pontoon are usually decided according to athlete rankings coming into the event.

Race strategy

Every swimmer has different physical and psychological strengths, which affect whether they prefer to forge ahead at the start and swim steadily, hang back a bit until the second half, rely on a fast finish or use some other tactic. Over time, you build up an understanding of what suits you. Split times are helpful in working out your best strategy: to swim a given time, how fast was each 500m, or even each 100m? Did your speed drop off or remain steady? Understanding this will help you adapt your strategy and training. In the past, getting this information required a mate with a stopwatch (and possibly a boat). Today, various wearables will do the job.

Exhaling

Breathing out effectively while your face is in the water expels the maximum amount of CO_2. This clears your lungs for more oxygen uptake, and helps flush lactic acid from your system. So:

REMEMBER TO BREATHE OUT.

The breathing exercises on pages 62–7 will help increase your breathing ability, but this is something to focus on while swimming in every training session, too.

Triathlon strategy

Triathlons are *never* won on the swim leg. In a triathlon, you need to fit your swim into your overall performance. You need to balance two key elements: finishing position versus energy expended. Pushing yourself to keep up with a fast group may leave you too tired for the bike and run legs. It's better to finish the swim feeling somewhat within yourself than about to throw up from the effort. Save that for the run. This sounds utterly obvious, but it's very easy to get overexcited at the start of the swim and go too fast. The pacing advice and practices on pages 121 and 130 will help you bed in the ideal speed.

T1

T1 is the first transition phase in a triathlon, where you change from swim to bike. If you're competing, significant time can be lost or gained here. From a swimming point of view, the crucial elements of the transition are a) exiting the water and b) getting your wetsuit off.

The best practice for exiting the water is to try it on the race's exit ramp. This isn't always possible, so you may have to adapt to the conditions as you find them. There are three basic choices: dolphining (see page 133); stand up and run through the water; or swim as near as possible to shore. Which is best usually depends on how deep the water is and how steep and slippery the exit ramp is.

GETTING IN AND OUT OF YOUR WETSUIT

Key aim: *To improve T1 speed*

The only way to develop a smooth, fast wetsuit-shedding technique is to practise. Take your chances to do this in similar situations to a race, such as climbing up a beach or lakeside at the end of open-water training sessions.

1 As soon as you emerge from the water, start running towards your bike. Reach behind and grab the puller ribbon on your wetsuit.

2 With the other hand, undo the Velcro tab that holds most wetsuits closed. Next, pull down the zipper.

3 Peel off first one arm, then the other. Then peel the suit down to your waist. The wetsuit will be half inside-out at this point.

4 When you reach your bike, bend over and peel down/ step out of the wetsuit legs.

Open-water strategy

Your key requirement for most of the swim is to stop lactic acid building up and hampering your performance. Of course, open-water racing is different from triathlon: you don't have to do a bike and a run afterwards. This raises the possibility of a sprint for the line. If you feel strong enough, you can raise your pace as much as 500m (or more) from the finish. Be careful when trying to sprint at the end of a long swim, though: it's easy to lose your technique, which will be counterproductive.

Refereeing

In open-water swimming, including in triathlon, physical contact is part of the sport. If you're swimming in a pack, you will – as a minimum – get bumped, have your feet tapped and have swimmers veer across your path. Usually it's unintentional, a product of swimming in a pack. There should be referees watching to make sure there's no foul play or cheating; in bigger races they will be helped by transponders worn by each swimmer.

The referees have an unenviable job, akin to refereeing a water-polo match with the players spread out over a lengthy course. Inevitably, a lot of contact goes unnoticed – at least by the referees. If you regularly initiate contact with other swimmers, though, don't expect to get away with it entirely: some sort of retribution will probably come your way. If referees do see misdemeanours, they have three tiers of sanction available:

Referee's action	Reasons
WARNING WHISTLE	Indicate unsafe conditions ahead Swimming too close to another swimmer Swimming too close to official boats Bumping another swimmer Locking arms with another swimmer Touching or tapping another swimmer's feet
YELLOW CARD (a caution)	Intentional or unintentional contact that impedes another swimmer Intentional interference (cutting off or veering into another swimmer) Swimming crookedly into another swimmer Swimming over the legs or lower back of another swimmer Intentionally drafting an official boat
RED CARD (disqualification)	Unsporting conduct (e.g. punching, elbowing, kicking) Walking on or jumping off the bottom (this is allowed only at the finish and some starts) Pulling another swimmer's legs Pushing another swimmer underwater Intentional interference when swimmers are approaching the finish Accumulation of two yellow cards

Key skills

- *Pick an event that suits your level of experience and confidence.*
- *Prepare so that there are no surprises on the day.*
- *Don't get overexcited and sprint off from the start.*
- *Swim hard but fair.*

09

SKILLS AND FITNESS

skill *noun* ability to do something well
fitness *noun* condition of being physically
fit and healthy; ability to perform
a specific function or act

117

SKILLS AND FITNESS

The obvious difference between open-water and pool swimming is the lack of turns. In an open-water event you may swim a kilometre or more without interrupting your rhythm. It's pretty relentless, and if you don't practise for it, it comes as quite a shock. But few of us can do all our training in open water (and anyway, its choppy, inconsistent conditions aren't conducive to developing your technique). This is where POW training comes in.

POW training

POW is a happy acronym for Pool Open Water. It developed as a way of mimicking many of the physical challenges of open water, but in a

controlled environment. It allows you to develop the fitness and skills of a specialist open-water swimmer, but in a pool.

Ideally, the swimmers need access to a whole pool, though a couple of lanes is enough. You set up buoys in the corners or either end, then swim without touching the walls, turning around the buoys. POW training groups work best when the swimmers have similar speed and endurance. They allow you to work on:

- Swimming the race distance without stopping
- Turning round a buoy, to the right and the left, solo and in a group
- Swimming in a pack, in a variety of positions
- Drafting
- Dealing with physical contact
- Changing pace during a swim

▶ If you have access to a whole pool, positioning turn buoys at the corners gives you a big area of water to work with. You can swim along the edges, between the corners in an X shape, in a Z pattern – wherever your imagination (or your coach) leads you. Even if some of the pool is taken up with other swimmers and you can only get a couple of lanes, a pair of turn buoys give you many of the same options.

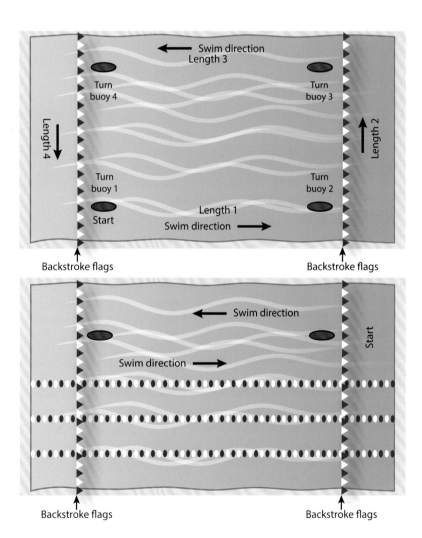

SAMPLE POW IDEAS

Key aim: *To improve open-water swim skills and endurance*

What you need:
- *A pool or section of pool set up for a POW session.*
- *A group of swimmers (between 6 and 12 is a good number, but more or fewer will also work)*

There are lots of ideas here: you wouldn't necessarily put all of them into one session. The numbers are based on having four buoys in a whole 25-metre pool.

Warm-up	2 x clockwise circuits; 2 x anticlockwise circuits; repeat. Every third 'length' to be swum as Tarzan and Jane (see page 88–9).
	2 x clockwise circuits kicking; 2 x anticlockwise circuits kicking. Swim every third length doing the simple rotation drill from page 54.
	2 x clockwise circuits and 2 x anticlockwise circuits full stroke. On the first circuit, the first length is fast, the rest steady; on the second circuit the second length is fast, and so on.
Main set	Swim in a paceline (see page 130) for 8 x 1 circuits, changing the lead swimmer every length.
	Swim 8 x 1 circuits in groups of three, with the first circuit swum three abreast and the second circuit raced. Change positions in the abreast line after each circuit.
	Swim 8 x 1 circuit aiming for the same time on each circuit.
Speed work	8 x 1 circuits with at least a minute's rest between each circuit. On even numbered swims the first and third lengths are sprints after the turn; on odd numbered swims, the second and fourth lengths are sprints.
Cool-down	Minimum five minutes' steady swimming, to include some backstroke.

Skills: pacing your swim

Pacing a swim is something very few people can do intuitively. Most swimmers start too fast and finish less strongly than they might. Going too fast at the start of a triathlon, even if it's only a 400m swim, can be spectacularly disastrous.

Many swimmers find that a combination of a Tempo Trainer and critical swim speed (CSS) training helps them build a sense of how fast they can go over distance. CSS involves putting your 400m and 200m times into an online calculator, and training to the times the calculator suggests.

Skills: drafting

Drafting works the same in the water as it does on land: you tuck in close behind or beside someone and get, effectively, a tow. The faster the other person is moving, the more effective the tow. (In some races drafting is not allowed: always check.)

For swimming, the best drafting position is usually behind and close to the side of another swimmer, with your head more or less level with their thigh. You can save a lot of energy here (or swim faster than your true pace). Side drafting doesn't require you to look forward and compromise your streamlined body position, because you can keep track of the other swimmer when you breathe.

DRAFTING PRACTICE

Key aim: *To improve understanding of drafting*

What you need:

- *An empty lane or open water*
- *At least three swimmers*

A race or organised swim probably isn't the best time to learn about drafting. Fortunately it's easy to prepare beforehand. One way is through paceline training (see page 130), but that mainly gives you a feel for rear drafting. This exercise is good for side drafting practice.

1 Set off three abreast, but with a plan for one swimmer to be ahead for the first minute. The other two swimmers side draft the leader. (This is easiest if you're able to match stroke rates, but don't compromise your own stroke efficiency trying to do it.)

2 After a minute (set a Tempo Trainer or watch to tell you when the time has come), a pre-planned second swimmer moves forward. The other two adjust their positions accordingly.

3 After another minute, the process repeats with the third swimmer in the lead and the others drafting.

4 At the end of that minute, stop at the end of the next length (if you're in a pool), change positions and repeat.

Of course, in a race, few people like it when someone drafts off them, and typically they try to shake you off. Mimic this by having the lead swimmer change speeds and, if there's room, direction.

Skills: sighting

For most swimmers a streamlined head position looks more down than ahead. In open water this causes an obvious problem: however good you are at swimming in a straight line, you do need to check where you're going from time to time. To get around this, you need to learn to 'sight' – lift your head to see whether you're on course for the turn or finish you're aiming at – without interrupting your stroke.

SIGHTING

Key aim: *To maintain swimming speed when sighting*

The key to this technique – which requires diligent, regular practice – is not to confuse sighting with breathing. They're two separate skills, and trying to mix them together slows most swimmers down.

1 Finish breathing out until your leading hand enters the water.

2 Lift your chin so that you look forward, while pressing down (rather than pulling back – this is the only time pressing down is allowed!) with your leading hand. At the same time, kick a little harder.

3 As your head rises, take a mental photo of the course, and immediately drop your head back down into the streamlined position. Don't take a breath – if your head comes out that high, you've lifted it too far.

4 Take an arm stroke or two, during which you can process the 'photo' and then take a breath.

Skills: turns

Turns offer competitive swimmers an opportunity to gain time on other racers. Turning as close as possible to a buoy, without losing speed, can gain you several metres. Of course, that means the area close to the turn buoy becomes a pinch point, which can be a bruising experience. If you're not competing, and prefer to avoid flying elbows, scratches, tugs on your legs, etc, you may decide it's a good idea to give the buoy a slightly wider berth.

ROUNDING A BUOY

Key aim: *To improve speed and confidence while rounding a buoy*

You will need: *Ideally, an anchored buoy*

This is a good exercise for competitors. Practising this will get you corkscrewing round a turn buoy very quickly.

1 Swim at the buoy, sighting a couple of times as you get close to it.

2 Aim to swim very slightly past the buoy, taking a stroke with the arm closest to the buoy (your left) as you come past.

3 Instead of taking another front crawl stroke, continue the roll of your body so that you turn on to your back. As you do this, twist slightly towards the buoy.

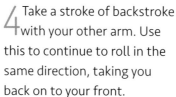

4 Take a stroke of backstroke with your other arm. Use this to continue to roll in the same direction, taking you back on to your front.

With practice, this will get you round a 90° turn very quickly, without the need to lift your head, do a little bit of breaststroke, etc.

Skills: rough-water confidence

For some swimmers, even strong ones, open water is at first quite nerve-wracking. Rougher water, in particular, is so different from the pools in which most of us learn to swim and train that it can induce near-panic. In a race or event, this kind of tension will affect your breathing, and therefore your performance. Fortunately, training can help most people overcome rough-water nerves.

ROUGH WATER PRACTICE

Key aim: *To improve confidence in rough water*

If you're nervous of open water, it's easy to put off training in it. 'Next week... No, on Wednesday... No, next weekend... Actually, after that big bike ride...' – the list goes on, and suddenly it's two weeks until the event and you're feeling more nervous than ever.

Facing and conquering a fear is an intensely personal thing, but these tips should help:

1 Arrange visits to open water with a patient, confident companion. You'll feel safer, and it's harder to back out.

2 Take baby steps, and take them often. Don't try to get in and do race distance first go, however fit you are. On your first session, focus on getting in and out. Second time, swim a bit. Third, swim a bit more. Adjust to suit the conditions: if it's like a millpond on your first go, and you feel like it, swim a bit. If it's windy and choppy second time, just bob about for a while in the rough water, then come in.

3 If you plan to do an open-water session, stick with the plan. It's fine to adapt to the conditions, as above. But do get in.

4 When the day of the swim actually comes, have a little swim before the start. Concentrate on your breathing and technique, and realise that your training has equipped you for this challenge.

Mind your t & q

However much you're focusing on training hard and building strength and endurance, always remember:

LEAVE TIME FOR TECHNIQUE

Include some technique drills in every session: the beginning, when you're not tired, is generally the best time for these.

Always try to maintain your technique, especially when you're tired, so that you will do the same in a race. Try to end every training session with a few lengths of perfect technique, reinforcing muscle memory and setting you up for your next swim.

Fitness: training cycles

All athletes benefit from training in cycles, rather than doing the same thing week-in, week-out, month after month. Olympic athletes tend to think first in four-year cycles. They break these down into years, then periods of the year, weeks within each period and days within the weeks. At each stage, they mark where their performance needs to be, and constantly adjust training accordingly.

For most of us this Olympian approach isn't necessary, or even possible, but planning your training in some detail is still productive. Planning a three- or four-month training period before an event works well for many people; within this, mix up your swimming but aim to include:

▼ Whatever point you're at in your training cycle, and however far you are swimming, always try to maintain good technique. If you drop it in training, you'll almost certainly drop it in a race too.

1 Base endurance work, at relatively low heart rate but high volume. This means swimming mainly within yourself, but with short rest intervals

2 Speed endurance work, which includes periods of working at higher heart rates followed by base-endurance-type recovery swimming

3 A short taper, where the balance shifts towards higher speeds and longer rests, but still with some recovery swimming

Keeping a training diary will, over time, let you see how to strike the best balance between these three types of training. A starting point for a 17-week training block: nine weeks on base endurance, five on speed endurance and three easing into a taper.

Fitness: land training

All elite-level triathletes and swimmers include land training in their swimming-specific programmes. In particular, using a swim bench or stretch cords is a good way to build strength for a high-elbow catch. A company called Halo makes a training device that, combined with a swim bench, teaches you to pull with a high elbow.

More generally, land training is a benefit: building good abdominal strength will help you maintain technique and a streamlined body position in a fluid environment. A combination of push-ups, squats, abdominal crunches, planks and Swiss ball hamstring curls is a good basic strength-training programme for swimmers.

PUSH-UPS

Key muscles: *biceps and triceps, pectorals, abdomen, abductors, quadriceps and hamstrings*

1 Balance on your toes and hands, with hands a little over shoulder-width apart, and a straight back and legs. Breathe in and bend your elbows to 90° to lower your torso towards the floor. (Engaging your abdominals helps keep your legs straight.)

2 Breathe out and push back up to the starting position.

Quantity: Build up to 3 x 15 push-ups, with 45 seconds rest between each set (start with 3 x 5).

SQUATS

Key muscles: *hamstrings, quadriceps, gluteals, calf muscles, trunk and lower back*

1 Stand with feet shoulder-width apart. Relax, especially the neck and shoulders, and lengthen your torso without losing your spine's natural S-shape.

2 Contract your abdominals and breathe in. Relax your knees until they are over your toes and your thighs are parallel with the ground. Keep your back straight, hold your arms out in front of you for balance, and keep your heels on the ground and the weight over the back of your foot. Keeping your tongue on the roof of your mouth will activate the neck's stabiliser muscles.

3 Breathe out and press through the heels to return to the start position.

Quantity: Build up to 3 x 30 squats, with 45 seconds rest between each set (start with 2 x 15).

ABDOMINAL CRUNCHES

Key muscles: *abdominals*

1 Lie on your back with knees bent, feet flat on the floor and hands by your ears.

2 Keeping your lower back on the floor, curl your shoulders forwards. Tense your abdominals, breathing out as you lift up and in as you lower. Keep your head in line with your spine: don't let your chin drop towards your chest.

3 Each rep should take about four to five seconds.

Quantity: Build up to 4 x 25 crunches, with 45 seconds rest between each set (start with 2 x 20).

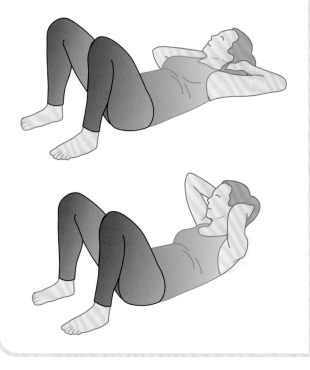

THE PLANK

Key muscles: *abdominals, core muscles, biceps and triceps, calf muscles, quadriceps, hamstrings*

1 From lying face down, push up on to your elbows and feet. Keep a straight line through the head and hips and down to your feet. If you feel any tension in your back, lift your hips a bit.

2 If this movement is difficult, perform the hold with your knees, rather than your feet, on the floor.

3 Hold for 45–60 seconds. Gradually build up the length of time you can hold the position.

SWISS BALL HAMSTRING CURL

Key muscles: *hamstrings, quadriceps and core muscles*

1 Lie on your back on a mat and press your heels into the middle of the ball. Extend your legs with your feet together and pointed toes.

2 With your shoulders on the floor, arms out and palms facing up, breathe out and lift your hips off the ground by engaging your abdominals.

3 Pull the ball towards your bottom until your feet are flat on its surface. Inhale and push the ball back to the start position.

Quantity: Build up to 3 x 15 curls, 30 seconds rest between each set (start with 2 x 10).

PACELINE TRAINING

Key aim: *To develop endurance and ability to swim in a pack*

Training in a paceline is great practice for open-water swimming, which is often done in a pack of swimmers all travelling at a similar speed. You need at least three swimmers, and ideally no more than six. The paceline allows everyone to build endurance, even in a mixed-ability group.

1 Set off in a line, with each swimmer right behind the one in front, almost touching their feet.

2 After a set distance or time, the leader pulls off the front. In a pool, it's best just to stop after, say, 50m and let everyone else go by; in open water, the leader can just drift back after a minute on the front, then tag on to the back of the line. (If you've got a kayaker or someone who can blow a whistle at one-minute intervals, it makes this a lot easier.)

3 The new leader swims the same distance or time, before rotating back and allowing the swimmer behind to come through.

All the swimmers need to have similar abilities, but you can make adjustments to fit quite a wide range. If stronger swimmers take longer pulls on the front, and weaker swimmers either take shorter turns or miss them, a fairly mixed group can train together.

Fitness: training for a fast start

In triathlon and open-water races, the start is usually fast and furious. It's generally a bad idea to get too caught up in this: there's a price to pay later for burning off big chunks of muscle energy so early in the swim. Even so, being able to fight your way forward from a bad starting position can sometimes be useful, so it's a good idea to train your body to continue at race pace after a sprint.

FAST STARTING

Key aim: *To practise distance pace after a fast start*

Towards the start of the session is probably the best time for this kind of practice, as it's when your body will best engage the same energy systems as at the start of a race.

1 SET: 5 X 4 LENGTHS – swim the first length at a flat-out sprint. Stop for 10 seconds, then push off into three lengths at your normal race pace. Take a one-minute rest between each swim.

2 SET: 3 X 6 LENGTHS – swim the first length at a flat-out sprint, take a 5-second rest, then push off into five lengths at race pace. Take a minute's rest between each swim.

3 SET: 1 X 12 LENGTHS – swim the entire distance at race pace.

Fitness: training for a fast finish

The key to a good finish is pacing the rest of the swim well (see page 121). Few swimmers do this, especially in triathlons, so being able to pick up your speed in the last few hundred metres will allow you to pick up a lot of places and improve your position.

You can improve your finishing speed by adding changes of pace to a training swim. This helps condition your body to be able to sprint when tired. One way to do this is fartlek training. Swim non-stop for, say, 15 minutes, aiming to maintain your race pace as the minimum speed throughout.

At pre-planned times or distances, add sprints. You could sprint every sixth length or, if you're swimming in a group, race for every fifth minute. Then drop back down to race pace again.

Open-water race finishes

Most open-water events record your place and finish time after you have left the water. In major races, though, you register a finish by slapping a touch pad hanging above the finish line. Just crossing the line does not register: you must touch the pad. The finishes are often close, and sometimes the ability to reach out ahead of your body and tap the pad is the winning margin.

DOLPHINING

Key aim: *To improve start/finish speed in shallow water*

In shallow water starts and finishes, you can gain position by using a technique called dolphining. Every kid who's ever run into the sea has probably done a version of this:

1 For a start, run in and dive forward when the water depth stops you running.

2 As soon as your momentum through the water drops, push down with your hands and bring your legs and feet up and under you.

3 Plant your feet on the bottom and dive forward again.

4 Repeat until the water is too deep (or shallow at the finish).

▼ You can practise dolphining in a pool, in water anything less than rib-deep.

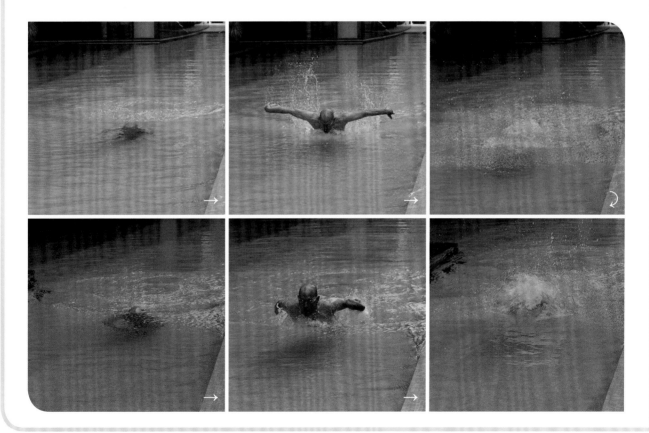

Skills: race navigation

Race navigation can make the difference between a good swim and a disappointing one. Stopping to see where you are breaks your rhythm and slows you down. Even in a river swim, navigation is important. The best swimmers don't just follow the banks – they look for the faster water on the outside of each bend. Without knowing exactly where you are, this is impossible, or at best a matter of luck. The skills you need are the ability to swim straight, plus smooth, efficient, infrequent sighting.

Swimming straight

There are various ways to test whether or not you're swimming straight. One of the easiest is to pull a swimming hat over your goggles and swim blind down the lane. (Obviously make sure no one is coming the other way.) Do this five times, without consciously trying to correct for which side you hit the lane rope last time, and it will show you whether you tend to steer to the left or right. If you do, the reason will be found in your technique, usually either in your breathing technique or the efficiency of one arm's stroke versus the other.

NAVIGATION PRACTICE

Key aim: *To improve open-water navigation skills*

You will need:

- *A small cone*
- *A coach or helper on poolside*

Swimming straight for 25m, then efficiently sighting, will make any open water swim easier. Over time, this exercise will help you develop the necessary skills to do this.

1 Position your coach or helper, armed with the cone, as far away as possible. (This exercise is ideally done in an empty pool, but can also be done 25m or so out from the bank of a river, lake, etc.)

2 Push off the wall and start swimming. While you are underwater, your assistant will be putting the cone down somewhere along the far edge of the pool.

3 Once you've taken a few strokes, sight as on page 123, looking for the cone.

4 Swim to the cone without sighting again, aiming to finish your length as close to it as possible.

ODD-NUMBER TRAINING

When training in a pool, it's easiest to set yourself training swims that fit into an easy number pattern. For example, 10 x 100m, going every 1.45, is easy to follow on the pace clock. Basing part of your session around odd numbers is a good way to force yourself to concentrate.

So, for example:

~~10 x 100m on 1.45 turnaround~~

becomes

3 x 100m on 1.41 turnaround
3 x 100m on 1.43 turnaround
3 x 100m on 1.47 turnaround

Sprint the second length of the first 100m, the third length of the second 100m, the fourth length of the third 100m, and so on through the sequence.

~~800m at 90% race pace~~

becomes

800m at 90% race pace. Do a push-out (both hands on the side of the pool, pull yourself up until your torso is out of the water and your arms are straight) after every prime-number length (so, after lengths 1, 3, 9, 11, 13, 17, etc).

Add one push-out each time you do them until you get to 9, then decrease by one each time until you get to 1, then start to increase again, etc.

Skills: race concentration

Open water swims can take a long time. Even 1500m takes many people 25–30 minutes or more; a 3.8k can be well over an hour, and true marathon swims are hours long. Unlike biking or running, there may be few sights on the way to help you maintain concentration. Swimming the Alalakeiki Channel from Kaho'olawe to Maui, for example, is basically a matter of keeping going, wondering about pronunciation, and waiting for Maui to get bigger/nearer: there aren't really any waymarkers. In circumstances like these, it pays to keep your concentration.

Replicating the required concentration in training will make concentrating easier in the swim. Otherwise there's a possibility you will drift off: either literally off course, or off your intended pace. Always being conscious of your rhythm and stroke, particularly the high-elbow catch, will help. Forcing yourself to maintain concentration in training will also improve your ability to focus.

Key skills

- *Use POW training to practise separate race skills multiple times in a controlled environment.*
- *Don't wait until race time to try drafting or sighting – practise them constantly in training.*
- *Learn to swim straight without sighting – few people master this, but it gives you a massive advantage.*

10
FLEXIBILITY

flexible *adj.* lissom, supple, elastic, able to bend or be bent repeatedly without damage or injury

FLEXIBILITY

If you lack flexibility, there are some elements of an effective front-crawl swimming technique you'll never be able to manage. People with stiff neck, shoulders and back find it particularly hard to master technique, but overall flexibility is important in swimming. The stretches in this section are a starting point: use them as a springboard to find the particular stretches and exercises that work for you.

Using your breathing

When you've taken a static stretch as far as is comfortable, concentrate on breathing deeply, from your stomach rather than your chest. This should help you to relax and get a little more from the stretch.

Stretching techniques

Never do any stretch to a point where it's painful. You need to be able to feel a bit of pull in the muscles you're stretching, but if it starts to hurt, gently ease out of the stretch and try again. It's best to time your movement into the stretch to happen as you breathe out. If you need to take a breath, stop moving while you breathe in.

Increasing flexibility

For most people, improving their general flexibility has a benefit for their swimming. Triathletes also find that better general flexibility helps them adapt more easily to the demands of three different disciplines.

The exercises on the following pages are mainly targeted at swimming (apart from the Sun Salute on pages 142–3). They don't have to bite into your precious training time too much, because you can do them just about anywhere: sitting in front of the TV, on the poolside, out in the garden. Try to do some flexibility work every day – 15 minutes spent on this pays dividends in the pool (and on the road when you're cycling or running, too).

Warming up and warming down

Ten minutes stretching at the start and finish of every session is time well spent. At the start, it prepares your muscles for what's coming; at the finish, it will reduce any muscle soreness and fatigue you feel the next day. Dynamic stretches (see page 148) are currently held to be best for warming up, while static ones are better for warming down. Dynamic stretches can increase heart rate and blood flow to active muscles, preparing them for training.

General flexibility – sun salutes

Yoga is a simple, time-effective way of improving your general flexibility. In particular, try following the lead of millions of people who start each day with a sun salute or two. There are slightly differing versions of the sun salute: what's shown here seems to work well for swimming and cycling. Steps 1 and 2 alone are an excellent stretch to do as a way of relaxing your jaw, neck and back muscles.

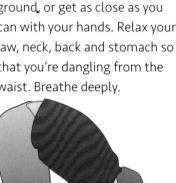

1 Stand up straight, heels on the floor, feet shoulder-width apart. Be careful not to stick your bottom out. Reach your arms above your head and extend them directly upwards, but without altering your body position.

2 Bend forward from the waist, keeping your arms stretched out and your feet flat. Touch the ground, or get as close as you can with your hands. Relax your jaw, neck, back and stomach so that you're dangling from the waist. Breathe deeply.

3 Place your hands on the floor, bending your knees a little if you need to. Bend one leg, and lunge back with the other one, placing it directly behind you. Drop your hips (make sure not to twist them sideways), and feel the stretch in your groin.

4 Step the bent leg back beside the extended one, so that you end up in a dead-straight press-up position. Hold this – which can be a bit of a trembler – for two or three breaths.

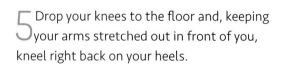

5 Drop your knees to the floor and, keeping your arms stretched out in front of you, kneel right back on your heels.

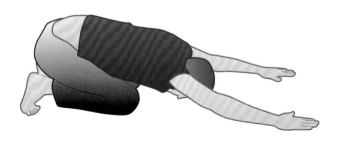

6 Pivot forward on your knees and drop your hips to the floor, arching your lower back while extending through the shoulders and neck and pushing up with straight arms. Imagine your head is lifting upward, and avoid throwing it backwards.

7 Push up and lift your knees from the ground until your legs are straight (or as straight as you can get them) and your bottom is high in the air. You're aiming to make an upside-down V shape. Keep your legs and arms as straight as possible, and, if you can manage it, have your feet flat on the floor (this isn't crucial). Relax, especially your shoulders, neck and jaw. It should feel as if your head is dangling loosely between your shoulders.

8 Lunge forward with the same leg as stepped back in step 3. You should find yourself in a mirror image of the position from step 3.

9 Bring your back leg forward to join the front one, and bend at the waist to return to the same position as in step 2.

10 Curl slowly back up to a standing position. Try to imagine each individual vertebra straightening one at a time, starting from the very bottom of your spine. Let your arms dangle loosely, and keep your neck and jaw relaxed.

Hold each pose

Spend a little time in each pose. Holding each one for about five deep, long breaths is usually about right.

Hips and torso

Tightness in this area, in the middle of your body, affects your ability to rotate from side to side while maintaining a steady kicking action. These stretches improve flexibility in the hips, groin and related muscles.

Hip stretch 1

Sit down with your legs out straight in front of you. Bend and lift your right leg, placing your foot on the outside of your left knee. Turn to the right, keeping your hips level and your bottom flat on the ground. Place your left forearm outside your right knee then gently move your right knee outward. Hold for five deep breaths, then repeat on the other side.

Hip stretch 2

From a standing position, take a lunge step forward. Kneel on your rear knee: this knee needs to be behind your hip. Cup your hands over your front knee, then move your hips forward until you feel the stretch in your hip and upper thigh. Your front knee should be at an angle of at least 90°. Repeat with the other leg.

Side stretch

Stand in the starting position for the sun salute (see page 142). Make sure your hips are tucked in and relaxed, and your feet shoulder-width apart. Bring your arms above your head, and hold your right wrist with your left hand.

Lean to the left: take care to keep your body facing forward, don't let yourself turn your shoulders or hips in the direction of the stretch. When you feel a stretch down your side, hold the position for several deep breaths, then return to the starting point. Repeat for the other side.

Shoulders and neck

These two stretches help with shoulder mobility, which is crucial for swimming front crawl. Don't worry if you find these stretches easier on one side than the other: almost everyone does. Balance would be ideal – but in stretching, as in life, the ideal is rarely possible.

Crossed-forearms stretch

1 Stand or sit upright looking straight ahead, with your shoulders relaxed. Bring bent arms up and forward, and cross them at the elbows.

2 Bring the forearm of the lower arm inward, and cup your fingertips in the heel of the other hand. Relax your jaw and shoulders, letting the shoulders drop.

3 Slowly lift your elbows up and forward (don't forget to keep your shoulders relaxed). As your elbows rise, you should feel the stretch engage between your shoulder blades. Move your elbows steadily up and down slowly several times.

4 Release, and repeat with the opposite elbow highest.

Reach-behind stretch

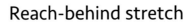

1 Relax your jaw and shoulders, and let your shoulders drop. Lift one arm up and put your hand behind your head, aiming for your forearm to be dangling down the line of your spine.

2 Bring your other arm behind your back and work your hand up the line of your spine. You're aiming for the back of your hand to be resting between your shoulder blades.

3 Try to place the palms of your hands together; you may not actually be able to touch your hands at all, but this will improve with practice.

Legs

Relaxed, flexible legs are important for front crawl; stiff ankles, in particular, will cause significant drag because they make it impossible to point your toes back into a good streamlined position.

Leg stretch 1

This one is good for your hamstrings if you've ridden a bike to the pool. Sit up straight, with your legs out in front of you and your toes pointing up in the air. Move one foot back, turning the knee outwards and sliding the sole along the calf and thigh of your other leg.

Staying upright, reach forward with both hands and place your fingertips on the toes of the foot pointing up in the air. Hold the stretch for five deep breaths or so, return to the starting position, and repeat for the other leg.

Leg stretch 2

Stand upright, next to a wall if your balance isn't great. Lift one foot behind you, hold it with your hand, and press your heel into your bottom. Here you might need to grab something for balance. Hold the stretch while you breathe deeply several times, release your foot and let it swing gently forward. Repeat using the other leg.

Take care with this stretch not to arch your lower back when you pull your foot in: your hips should stay level with the ground.

Ankle stretch

Kneel down with your legs tucked under you, toes pointing back. Ease backward, lifting your knees, so that your weight is taken by the tops of your feet. You can do this one leg at a time or both together. This stretches the fronts of your ankles. (Go steady if you're a runner, to give yourself time to adjust to the greater ankle flexibility.)

Warming up

Stretching has a part to play in warming up before a training session. It prepares your body for exercise, making injury much less likely.

Warming up – legs

A great way to get your body systems going before training is to cycle to the pool. A 10km ride will prepare the joints in your hips, knees and ankles and lift your heart rate. As an alternative, try 10 minutes on an exercise bike, or skipping.

Warming up – shoulders and upper body

Warm up your shoulders with more active movement. A good basic beginning is to windmill your arm backward; start really slowly, trying to relax your shoulder so that there's no creaking, clicking or straining. Steadily build up the speed until you feel a slight tingling in your fingertips, then maintain the movement for 10 full windmills. Repeat with the other arm; then do the whole thing again with each arm windmilling forward.

▶ Dynamic stretching like this arm windmilling is ideal for warming up before you get in the pool. Remember, your movements shouldn't be too sudden or severe.

Warming down

Including a good warm-down in your swimming routine will prevent or ease the muscle soreness you feel later. Start with dynamic movement and move on to static stretches.

For swimmers, the two parts of the warm-down could look something like this:

1 Swim a reasonable distance (for most people, between 200m and 400m is about right) at a steady pace. Don't crawl along so slowly you're practically sinking; just don't push things. Concentrate on keeping your stroke balanced and steady, with perfect technique. Using your muscles in this way will help flush out waste products and improve recovery

2 Do a few key stretches. My favourites are the shoulder stretches from page 146, pose 7 from the sun salute sequence on page 143, and the leg/hamstring stretch from page 147. That last one is because my hamstrings are shorter than Ronnie Corbett (RIP) and I need to work on them whenever I can. You'll find the ones that work for you: the areas where you tend to feel muscle soreness will guide you, but don't forget that this will change as your stroke develops

▼ Static stretches like this are often used for warming down, but some swimmers also include them in their warm-up.

▲ Most people have one area of their body that needs a little extra flexibility work. If you're a keen cyclist it may be your hamstrings. If you sit at a desk all day, that can result in tight hip flexor muscles. If you do have an area of particular inflexibility, it's worth getting expert advice about how to address it, because the problem doesn't always originate from the place where you can feel the stiffness.

Key skills

● **Make sure your flexibility training encompasses your whole body, not only specific areas where you feel weak.**
● **Work flexibility exercises into your daily routine: get into the habit of doing them when a particular TV programme starts or finishes, or before breakfast, for example.**
● **Include stretching in your swimming sessions: dynamic stretching at the start and static stretching at the finish.**

GLOSSARY

Abandon Retire from a race

Acclimatise Adapt to warmer or colder water temperatures and conditions

Blown Completely out of energy

Boxed Caught in between and behind swimmers so as to not be able to swim with the desired direction or pace

Break Gap to the rest of the field, made by increasing your speed

Chafing Irritation due to repeated rubbing of skin against swimsuits or other items

Chop Small, irregular waves caused by wind

Course Direction or route taken by swimmer/s

Cut Fail to turn properly round a required **turn buoy**

Draft Swim close behind and/ or beside another swimmer or swimmers

Escort Person or group of persons in a craft accompanying or leading swimmer/s

Feed Eat or drink during a race

Feeding pole Long pole used to pass food or water to a swimmer

FINA (Fédération Internationale de Natation Amateur) International governing body of swimming, water polo, diving, synchronized swimming and open-water swimming

Impede Obstruct, interfere or retard in movement or progress other swimmers during a race

Lap One complete round, length or circuit of a race course

Lead pack First group of swimmers in a race, all swimming closely together.

Positioning Placement of a swimmer in the course of an open-water race

Rabbit Swimmer whose goal is chiefly to set a fast pace, either to set a record or to exhaust a specific competitor so that a teammate can win

Starting platform Dock, pier or other floating structure where the swimmers stand to start an open water race; each swimmer is given about 60cm of space on the starting platform

Strung out Widely separated from one another

Turn buoy Distinctive buoy, anchored to mark the course for swimmers

ABOUT THE AUTHOR

Paul's swimming ability first became obvious to his dad (if no one else) when he placed 16th in the national age group championships at the age of 11. Two years later Paul won his first international race, at a home nations meet in Scotland. He broke into the national junior team, and went on to race in the pool for two more seasons.

During this brief international career Paul held national 100m and 200m titles, raced in the European championships and finally became – according to his coach – the third-fastest 15-year-old in the world. Recognising an unrepeatable peak when he saw one, Paul immediately retired from swimming and went in search of the ultimate mountain-bike singletrack, the perfect wave and a girlfriend who didn't smell of chlorine.

Paul later found his way back into swimming via triathlon, and started working with other triathletes who wanted help to improve their technique. Gradually these pieces of ad hoc coaching morphed into the Swim Better Fast clinics. Here are a few quotes from swimmers Paul has coached:

'It all now seems less complicated than I've been making it.'

'I've improved my open water swim time by 12 per cent.'

'I normally dread swimming sessions, but yours showed us how to use our training to better effect, rather than just slogging up and down the pool.'

'It's like a new beginning. I felt before that I needed to get fitter and stronger to improve my swimming. Now I know the truth.'

'One of the lifeguards has just told me how well I'm swimming compared to when he'd last seen me. I gave you full credit!'

Paul still swims most days, competes over distances from 50m to 3.8k, and coaches swimmers ranging in age from 8 to 84. He also works as a writer: his articles on swimming have regularly appeared in the *Guardian*, and his children's books – on important subjects such as whether you could fill an Olympic swimming pool with a lifetime's spit – are regularly nominated for awards. In his spare time he's a keen surfer, cyclist and snowboarder.

▶ He went in full of confidence and vim, and came out looking like this. The author at the end of a 3.8k swim in 2016.

Swimming for Triathlon and Open Water

ACKNOWLEDGEMENTS

Every swimmer starts somewhere; early in my swimming career, my dad was my top supporter. Only now do I realise that it can't have been pure pleasure to wake me up at 5.15 every weekday for Shreddies and training. He used to co-opt members of his extended family as reserve cheerleaders: no distant second place ever got a more raucous cheer than mine at the National Age Group Championships in Leeds. (He also got overexcited and entered 11-year-old me for that disastrous pier-to-pier race, of course – it wasn't all good.) I know he'd have enjoyed seeing me putting something back.

Today, every session I coach, I learn something – whether it's from other coaches or the swimmers themselves. So, a big thanks to everyone I've worked with so far – in particular Darren Sims, who was kind enough to look through proofs of the book and offer me his advice (any errors are, of course, my own).

The photos in this book would have been impossible without other people. Above all, my wife Emma helped with most of the shoots; without her patience and enthusiasm they just wouldn't have got done. Thanks also to my brother Dan, who set up the photos in Singapore, and to the swimmers who repeated drills and exercises again and again: Adam, Amber, Bethan, Emma, Esca, Kim, Oscar and Paul.

The photos were taken at a variety of facilities: thanks, then, to Arena Biarritz, France; One Shenton, Singapore; Quinta Raposeiros, Portugal; the beautiful outdoor pool at Petersfield (www.petersfieldpool.org) / Northlands Farm / The Witterings / Chichester Harbour, England.

◀ Thanks to all the swimmers who helped with the photos in this book – especially Adam, Amber, Oscar, Esca (shown left) and Bethan, who all braved the murky, giant-carp-haunted waters of Northlands Lake.

INDEX

slow kick practice 74
streamlined body position 70, 71
timing strokes 70, 71
vertical kicking 77
leg stretches 147
legs, warming up 148
lung function, improved 66–7

m

massed starts, open-water events 111
Millar, Robert 82
motivation 12
muscle memory exercises 41, 48, 73
muscle soreness, preventing 149

n

navigation 135
neck flexibility 146
Newton, Sir Isaac 28, 48
noseclips 17
nutrition 110

o

odd-number training 136
Olympic Games 9, 14
open-water events
  choosing an event 108
  open-water strategy 114
  pacing yourself 110
  preparation - equipment 109–10
  preparation - fuelling 110
  preparation - the course 109
  race finishes 132
  race strategy 112
  referees 114–15
  registration and mustering 110
  starts 110–11
  T1 - triathlon transition phase 112
  triathlon strategy 112
  warming up 110
  wetsuit changes 113
open-water turns 96

p

paceline training 130
pacing yourself 110, 121, 132
packs, swimming in 114–15, 130
paddleboarders 10, 12
paddles, hand 17
partners, training 10, 12
Payne, Keri-Anne 91
petroleum jelly 14
physical contact 114, 115
plank 129
Pool Open Water (POW) training 118–20, 137
pull, arm stroke 22, 25, 31, 35, 45, 86
pull buoys 17
push-ups 127

r

race strategy 112
recovery, arm stroke 22, 32, 44
red cards 115
referees 114–15
relaxation in the water 23, 33, 44, 60
reverse catch-up drill 84

rhythm of leg kicks 25, 70
Roche, Stephen 82
rotation, body 50
  breathing technique 60
  reverse catch-up 84
  rotation drill 1 51
  rotation drill 2 52–3
  rotation drill 3 54
rough water practice 125

s

safety tips 10
  natural hazards 11–12
  training partners/groups 10, 12
sealife 12
shoulder flexibility 56, 57–8, 146
shoulders, warming up 148
side drafting 121
side stretches 145
sighting 123, 137
6-beat kick 70, 71
skills and fitness
  concentration 136, 137
  dolphining 133–4
  drafting 121–2
  fast finishes 132
  fast starts 131
  land training 127–9
  navigation 135
  paceline training 130
  pacing your swim 121
  POW training 118–20
  rough-water confidence 125
  rounding a buoy 124
  sighting 123
  training cycles 126–7
  working on technique 126